D1600704

THE I TATTI
RENAISSANCE LIBRARY

James Hankins, General Editor

SCALA

ESSAYS AND DIALOGUES

ITRL 31

BARTOLOMEO SCALA

✦ ✦ ✦

ESSAYS AND DIALOGUES

ENGLISH TRANSLATION BY

RENÉE NEU WATKINS

Introduction by Alison Brown

THE I TATTI RENAISSANCE LIBRARY

HARVARD UNIVERSITY PRESS

CAMBRIDGE, MASSACHUSETTS

LONDON, ENGLAND

2008

Series design by Dean Bornstein

Library of Congress Cataloging-in-Publication Data

Scala, Bartolomeo, 1430–1497.
[Selections. English & Latin. 2008]
Essays and dialogues / Bartolomeo Scala ;
translated by Renée Neu Watkins ; introduction by Alison Brown.
p.   cm.
Latin text and English translation;
introduction, notes, and commentary in English.
Includes bibliographical references and index.
ISBN-13: 978-0-674-02826-5 (cloth : alk. paper)
1. Scala, Bartolomeo, 1430–1497.
2. Florence (Italy) — Politics and government — 1421–1737.
3. Italy — Intellectual life — 1268–1559 — Sources.
I. Watkins, Renée Neu.   II. Brown, Alison, 1934–   III. Title.
PA8570.S54A2 2008
945′.5105092 — dc22   2007041356

Contents

⚜

Introduction   vii

Introduction

Bartolomeo Scala's life is familiar to us in outline, as are his writings.[1] He was born the son of a tenant miller in the provincial town of Colle Val d'Elsa in 1430. After graduating as a lawyer in Florence's studium, he spent a year in Milan with the Borromeo family and returned to Florence in 1455 to begin his rapid ascent to power as a new man. He first worked as Pierfrancesco de' Medici's secretary; in 1459 he was appointed chancellor of the Guelf Party; and six years later, in 1465, he was appointed first chancellor of Florence, the top administrative job in the city-state. He was later awarded citizenship, knighted by the pope in 1484, and two years afterwards drawn for the top political office as Gonfalonier of Justice, "to the great anger and indignation of all men of good birth," as Francesco Guicciardini famously commented.

By then Scala was living in his classicizing palace in Borgo Pinti, which too was derided by envious contemporaries like the scholar Angelo Poliziano, who called it "an urban villa with open fields in the safe pomerium inside the city walls." Yet this palace is emblematic of Scala's achievement not only as humanist but also as a public official. Built on the classical model, its atrium has a frieze based on Scala's own fables, where leading literati gathered for learned discussions and to watch Scala's children performing Greek plays in the original. More details are emerging about the avant-garde culture of Scala's palace, as we shall see below. They provide an important link between his public role in Florence and his more private writings that are the subject of this volume.

Both Scala's professional writings as chancellor and his personal treatises, fables and dialogues were deeply indebted to classical models and rhetoric. In 1493, Poliziano again mocked him for hav-

ing "written a lot but published little known to the public." It is true that only four of his writings were printed during his lifetime, all of them official writings (the last, his 1496 *Defense against the Detractors of Florence*, is translated in this volume).[2] But other unprinted writings were also read and admired by his contemporaries. We know, for example, that the cardinal Francesco Gonzaga wanted a copy of Scala's first *One Hundred Fables* and that the future Pope Paul III, Alessandro Farnese, liked them for their blend of humor and seriousness. Others admired his ongoing *History of Florence*, and the humanist Bartolomeo Fonzio paid homage to Scala's learning by quoting in his *Dictionary* passages from two writings, both translated here (*Whether a Wise Man Should Marry*, written in the late 1450s, and the 1483 *Dialogue on Laws and Legal Judgments*).[3] In such a wide gamut of writings, dating from the 1450s to 1496, the penultimate year of Scala's life, what are the qualities that make them still valuable today ?

The earliest essays and letters are valuable as evidence of the literary culture of Florence in the mid-Quattrocento. Both Cristoforo Landino and Scala were pupils of Carlo Marsuppini in the Florentine Studio (or university) and both competed for his chair of oratory and poetry after his death — which Landino eventually won in 1458. It seems that Scala's *Letter on the Philosophical Sects*, written in the same year, as well as other similar essays on ancient philosophical sects at this time (including one by Marsilio Ficino), are to be associated with Landino and his lectures on Cicero's *Tusculan Disputations*.[4] Accepting Landino's definition of philosophy as the love of wisdom, Scala is novel in his use of less familiar sources, such as Cicero's *Prior* and *Posterior Academics*, Diogenes Laertius's *Lives of the Philosophers* and Lucretius's recently rediscovered *De rerum natura*, which both he and Ficino quoted from in their essays. As Garin has acknowledged, both are innovative, Ficino for writing in greater detail about Epicurus, and Scala for saying Epicurus wrote "quite divinely" about some things.[5] As

Epicurus and Lucretius were materialists who denied the existence of the soul and questioned the value of organized religion, Scala was taking something of a risk in praising them.

Scala's second essay, written around the same time, *Whether a Wise Man Should Marry*, adopts the same philosophical stance and is also novel in borrowing its theme and its opening discussion from Diogenes Laertius's *Life of Epicurus* as well as from Quintilian. For Epicurus, the issue of marriage was ambiguous—to be avoided by a wise philosopher and yet necessary for procreation, so a good topic for debate *in utramque partem*, on both sides of the question. Thus after drawing much of its ammunition from the misogynistic St. Jerome and Juvenal, it recants ("like Plato in the *Phaedrus*") by concluding in favor of marriage on the grounds of natural self-survival.

A poem addressed to Pius II in 1459–60 reflects the same interests but tailored now for a papal monarch. Praise for Pius's learning in mastering the ancients (from Pythagoras and the Greeks to Cicero and Virgil in Rome) is preceded by criticism of Epicurus and Lucretius for their atomism and negligent gods: far better, Scala declared, is a world ruled by the supreme reason of the masculine Stoics. When the same themes reemerge in his next essay—the letter of consolation addressed to Lorenzo de' Medici in December 1463, on the death of his uncle Giovanni, the third writing translated here—we find them presented for the first time in dialogue form. In the dialogue, which purportedly describes Scala's attempt to console Cosimo on his son's death, Cosimo is the Christian and Epicurean, countering Scala's Stoic counsels of fortitude with three direct quotations from *De rerum natura* to demonstrate the inability of wealth and possessions to mitigate grief and the fear of death. Since one of them had also been quoted by Ficino in his treatise *De voluptate*, it seems likely that both Ficino and Scala—as fellow students and intimates of the Medici palace at this time—used the Medici's own copy of this

still little-known text. Nor is this the only unfamiliar text to be quoted in the *Consolation,* since there are also quotations from Hermetic writings that had reached the Medici library in the year before Scala wrote this dialogue—including the manuscript that Cosimo urgently wanted Ficino to translate for him before he died.[6]

The death of Cosimo less than a year later, in August 1464, provided Scala with the opportunity to write to Lorenzo again. This time he sent him a collection of praises of his grandfather, partly drawn from books in the Medici library, which he prefaced with the fourth writing translated here. More like a Festschrift than a history (which would have been tactless in this republican city), the volume nevertheless plays the role of a history in eulogizing Cosimo's life and achievements, especially his role as a patron of learning—a theme that allowed Scala to draw on Cosimo's growing collection of manuscripts, Hebrew, Arab and oriental as well as Greek and Latin, in order to praise his patron's classical learning and also to demonstrate his own.

The value of this short preface and his other essays is to show how deeply Scala's later achievements were rooted in this early period of his life. As intimates of the Medici palace, both Scala and Ficino were familiar with the newly acquired manuscripts in Cosimo's library which took Florentine humanism in a new direction—not only Lucretius's *De rerum natura,* which they used and quoted in the 1450s before other humanists, but also Plato's dialogues, ten of which Ficino had translated and read to Cosimo before he died (later thanking Scala among others for help with the translations), and the Hermetic writings Cosimo acquired in 1462 and asked Ficino to translate at once, encouraging a new interest in *prisca theologia* that influenced not only Scala and Ficino but also their future friend, Giovanni Pico della Mirandola.

A year after Cosimo's death, Scala was appointed first Chancellor of Florence, leaving him little time for private scholarship until

the successful conclusion of the Pazzi War more than fifteen years later. By then, he was a mature writer, composing ironic and witty fables that were admired in learned circles outside Florence and a dialogue reflecting his new thinking on law and morality. He dedicated his first *One Hundred Apologues* to Lorenzo de' Medici in September 1481, later describing these fables as an annual tribute to his patron that he continued with Piero, his son.[7] His next substantial writing, the *Dialogue on Laws and Legal Judgments*, was sited in his elegant villa in Borgo Pinti, where he lived with his wife and six children. This time the dialogue purports to represent a debate about law with his fellow jurist, Bernardo Machiavelli (Niccolò's father), while marooned at home with gout during Lorenzo's absence at a congress in Cremona in 1483. In it, Bernardo, the practicing lawyer, argues that law should be codified; Scala, the pragmatist, that it should be interpreted flexibly by a good man or judge as arbiter.

The topicality of the debate is obvious, at a time of growing Medici power and growing criticism of the law's delays. The argument is nevertheless wide-ranging. Still influenced by the ancient philosophers and theologians he had discussed in his early writings, using Cicero, Lucretius, the Hermetic writings and Platonic dialogues translated by Ficino, especially the pseudo-Platonic *Minos*, Scala now expanded his interest to the cultural practices and beliefs of other regions in the world, using Livy and Herodotus as his guides. Whereas in the dialogue it is he who points out the common ground shared by men and animals in following a universal law of nature and Bernardo the differences among men's customs, both men agree that the purpose served by giving law a divine origin — by lawgivers ranging from Zoroaster, Trismegistus and Moses to Numa Pompilius and Muhammad — was not only to make people more obedient but also to suggest that law was based on nature and "dictated by right reason, which is the likeness of divinity within us." This comparative approach to

religion as well as law anticipates Scala's last writing, defending Savonarola from his critics, and also looks forward to Niccolò Machiavelli.

New light is thrown on this dialogue by the recent discovery that in February 1480, three years before writing it, Scala purchased "two spheres, one of the heavens, the other of the earth" — that is, the Zodiac and a Mappamundi — from the heirs of the eminent printer and astrologer in Florence, Donnus Nicolaus Germanus.[8] Nicolaus was famous for replacing the so-called cylindrical and conical maps of Ptolemy's quite newly recovered and translated *Geography* with the more accurate "trapezoid" projection, which would surely have been the basis for the globes acquired by Scala. It was Donnus Nicolaus who commissioned Bernardo Machiavelli to prepare an index for his printed edition of Livy in 1475, for which Bernardo then borrowed a copy of Ptolemy's *Geography* from a friend to help him compile the index, retaining the Livy as payment for his labors.[9]

Scala already had his own copy of Livy and, as chancellor of the Guelf Party, which took over control of maritime affairs while he was its chancellor, had long been involved in overseas affairs. Nevertheless, it seems very likely that his renewed interest in the wider world, and especially his acquisition of the novel double globes, was stimulated by his friendship with Bernardo Machiavelli at the time Bernardo was working for Donnus Nicolaus. We know, moreover, that shortly after Bernardo completed his index in 1476, Scala was in communication with the humanist Francesco Berlinghieri, then versifying Ptolemy in *Le septe giornate della geographia* and about to go to Rome to meet the printer Conrad Sweynheym about his edition of Ptolemy's *Geography*.[10] So his discussion in the dialogue of the customs of the "previously unknown people" in the islands discovered by John of Portugal and the contrasting practices of Muslim Turks, Arabs and Indians was

soundly based on his own experience as well as reflecting his humanist interests.

The next decade saw Scala engaged in writing his arduous (and incomplete) *History of the Florentine People*, as well as writing another hundred fables for Lorenzo de' Medici. The atrium of his palace was now being adorned by a frieze based on his first collection of fables. It was autobiographical in describing the poor man's social ascent through hard work, a theme of nearly all his writings, especially his preface to the *Collectiones Cosmianae*. And by referring overtly to Lorenzo and his growing collection of antique gems, he added the luster of antiquity to his own palace, which became a center for cultural gatherings attended by leading literati.[11] In the early 1490s the atrium served as the backdrop for a performance of Sophocles' *Electra*, in which the lead roles were played by Scala's bluestocking daughter Alessandra and his son Giuliano.[12] The audience included one of Alessandra's tutors, Angelo Poliziano; doubtless Marsilio Ficino, too, as a friend and frequent visitor to the palace; and perhaps Giovanni Pico della Mirandola, who we know delivered an oration on friendship in the gardens of Scala's palace on another occasion. As a visitor to the palace, it seems likely that Pico knew Scala's two globes, which may in turn have contributed to the novelty of his *Heptaplus*, with its description of the creation of four spheres or worlds, the "celestial" and "elementary" worlds separated from the "intellectual" and "human" worlds, to which Scala paid tribute in his fable "World."[13]

Although Scala initially lost his office as First Chancellor on the fall of the Medici in November 1494, he was reappointed shortly afterwards as joint-chancellor, dying in office in July 1497 in the middle of writing a long Lucretian poem *On Trees* dedicated to the son of his former patron, Lorenzo di Pierfrancesco de' Medici. The most important writing of this period in his life, however, was his *Defense against the Detractors of Florence*, the last

writing translated here. Its principal themes were dictated by its official function, to defend the city from the charges of losing its empire, of being too populist and too influenced by religious sectarianism under the aegis of Savonarola. Its opening salvo was to attribute Florence's recent loss of cities like Pisa and Montepulciano to the play of fortune, introduced by a surprising reference to Epicurean atomism. Although Scala admitted to being far from convinced by the theory that the world was created by the chance meeting of atoms — as, he wrote, Greek and Latin philosophers like Lucretius believed — by giving it prominence in his printed *Defense*, he nevertheless introduced a theme that had an important influence on his successors in the chancery, Marcello Adriani and Niccolò Machiavelli.[14]

The same is true of his defense of Florence's popular government, which has been called "a key moment of transition to the modern language of republicanism" for defining it as a constitution in which all the citizens rule.[15] To the charge that the vastly expanded new legislative council was unwieldy and incompetent, Scala responded by claiming that of the three accepted types of classical republican government, only popular government was "properly called a republic," since it alone had liberty and the common interest as its objectives, the latter being better defended when a large number of people identified it with their own self-interest and when decisions were voted on by those most affected by them. Since he was not writing about government "as philosophers do," he was equally pragmatic in defending less popular aspects of the new regime, as in distinguishing the people's function of "filling the civil offices," by election or by lot, from that of a senate of selected older citizens, who enjoyed a consultative and advisory function and were thus equally essential (he tells us) to republican government. And as this republic was in any case the second best, since in the state of nature before the Fall we would have lived happily under the guidance of a leader, Scala cannot be

said to have been an unconditional admirer of popular government.

The third important theme of his *Defense* concerns the role of religion, which Scala was surprised to find little discussed by political writers. Since no one disputed Florence's cult of religion as evidenced by her numerous churches and religious works of art, he addressed his remarks to those who criticized the role of the religious in secular society, especially — of course — preachers like Savonarola, who had aroused such enthusiasm both as a prophet and as a lawgiver that Florence had become the laughingstock of Italy. Scala centered his defense on a broad interpretation of religion as something common to all people, even barbarians, sacred rites being observed by Romans and Jews alike, while prophecy as foreknowledge was also practiced by ancient Greek and Hebrew seers and oracles as well as among "us" Christians (here quoting from the Bible as well as from more recent Christian history). In this context, he did not repeat the functional view of religion described in his *Dialogue on Laws and Legal Judgments* (which Niccolò Machiavelli later followed), but by treating it almost anthropologically, as something shared by all peoples, he managed to defend Savonarola's far from tolerant regime by adopting the same comparative standpoint that he had developed towards the early Greek and Hermetic philosophers.

Disparate though the writings in this volume are, they share common themes that run throughout Scala's life from his earliest essays in the late 1450s to his late *Defense* in the year before he died. They provide an interpretative thread not only for his own life but also for the literary culture of the second half of the Quattrocento, in which Scala played an important role. Since he believed that letters were more immortal than "those superior beings which some defend" in alone surviving when everything else dies and disappears, I hoped ten years ago that he would be ensured immortality by my edition of his *Humanistic and Political Writings*,

and doubly so now that so many of them have been translated with parallel texts in this splendid I Tatti Renaissance Library series. A special debt of gratitude is owed to Renée Watkins for her skill in undertaking this difficult task, to David Marsh for contributing his translation of *Dialogue on Laws and Legal Judgments* republished here, and above all to the series' General Editor, James Hankins, who planned and oversaw the volume.

Alison Brown

NOTES

1. On his life, see Brown, *Bartolomeo Scala* (Italian translation Florence, 1990); on his writings, Scala, *Humanistic and Political Writings*. (For full citations, see the Bibliography).

2. Angelo Poliziano, *Opera omnia* (Venice, 1498), fol. f4r (Epist. V, 1): "Multa tu quidem, credo, scripsisti, non multa adeo tamen edidisti quae volgo ferantur." Scala's two printed orations in 1481 and 1484 and his two defenses of Florence in 1478 and 1496 are in Scala, *Humanistic and Political Writings*, pp. 215–231 (III, 4 and 5), 199–202 (II, 6), and 394–411 (V, 8). The *Defense* translated below as Text 6 reveals in its prefaces and postface that Scala had a certain prejudice against printing as potentially "plebeian" and "rustic."

3. Brown, *Scala*, 209–11.

4. Ibid., 263–265; Arthur Field, *The Origins of the Platonic Academy of Florence* (Princeton, 1988), 234–236, 242.

5. Alison Brown, "Lucretius and the Epicureans in the social and political context of Renaissance Florence," *I Tatti Studies* 9 (2001): 26–27, citing Garin in n. 42.

6. Eusebius, *Preparatio evangelica*, translated by George of Trebizond, was acquired by the Medici library in 1462, when Ficino was translating from the Greek manuscript of Hermes Trismegistus brought to Italy in 1460. See Brown, *Scala*, 268–269, citing D. P. Walker, *The Ancient Theology* (London, 1972), 28; Frances Yates, *Giordano Bruno and the Hermetic Tradi-*

tion (London, 1964), 12–13; on the dialogue, see Brown, *Scala*, 36–37, and eadem, "Lucretius and the Epicureans," 28–29.

7. See his letter to Piero (2–3 November 1492) in *Humanistic and Political Writings*, 170 (no. 211); for the first and second books of apologues (1481 and ?1488) ibid., 305–337, 364–393 (V, 5 and 7), reprinted with translations and notes in *Renaissance Fables*, 86–271.

8. I am indebted for this information to Lorenz Böninger, *Die deutsche einwanderung nach Florenz im spätmittelalter* (Leiden, 2006), 339–341. On the globes, which must have been similar to the two Vatican globes acquired by Sixtus IV from Donnus Nicolaus in 1477 for 200 ducats, see J. Babicz, "The Celestial and Terrestrial Globes of the Vatican Library, dating from 1477, and their maker, Donnus Nicolaus Germanus," *Der Globusfreund* (June 1987): 35–36, and (1987–89): 155–168 (described by Isabella d'Este [163] when asking for a copy of the Vatican globes, as "in una è depicto el Mapamundo, in l'altra i signi celesti, cioé el Zodiaco").

9. See Bernardo Machiavelli's *Libro di Ricordi*, ed. C. Olschki (Florence, 1954), discussed by C. Atkinson, *Debts, Dowries, Donkeys: The Diary of Niccolò Machiavelli's Father, messer Bernardo, in Quattrocento Florence* (Frankfurt, 2002), 142–144, 167–168.

10. Partly edited in the *Inventaire des autographes . . . composant la collection de M. Benjamin Fillon*, I (Paris-London, 1878), 233, no. 818. The letter from Berlinghieri to Scala, dated 10 September 1476, is cited by Sebastiano Gentile, ed., *Firenze e la scoperta dell' America: Umanesimo e geografia nel '400 Fiorentino* (Florence, 1992), 234.

11. James David Draper, *Bertoldo di Giovanni, Sculptor of the Medici Household: Critical Reappraisal and Catalogue Raisonné* (Columbia, Missouri, 1992), 224, 241; Laurie Fusco and Gino Corti, *Lorenzo de' Medici: Collector and Antiquarian* (Cambridge, 2006), 124, 207, figs. 128–130; see Melissa M. Bullard and Nicolai Rubinstein, "Lorenzo de' Medici's Acquisition of the *Sigillo di Nerone*," *Journal of the Warburg and Courtauld Institutes*, 62 (1999): 283–286.

12. Discussed by Paola Ventrone, *Gli araldi della commedia: Teatro a Firenze nel Rinascimento* (Pisa, 1993), 28–29.

13. Pico della Mirandola, *Heptaplus*, in his *Opera omnia* (Basel, 1557; anastatic reprint, ed. C. Vasoli, Hildesheim, 1969), 1: 34, the preface to the fifth exposition, "De omnibus mundis divisione"; translated by Douglas Carmichael (New York, 1977), 70. For the fable "Mundus," see Scala, *Humanistic and Political Writings*, 392–393; translated by David Marsh in *Renaissance Fables*, 268–268; and on Pico's oration, ibid., 392, note (e). Brian Copenhaver has pointed out to me a possible source for Pico's reference to ascent from "center to center" in his *Oration* (*Opera*, ed. Vasoli, 1: 317); see his paper, "Maimonides, Abulafia and Pico: A Secret Aristotle for the Renaissance," *Rinascimento* (forthcoming), which he kindly sent me before publication.

14. See Alison Brown, "Reinterpreting Renaissance Humanism: Marcello Adriani and the Recovery of Lucretius," in *Interpretations of Renaissance Humanism*, ed. A. Mazzocco, (Leiden, 2006), 267–291; eadem, "Philosophy and Religion in Machiavelli," in *The Cambridge Companion to Machiavelli*, ed. John M. Najemy (forthcoming).

15. By David Wootton, "The true origins of republicanism, or *de vera respublica*," in *Il repubblicanesimo moderno: L'idea di repubblica nella riflessione storica di Franco Venturi*, ed. M. Albertone (Naples, 2006), 292–293, 296–300.

ESSAYS AND DIALOGUES

Epistola de sectis philosophorum

1   Philippo Borrhomeo Comiti salutem dicit.

Scribis audivisse a nonnullis, qui hinc ad te quotidie veniunt, philosophari me coepisse, nec paucis, ut Neoptolemus apud Ennium, sed hisce studiis totum esse deditum; proptereaque a me petis ut quam potissimum opinionem sequar quamque in familiam philosophorum memet contulerim certiorem faciam. Existimas enim, ac vero quidem, id esse iam pridem mihi constitutum. Nam quacunque agas de re, nisi principio finem quendam et tanquam signum ad quod referas omnia statueris, errans ac tanquam peregrina omnis est semper futura investigatio. Addis in postremis ut, nisi laboriosius mihi videatur onus a te esse impositum, de nobilioribus philosophorum sectis deque earum inter se differentia aliquid ad te scribam. Videntur enim adeo similes atque implicitae inter se ut etiam diligentissime consideranti in quo maxime discrepent non facile appareat.

2   Nam et Leonardus Aretinus, vir sane doctus et elegans, in libello quem appellavit Graeco vocabulo *Isagogicon,* conciliationem quandam fecit philosophorum atque illorum maxime quorum putatur sententia praestantior. Mihi vero laboriosum videri nihil potest, cum sum in hominem amicissimum obsequium collaturus, ac res ipsa, de qua scribi a me vis, non indigna esse videatur quam omni studio indagemus. Non enim parum conferet ad inveniendam veritatem ea cognoscere quae a multis excellentissimis viris diversa et plane contraria de vita et moribus, de occultissimis naturae rebus, deque ea ratione quae tota est in disputando (nam in tris has partes omnis est philosophia distributa) explicata sunt infinitis paene voluminibus.

Letter on the Philosophical Sects

Greetings to Count Filippo Borromeo:[1]

You write that you have heard from some who come to you daily from here that I have begun to devote myself to philosophy, not just a little, as Neoptolemus did according to Ennius,[2] but wholeheartedly; and on this account you ask me to tell you what opinion I accept as most convincing, and which philosophical family I take for my own. You rightly think I long ago made such a choice. In any undertaking, it is true, unless you have from the beginning some end in view, some standard to judge by, your investigation will always stray and remain that of an outsider. And to prevent me feeling that you have imposed a too heavy burden on me, you add, finally, that you would just like some sort of account of the more famous philosophical schools and their differences. For they seem so similar and interwoven that even careful study does not make it easy to see the main disagreements.

Leonardo of Arezzo, a truly learned man and an elegant writer, in the little book to which he gave the Greek title *Isagogicon*, reconciled the philosophers, especially those whose views are considered the most important.[3] Of course nothing that you ask could seem too much effort to me, considering my most affectionate veneration for you who ask it, and considering too that the subject seems not unworthy of the most zealous investigation. For it must help us substantially to learn the truth if we know the various and plainly contradictory views that excellent men have set forth in an almost infinite number of books about life and morality, the secrets of nature, and the reasoning used in philosophical argument — for these are the three parts of philosophy.[4]

3   Verum hac in re molestum, id est rem peti a te supra meas vires. Cum enim vix adhuc primis, ut aiunt, labris ista degustarim, vereor ne possim et desiderio tuo et voluntati meae satisfacere. Conabor tamen quantum potero, quantum epistola, quae brevior esse debet, patietur, ut ex his quae maxime probantur disciplinis quid maxime secuti sint hi qui principes et quasi totius domus patres extitissent aperire, si tamen prius quae huiusmodi de rebus a Varrone dicuntur breviter percurrero. Varro igitur LXXXVIII supra ducentas, non quae iam essent, sed quae esse possent, sectas acutissime explicavit. Cum enim voluptatem, quae sensus movet corporis, quietem, utrunque, et prima naturae, quae appellat primogenia, exequitur docetque quatuor haec natura ipsa, nullo praeceptore, nullis vivendi adminiculis, appetere cunctos mortales, in quattuor primum partes ostendit omnium secari opiniones oportere. Rursus cum aut virtutem, quae postea discitur, propter ista aut ista propter virtutem aut utraque propter se esse expetenda disseritur, triplicari numerum atque ex quattuor XII effici sententias. Aut enim voluptati antecellere virtutem aut servire virtutem voluptati aut aequalem inter se dignitatem voluptatem obtinere ac virtutem. Ita trifariam variata prima parte, tres fieri ex ea sectas, necnon idem facere quietem, idem utrunque, idem primogenia.

4   Praeterea quoniam quae natura expetantur, aut solis expetantur nobis aut etiam caeteris, duplicantur sectae fiuntque ex XII, quattuor et XX. Ad haec cum defendantur vel tanquam certa, ut Stoici, vel tanquam incerta, ut novi Academici, iterum duplicatur numerus fiuntque octo iam et quadraginta. Insuper quando huiusmodi de rebus vel Cynicorum habitu vel caeterorum disputari philosophorum potest, augetur numerus et sex habentur iam et nonaginta. Demum quoniam illa vel ut otiosi (sicut qui doctrinae penitus se dederunt), vel ut negotiosi (quemadmodum qui philo-

The only trouble is that what you ask lies beyond my ability. As 3
I have only attempted to taste these matters with, as they say, the
tip of my tongue, I fear that I shall not be able to satisfy your desire and my own wishes. I shall try what I can do, however — insofar as a letter, which has to be brief, permits me — to set forth
what was approved by those who were foremost in the most respected teaching traditions and became, as it were, the fathers of
the entire household. But first let me quickly summarize Varro on
the subject.[5] For Varro very cleverly showed, not that there were,
but that there could be 288 philosophical sects. For Nature herself,
without teachers or helps, acts on all mortals and instructs them
to pursue four things: the pleasure toward which our physical
senses urge us, and repose, and these two together, and certain innate natural principles (he calls these the *primogenia* or primordial
seeds), and he showed that by these the opinions of men are first
divided into four sects. Then again, virtue, which is subsequently
taught, arises because of these or they derive from it, or, as some
say, each is independently pursued, by which the number of philosophical sects is trebled from four to twelve. Again, either virtue
takes precedence over pleasure, or virtue serves as a means to pleasure, or they are of equal importance. This is a triple division
which applies to each sect, whether it posits the primacy of pleasure, of repose, of both pleasure and repose, or of primordial
seeds.

Further, we pursue our natural ends either for ourselves only or, 4
on the other hand, for others as well, by which the twelve sects are
doubled to twenty four. In addition, whether we maintain our position as certain, with the Stoics, or uncertain, with the New
Academy, the number doubles again to forty-eight. When we discuss such matters, moreover, we can do so in the manner of the
Cynics or in the manner of all other philosophers, which swells
the number to ninety-six. Then, since philosophers may be men of
leisure who devote themselves to it alone, or men of affairs who

sophantes administrationibus quoque se admiscuerunt rerum publicarum), vel ut qui pro temporum conditione utroque in studio occupatissimi fuerunt persequuntur, necesse est ut triplicato numero LXXXVIII supra ducentas sectas habeamus. Verumtamen nos hanc Varronis subtilissimam explicationem omittamus, praesertim cum ab eodem confutentur praeter tres quasdam ex primis duodecim, quae ex primis manabant naturae. Nulla enim inquit dici vere secta potest in qua de summo hominis bono nihil disputetur. Haec enim vel praecipua causa fuit omnibus philosophis universam in studiis aetatem, id est in summo investigando bono, conterendi. Quod quoniam in obscuro latet omne praeter nomen difficillimeque inveniri quod omnes praeter cetera concupiscunt potest, varios ac paene contrarios eosdemque laboriosissimos infinitorum fere hominum conatus irritos tandem nova hac philosophia, quam Christianam vocant, factos fuisse manifestum est.

5 Verum haec posterius. Nunc unde habuerint initium sectae, et quae ex multis nobiliores fuerint dicendum breviter. Plato igitur Atheniensis, vir summo ingenio atque eloquentia singulari, cum ea quae audivisset ab praeceptore Socrate, qui primus de bonis malisque rebus in vita disputavit, quod existimavit naturae aut deorum perplexam sane et multis involutam quasi nebulis quaestionem nihil conferre ad degendam vitam, et multis scripsisset libris et alios in Academia, ipsius gymnasio, edocuisset, reliquit tandem Speusippum, nepotem ex sorore, qui sibi hereditario quodam iure in Academia successit, et Aristotelem, qui seorsum Lycium sibi gymnasium delegit, in quo deambulando disputaret. Qui ergo Aristotelem secuti sunt ab deambulandi consuetudine Peripatetici, qui vero in Academia cum Speusippo, nihil ex Platonico praecipiendi et disputandi more commutato, fuerunt Academici nuncupati.

6 En habes initium sectarum et quasi philosophorum quandam seditionem, quanquam solo inter se nomine differentes eadem principia, eundem rerum fontem sectabantur. Aberrant enim qui

philosophize while taking part in the administration of the commonwealth, or alternate their time in each pursuit according to circumstances, it follows that the number is tripled to 288. But let us omit Varro's subtle elaboration of all this, especially since he himself throws out all but the three of those first twelve that concern the first principles of our nature. For he says that no sect can be called truly philosophical if it does not concern itself with man's highest good. This has always been the universal purpose of philosophy, that is, to track down with infinite pains the nature of the highest good. Yet since it remained hidden in darkness, aside from the name, and what men desire above all is most difficult to find out, countless men made strenuous attempts which led to varied and quite contradictory conclusions, until that new philosophy called Christian showed the futility of their striving.

But more of this later. Now we must speak briefly of how the 5 sects began and which among the many were most eminent. First of all, the Athenian Plato, a man of the highest intellect and of unequaled eloquence, propounded what he had learned from his teacher, Socrates, who was the first to discuss what are the good and the bad things in life, and who thought that the convoluted and, one might say, cloudy questions we have about nature and about the gods did nothing to help men manage their lives.[6] Plato produced many books, as did others in the school he founded, the Academy, which he left to Speusippus (his sister's son), whom he made his official successor by oath, and as did Aristotle, also, who founded his own separate school in the Lyceum, where he taught as he walked around. Those who followed Aristotle were called Peripatetics because of this habit of teaching while walking,[7] while those who followed Speusippus, who changed nothing in the Platonic way of teaching and debating, were known as Academics.

Here you have the beginning of sects and of something like dis- 6 cord among philosophers, though the parties differed only in name and derived from the same philosophical source and the same

putant veteres Academicos (sic enim dicti sunt propter novos, de quibus dicetur paulo post) ideo differre a Peripateticis quod illi antiquum Socratis morem omnibus in rebus continendi assensionem tenuissent, quod inveniri ab hominibus verum posse non putarent; contra vero hi, aliter iudicantes, et assentirentur aliis et ipsi quod dicerent pro certo confirmarent. Illam enim Socraticam dubitationem de omnibus rebus et nulla affirmatione adhibita consuetudinem disserendi, ut ait Cicero, etsi imitari videtur Plato in suis libris ut Socratem verius exprimat, quem frequentissime inducit disputantem, qui a Platone postea manarunt, reliquerunt. Ita facta est disserendi, quod minime Socrates probabat, ars quaedam philosophiae et rerum ordo et descriptio disciplinae, quae quidem primo erat duobus nominibus una. Nihil enim inter Peripateticos et illam veterem Academiam differebat. Abundantia quadam ingenii praestabat, ut mihi quidem videtur, Aristoteles, sed idem fons rerum erat utrisque et eadem rerum expetendarum fugiendarumque partitio. Solo igitur nomine differebant, quod hinc disputando deambulatio, illinc in quo Plato docuerat locus fecerat. Fuit enim inter eos rerum summa convenientia. Nam etsi videtur Aristoteles et ideas primus labefactasse et multis aliis in locis a magistro Platone dissensisse, dicit tamen divus Augustinus tertio *Contra Academicos* libro diligentissime atque acutissime interpretanti nullum fuisse inter hos duos philosophos discrimen apparere. Sit igitur haec nobis una secta, quoniam non putamus qui verbis tantum ac non etiam rebus inter se differant, etsi diversa sint appellatione, duarum esse sectarum. Quid enim aliud secta est, si a sectando, id est a persequendo, nomen ducit, quam electio quaedam eorum de quibus animus iudicat perseveransque sententia, quam complures

principles. Those persons are mistaken who think the Old Academy (as opposed to the New, of which we will speak shortly) differed from the Peripatetics because the former stuck to the old manner of Socrates, incorporating all his thinking, and continuing not to believe that the truth can be discovered by men, while the latter judged otherwise, granting their assent to other positions and declared as certain what they themselves believed. The Socratic way of arguing, with doubt about everything and no room for firm positive statements, was continued by Plato, as Cicero tells us, in the books where he expressed the ideas of Socrates most accurately, most often introducing him into the debate, but in Plato's later works, these postulates were given up.[8] Thus the practice of disputation was turned into something which Socrates did not approve of, namely, a philosophical technique, a system of nature and the codification of a teaching, which in the beginning had been one thing under two names.[9] For there was no difference between the Peripatetics and the Old Academy. Though Aristotle, it seems to me, was preeminent for the richness of his thought, he and the Academy sprang from the same source and he did not differ in what he thought should be sought after and what should be avoided. Only the name differed, because one group taught while walking about, and the other in one place, where Plato had taught. They agreed on a deep level. For even if Aristotle seems to have been the first to undermine the theory of ideas and departed in other ways from his teacher Plato, still Augustine in his third book *Against the Academics*, where he carefully and brilliantly interprets the two, says they did not really differ.[10] Thus for us this is one sect, because we think that two sects would have to differ not only in words, but in actual substance; otherwise their names differ, but they are not two sects. For what is a sect? If it takes its name from following closely (*sectando*) or conforming (*persequendo*), then it is nothing else but a kind of choice concerning things about which the mind judges, a steady conviction, which many persons

quasi quaedam familia persequantur? Non enim quod sentit unusquisque seorsum a ceteris, sive de principiis rerum sive de effecti-
bus, aut sectam fecit hactenus aut potest efficere. Hoc enim pacto
haud scio an magnum illum Varronis numerum de sectis non su-
peraremus modo, sed prae hoc etiam quam minimum redderemus.

7   Ut enim caetera omittam, quam ne in parvula quidem re sibi
consentit antiquissimorum turba philosophorum qui in naturae il-
lustranda obscuritate studia cuncta cunctamque vitam consumpse-
runt! Nam Thales, qui princeps eorum fuit qui septem apud
Graecos sapientum numero censentur, cum aquam principium ponit rerum ex eaque omnia creari dicit atque etiam mundum, manifestissime ab Anaximandro ipsius discipulo dissentit, qui principium dicit esse rerum naturae infinitatem nascique res omnes ex
suis propriis principiis. Mundos existimavit esse innumerabiles
eosque modo dissolvi, modo interire. Successit huic in schola
Anaximenes fuitque ipsius auditor, sed non naturae infinitati, verum infinito aeri causas rerum assignavit atque etiam deorum;
quae vero gignerentur definivit. Post eius auditor Anaxagoras *ho-
momeriam* quam appellant Graeci, ut ait Lucretius, materiam infi-
nitam, esse dixit ex qua fierent omnia similibus inter se particulis,
mente tollente divina confusionem quae antea inerat cunctis rebus.
Diogenes quoque, alter Anaximenis auditor, aerem dixit rerum
esse materiam, compotem divinae rationis, sine qua fieri nihil possit. At Xenophanes Colophonius, paulo etiam antiquior, unum
esse omnia et immutabile idque esse deum non natum neque cor-
ruptioni obnoxium figura conglobata; Parmenides duo elementa:
ignem qui moveat, humum quae moveatur formasque recipiat;
Leucippus plenum et inane ex his mundos fieri et elementa atomo-

conform to, like a family. For the mere fact that an individual thinks differently from others, whether about natural principles or their effects, in itself does not and cannot create a sect. For this reason, I suspect that we shall not only not exceed Varro's enormous number of sects, but even minimize the number of them by comparison.

To say nothing of other matters, the mob of philosophers who 7 consumed their lives and efforts in illuminating Nature's dark places did not agree about even the slightest detail. Thales, the first of those whom the Greeks counted as the Seven Sages, believing that water was the source of all things and even of the world, clearly disagreed with his disciple, Anaximander, who said that infinity was the principle of nature, and that all things were born each from its own principles. He believed that there are innumerable worlds which sometimes dissolve and sometimes pass away. His successor Anaximenes, who had been his student, did not assign the causes of things, and even of gods, to limitless nature but to limitless air; but limitless air limited the things that came into existence. After him, his student Anaxagoras, according to Lucretius, said that infinite matter displayed *homoeomeria* [similarity of parts], as the Greeks call it, and from it all things were made from particles similar to each other, the divine mind having taken away the primordial confusion of all things.[11] Diogenes too, another student of Anaximenes, said that air was the original substance of things, endowed with divine reason, without which nothing could come into being. A slightly older theorist, Xenophanes of Colophon, said that all things are one and immutable, and that this was a god, spherical in form, who was not born and not subject to corruption. Parmenides proclaimed two elements: fire which moves things, and earth which is moved and receives form. Leucippus thought that worlds were made by a combination of empty space and space packed with matter, and that the elements were produced by chance combinations of atoms, a

rum fortuita concursione, a quo quidem hac in parte non discrepat Democritus, quanquam est in ceteris abundantior; Empedoclis quatuor illa nota sunt principia cum amicitia liteque; Heraclito ignis placuit; Melissus hoc quicquid est infinitum esse dixit et immutabile fuisseque semper semperque futurum et immobile; motum enim videri, non esse asseveravit; de diis tacendum quod eorum cognitio esse nulla possit. Plato ex materia quae in se omnia recipiat mundum a Deo factum censet sempiternum. Pythagoras tandem ac Pythagorei omnes et numeris et mathematicorum principiis omnia tribuenda censuerunt.

8   Non ero in his enumerandis longior, cum haec ipsa quae dixi plura fortasse sint quam necesse fuit. Nam quis est, ne dicam mediocriter eruditus, aliquantulum discendi cupidus, qui non iam publicis in coronis viderit quanta sit inter philosophos de summo bono, de officiis, de moribus, quantaque cum diversitate contentio, ut si velis pro opinionum differentia sectas facere, non iam LXXXVIII et ducentae numerandae sint, sed paene infinitae. Quanquam non hae sunt tantummodo quae nobiliores putantur, de quibusque scribi a me petis, Academicorum veterum et Peripateticorum, de quibus est iam dictum; aliquid et dicetur deinceps Stoicorum, novorum Academicorum et Epicureorum. Has enim quatuor praestare caeteris putant. Verum addit Diogenes in *Vitis Philosophorum* Cyrenaicos, quorum Aristippus Cyrenaeus princeps fuit, Eliacos, qui manarunt a Phaedone Eliense, Megaricos qui ab Euclide Megarensi, Cynicos, qui fluxerunt ab Antisthene Atheniensi, Eretricos, quorum dux fuit Menedemus Eretricus, dialecticos, quibus Clitomachus praefuit Calcedonius.

view with which Democritus partly agreed, though he had more to say on other matters. Empedocles recognized four elements, adding friendship and enmity; Heraclitus liked the idea of fire. Melissus said that whatever is, is infinite and immutable, having always been the same and sure to be unchanged in the future; hence the appearance of motion and change was an illusion; and he was silent on the subject of the gods because he believed that knowledge of them was impossible. Plato thought that the world was made by God, was sempieternal, and was composed of matter which receives in itself all [the forms] of things. Pythagoras and all his followers thought that all things and the whole as well are to be explained by numbers and mathematical principles.

I shall not go on any longer listing these, since perhaps I have 8 already said more than was needed. For anyone who is, if not moderately educated, at least a bit curious to learn, will have noticed that there are enough conflicting philosophical opinions in the public arena about the highest good, the duties of men, and true morality, and so much disputation and diversity, that if you want to make differences of opinion the basis of philosophical sects, you will have not 288 but a nearly infinite number. But the Old Academy and Peripatetics, about whom I have already spoken, are not the only sects among those that are considered the finest (and that is what you've asked me to write about). Something must also be said about the Stoics, the New Academy, and the Epicureans, for these four are considered the most eminent. It is true that Diogenes in his *Lives of the Philosophers* adds the Cyrenaics, of whom Aristippus of Cyrene was the founder; the Elians, starting from Phaedo of Elis; the Megarians starting with Eucleides of Megara; the Cynics, whose founder was Antisthenes from Athens; the Eretrians, whose leader was Menedemus of Eretria; and the dialecticians, whose chief representative was Clitomachus of Chalcedon.[12]

9   Sed his in praesentia praetermissis, ad Academicos veteres Peri-
pateticosque reducatur oratio. Aristotelem audivit Theophrastus,
qui non solum, ut Varro apud Ciceronem ait, Platonis labefactavit
species, quod magister fecerat, sed et virtutem suo decore spoliavit
imbecillemque reddidit, quod negavit in ea sola positum esse beate
vivere. Eius autem discipulus Strato Lampsacenus ab eorum
consortio amovendus videtur, qui praecipue necessariam philosophiae partem de virtute et moribus deserens totumque se ad naturae vestigationem conferens, multis in rebus dissentit a suis.
Nam Demetrius Phalereus, etsi ingenio et doctrina praestitit, tamen rei publicae administrationem maxime sectatus a Theo-
phrasto magistro dissentire non videtur. Speusippus autem et Xenocrates Calcedonius, qui primi in Academia successerunt Platoni,
deinde Polemo, Crates et Crantor, nihil ex his quae acceperunt a
superioribus immutantes, in institutis quodammodo patriis diligentissime perseverarunt, nullusque fuerat qui a suis adhuc auderet penitus rebellare. Primus Zeno, cum Polemonem audivisset,
grandis iam natu et extranea imbutus disciplina, dissentire aperte
coepit certamque omnibus de rebus proferre sententiam. Quae
quoniam accommodatior multitudinis erat auribus — nihil enim
removebat a sensibus, nihil affirmans esse posse incorporeum,
neque deum ipsum, quem dixit esse ignem — multos habuit proti-
nus suae sententiae sectatores, qui sunt a porticu in qua disputare
frequentissime consuevere Stoici nuncupati.

10   Archesilas autem, Zenonis condiscipulus (audivit enim et ipse
Polemonem), cum videret approbari Zenonis sententiam de corporibus atque esse, ut ita dicam, popularem in diesque agere radi-
ces profundius, non invenit quonam pacto commodius posset ob-

But, leaving these out for the present, let us return to the Old 9
Academy and the Peripatetics. Theophrastus studied with Aristotle but, as Varro tells us in Cicero's account, he not only over-
threw Plato's concept of Forms, which his teacher had done, but
also stripped virtue of its dignity and made it seem a weak thing,
since he denied that it is in itself enough to constitute the good
life.[13] Straton of Lampsacus, a student of Theophrastus, seems to
have moved away from association with them, when he abandoned
the study of virtue and morals, an especially necessary part of philosophy, and devoted himself wholly to the investigation of nature,
disagreeing on many counts with his colleagues. Now Demetrius
of Phalerum, though he was preeminent in intellect and learning,
pursued mainly questions of government and does not seem to
have disagreed at all with his master, Theophrastus. Speusippus,
moreover, and Xenocrates of Chalcedon, who were the first successors of Plato in the Academy, and later Polemon, Crates and
Crantor, did not change what they had received from their predecessors but persevered diligently along the path of the fathers,
none of them daring to rebel to any extent against their teaching.
After Zeno had studied with Polemon and reached maturity, having absorbed other teachings outside the Academy, he was the first
openly to disagree with what he heard from Polemon, and to put
forward fixed views on all subjects. Since his ideas were more acceptable to the ears of the multitude—for he stuck close to the
senses, affirming that nothing incorporeal existed, not even god
himself, whom he declared to be fire—he quickly attracted many
followers, and his sect, because of the portico or stoa where they
regularly stood and argued, came to be known as the Stoics.

Arcesilaus was a fellow student of Zeno's, for he, too, had stud- 10
ied with Polemon. But when he saw that Zeno's thought about
corporeal reality was being accepted and, so to speak, taking root
daily in the popular mind, he found no way to oppose it more
effectively than by hiding his own beliefs. He found arguments

sistere Zenoni quam si sententiam occultaret suam. Contra omnia quae a Stoicis dicerentur disputaret; primusque dicitur consuetudinem in utranque disputandi partem induxisse. Itaque non tantum continuit assensionem, quod fecerat Socrates, cum unum se scire diceret quod nihil sciret, sed ne id quidem sibi relinquens, nihil etiam non[1] denegandum censuit. Ita enim putavit, omnibus quae dicerentur a Zenone confutatis, quid ipse sentiret esse homines requisituros. Hinc nova Academia est quae de omnibus dubitavit rebus. Huic enim necessitati veteres se non adstrinxerunt. Hanc nonnulli mediam appellant, Varro apud Ciceronem novam, dicitque usque ad Carneadem, qui quartus ab Archesila fuit, esse perductam; mihi vero placet appellari mediam. Video enim rerum ordinem ac varietatem ita deposcere.

II Carneades autem, lectis quae a Zenone praecipue Crisippoque scripta fuerant, iam non contra omnia disputabat, quod ante eum fecerant omnes ex ea disciplina, sed solos sibi Stoicos expugnandos evertendosque delegerat; cumque multi urgerent nihil acturum sapientem si rerum omnium contineatur assensus, si nihil, semper inquirens, unquam nacturus sit in quo possit consistere, invenit homo acutissimus quonam pacto haec argumenta declinaret. Esse enim non negavit quae sapiens sequi posset, sed ea non vera appellavit sed verosimilia, secutus, ut arbitror, Platonem, qui cum duos esse dixisset mundos, intelligibilem alterum, in quo ipsa veritas esset, alterum sensibilem, quem oculis tactuque sentimus, illum verum, hunc verosimilem nominavit. Itaque nullas esse in homine veras virtutes, sed omnes ad alterius cuiusdam verae imaginem esse factas. Quare videtur Carneades tertiam quandam posuisse Academiam, quam, si tibi videtur, appellemus novam. Nam quod Lacydem Laertius nova‹e› Academiae principem fuisse dicit, neque rationem suae sententiae affert ullam, non facile adducor ut

against every point made by the Stoics, thus introducing the philosophical custom of debating an issue from both sides. Not only did he maintain the Socratic assertion — that he knew one thing, which was that he knew nothing — but leaving himself not even that assertion, he believed that there was nothing that should not be denied. His idea was that, once he had refuted everything Zeno had said, men would embrace his own views. Thus began the New Academy, the school that doubted all things, for the older members of the Academy did not bind themselves to this necessity. Some call this school the Middle Academy, but Varro (as cited in Cicero) calls it the New, and he says that it lasted down to Carneades, who was the fourth head after Arcesilaus.[14] I prefer to call it the Middle Academy. I think the order and variety of things is best expressed in this way.

Carneades, however, having read both Zeno in the first instance and Chrysippus, now stopped disputing every single statement, as everyone of his school had done before him, but chose only to oppose and overturn the thinking of the Stoics. For when many pressed the point that the sage would be reduced to inaction if he withheld his assent in all things, if for all his inquiries he never hit upon anything upon which he could take a stand, this brilliant man found a way around the argument. While he did not deny that there were courses of action the wise man could follow, he called these "likely" rather than "true." He was, I think, following Plato, who said that there were two worlds, one intelligible, in which truth itself resides, and the other perceived by the senses, which we know by sight and touch; the former he named the true world, the latter the world of opinion. Thus, for example, true virtues do not exist in man, but all are made [in him] in accordance with the image of a certain true one. Therefore it seems that Carneades founded a sort of third Academy which, if you agree, we shall call the New Academy. Diogenes Laertius calls Lacydes of Cyrene the founder of the New Academy, but he gives no rea-

11

credam, praesertim cum scribat eum Cicero Archesilae discipulum
in magistri perseverasse institutis. In illa autem Carneadea disciplina maxime ex multis qui illum audiverunt Clitomachus excel-
luit. Clitomachum audivit Philo. Etsi eius discipulus Antiochus, a
suis desciscens, e nova se in veterem contulit Academiam, nonnullis tamen quasi coloribus infectus Stoicorum. Addiderat enim ad
Philonis disciplinam † omnes archistoici † praecepta nonnulla.

12   Quo tempore in primis M. Tullii novorum Academicorum est
praeclara defensio, qui adeo pervicit nihil posse comprehendi sed
verisimiliora ac probabiliora sequi oportere ut, penitus devictis
Stoicis, non multo post essent qui Platonis divinum illud os pur-
gatissimasque sententias suscitarent, vetusque rursus Academia,
cuius idem Plato auctor fuerat, revivisceret in Graecis Porphirio et
Iamblico et Apuleio Afro; praecipue tamen in Plotino, quem scribit Augustinus adeo illi similem fuisse iudicatum ut simul eos
vixisse putandum sit, tantumque intercessisse temporis ut in hoc
ille revixisse videatur. Ita usque in hodiernum diem vetus exsusci-
tata Academia maiore ex parte perdurat, etsi haec Platonis divinissima de philosophia praecepta nonnihil obscurasse videtur Aristoteles, quem quidam ob rerum maxime ordinem ita sequuntur ut a
magistro dissentientem, ut illis videtur, non tantum concordantem
anteponant, quanquam certo scio aliquando fore cum aut ambos
recte idemque sensisse, aut certe Platonem non male sensisse in
his quae ab illis, quos Aristotelicos vocant, male intellexisse insi-
mulatur, manifestum fiet.

13   Habes de Peripateticis, Stoicis Academicisque omnibus quae sit
nostra sententia. Restant autem Epicurei, quos fluxisse ab Epicuro
omnes norunt, qui Aristippi voluptatem amplexatus, extremum illam atque ultimum bonorum esse asseveravit; eaque ipsa nondum

son for his opinion and I cannot readily see one, especially as Cicero writes that Lacydes was the follower of Arcesilaus and perpetuated his teachings.[15] Of Carneades' many disciples, Clitomachus was the most notable. Philo was a student of Clitomachus. Although Philo's disciple Antiochus deviated from his teachers and returned from the New to the Old Academy, he nevertheless was tinged with a Stoic coloration. For he added to Philo's teachings some typically Stoic teachings.[16]

At this time, Cicero produced the most famous defense of the New Academy, and went so far as to say that nothing can be grasped, but that we must follow what is plausible and probable. Soon thereafter the Stoics were altogether defeated, and a revival occurred of the divine mouth and pure teachings of Plato, and once again the Old Academy, his creation, was reborn in the Greeks Porphyry and Iamblichus and in Apuleius of North Africa, but most of all in Plotinus, whom Augustine described as so much like Plato that one might easily think of them as contemporaries, and that only so much time had elapsed to allow the one to seem to be living again in the other.[17] Thus even up to our own time, the Old Academy, revived, largely persists, and though it appears that Aristotle has somewhat overshadowed the utterly divine teachings of Plato's philosophy. Certain persons follow Aristotle, most of all for his systematic rigor, regarding him as a thinker who disagreed with his master and who cannot be harmonized with him. But I am certain the time will come when it will be clearly shown either that both held the same correct views, or at least that Plato did not hold wrong beliefs on those subjects which the so-called Aristotelians allege he misunderstood.

Now you have had our thoughts concerning the Peripatetics, Stoics, and all the philosophers of the Academy. The Epicureans, however, remain to be discussed,. Everyone knows that they originated with Epicurus, who embraced Aristippus' idea of pleasure and declared it the ultimate and final good, an idea that is not yet

mortua est, atque haud scio an serpat in dies latius. Sed in ea profecto, si corporis significavit voluptatem — ut accusant omnes praeter Lactantium, qui animi voluptatem Epicuri, corporis Aristippi,
fuisse auctor est — ne mediocre quidem, nedum summum reperietur bonum. Quid enim esse magis abiectum potest magisque commune cum pecudibus? In animis profecto, in animis certa est sum-
maque hominis beatitas.

14   Nunc quae fuerint de omni philosophiae parte omnium principia, compendio brevissimo videamus. Epicurus, ut eum primo ab-
solvamus, tertiam philosophiae partem, quae disputativa dicitur,
cum dereliquisset, Leucippi Democritique minuta indivisibilia,
quas vocant atomos, persecutus est perque infinitum inane diversa
inter se figura concurrentes omnia quae videntur in natura creare
dixit. Deos vel sustulit vel profecto dormientes fecit. Eos enim inquit beatos, neque ex se habere negotium posse neque alteri exhi-
bere. Itaque ab illis removet curam humanarum rerum. Secundum
quam sententiam ait Virgilius:

> Scilicet is superis labor est, ea cura quietos
>   Sollicitat.

Animum, qui profecto divinum esse aliquid, nisi caeci omnino simus, intelligitur, expoliavit omni dignitate. Ita enim coniunctum
voluit esse corporibus ut nulla possit eo incolumi fieri separatio,
sed nasci simul cum corpore atque interire. Et haec quidem de natura, quae est altera philosophiae pars. De moribus autem (nam
haec restat tertia), ea praecipit quae, si homines sequantur, sublatis
e medio virtutibus vel certe pedisequis effectis voluptatis, non
modo non conservetur humanum genus, sed funditus evertatur.
Quis est enim qui referens omnia ad voluptatem tueri amicitiam
fidemque ac iustitiam colere, fortitudini obtemperare, sequi conti-

dead, and I suspect may be insinuating itself more widely every day. If this happiness is the pleasure of the body, this cannot be even a moderate good, let alone the highest. (Everyone says this in condemnation of Epicurus except Lactantius, who writes that Epicurus' idea of pleasure was the happiness of the soul while Aristippus spoke of the pleasure of the body.)[18] For what could be more base, more bestial? Certainly it is in our souls, in our souls, I say, that the surest and highest happiness for humankind lies.

Now let us survey briefly all the principles of each part of philosophy.[19] To deal with Epicurus first, he neglected the third part of philosophy, which is called dialectic. But he followed the doctrine of the minute indivisibles of Leucippus and Democritus, called atoms, and asserted that these, combining in the infinite void into diverse forms, produce all the visible things in nature. As for the gods, he either removed them from the world or regarded them as asleep: they are called blessed, he said, because they are not concerned for themselves or for others. Thus he removed from the gods any concern for humanity. As Virgil says: 14

> as if the peaceful state
> Of heav'nly powers were touch'd with human fate![20]

This philosophy strips of its dignity the soul, which (unless we are completely blind) is understood to be something divine. Epicurus insisted that the soul's connection to the body was such that there could be no separation that would leave it unharmed: hence it is born with the body and buried along with the body.[21] So much for nature, which is the second part of philosophy. As to the third part, ethics,[22] if men were to follow this philosophy — which eliminates the virtues, or at least makes them the servants of pleasure — the human race would not only not be preserved, it would be completely destroyed. For could anyone who made pleasure his only purpose maintain friendship and loyalty, work for justice, persist in courage, and exercise self-restraint? Of necessity, surely, either

nentiam possit? Necesse certe est aut nihil esse virtutem aut propter se, non propter voluptatem, esse expetendam.

15   Nunc principia dicam Peripateticorum ac veterum Academicorum, quos nomine dumtaxat differre inter se iam dictum est. Triplicem igitur philosophandi rationem, de vita et moribus, de natura deque veri falsique iudicio (id est de dialectica sive logica, ut
Graeci dicunt, nos de disputativa sive rationali possumus verbum e
verbo exprimentes dicere), acceptam a principe Platone servave-
runt. Beate vivere dixerunt omnia e natura esse consecutum, quorum erat tripartita ratio, animi, corporis et vitae. Animi bona in
duas dividebant partes ut essent quaedam natura, ut memoria et
discendi intelligendique celeritas, quaedam consuetudine, ut studia exercitationisque assiduitas et ratio (quae philosophia est), in
qua progressio quaedam est ad virtutem. Virtus enim ipsa perfec-
tio est omniumque rerum quas studio et assiduitate et ratione inquirimus consecutio. Ergo in ea esse beatam vitam voluerunt, non
tamen beatissimam, nisi corporis et quae ad vitam tuendam exor-
nandamque pertinent bona adderentur. Et corporis quidem bona
vel in toto esse dicebant, ut valitudinem, vires, pulchritudinem; vel
in partibus, ut in pedibus celeritatem, in manibus vim, in voce cla-
ritudinem, in oculis, auribus, naribus ceterisque sensibus integritatem quandam et praestantiam requirebant. Vitae autem bona
quae diximus, ea iam usitatiore vocabulo fortunae appellant, quae
si non beatam interturbare vitam possunt, beatissimam tamen, ut
dixi, et afferre possunt, si cum ceteris adsint, et auferre, si non adsint. Atque hoc quidem pacto veteres Academici de moribus; a
quibus si quid differre putent Peripateticos, longissime a vero ab-
sint necesse est.

virtue is nothing or it is pursued for its own sake, not that of pleasure.

Now let me state the principal doctrines of the Peripatetics and 15
the Old Academy, whose purely nominal differences I have already
explained. From their founder Plato they inherited and passed on
a threefold division of philosophy: moral philosophy, natural philosophy, and judging what is true and false, that is, dialectic or
logic, as the Greeks called it, which we may express literally as
"disputational" or rational philosophy. They said that to live happily comes from seeking all goods according to their natures, of
which there are three kinds: goods of the mind, of the body, and
of life.[23] They divided the goods of the mind into two kinds: natural ones like memory and quickness in learning and understanding, and acquired ones like study and zealous practice and rational
activity (which is philosophy), through which there is a certain
progress toward virtue. For virtue itself is a perfection and an or-
derly sequencing of all the things we apply ourselves to study and
think about. So they maintained that the good life consisted in
these things, but it was not perfectly good unless the goods of the
body and the things that preserve and enhance life were added to
it. The goods of the body they said either consisted in the body as
a whole — as in health, strength, and beauty — or were required in
its parts — as in, for example, the runner's speed, the strength of
one's hands, the clarity of the voice, and a certain soundness and
excellence of the eyes, ears, and nose, and other senses. As to the
good things in living mentioned above, these they call by the more
usual expression "the goods of fortune." While [the absence of]
these cannot disrupt the happy life, their presence can confer perfect happiness in life, and their absence can take perfect happiness
away. These were the views of the Old Academy on ethics, and
anyone who thinks the Peripatetics thought differently on these
matters is of necessity far from the truth.

16   Naturam autem, quae fuit secunda pars, bifariam considerabant. Illam enim in vim dividebant et materiam, alterumque dicebant in altero inesse, quod nulla materia sine vi aliqua neque vis intelligi sine materia ullo pacto possit. Quae ex his constarent corpora appellabant qualitates. Sic enim interpretatur Cicero quas illi vocant ποιότητες. Qualitatum autem alias primas esse, alias ex primis ortas. Primas dicebant ignem, aerem, aquam, terram, easque esse simplices et eodem modo. Ex his ortos animantes et cetera quae in terris videmus generata. Rursus ex primis simplicibus quaedam vim habere efficiendi, ut est ignis et aer, quaedam recipiendi et quasi patiendi, cuiusmodi aqua et terra est. Quintam quandam speciem, quam appellavit entelechiam Aristoteles, posuerunt, ex eaque mentes et sidera constare putaverunt, eamque esse semotam ab omni illa concretione et materia, quam qualitatem nuncupavimus. Factum mundum divina quadam vi quam eandem animam mundi dicunt et deum administrarique atque esse sempiternum. Quam illi vim modo necessitatem, modo fatum, nonnunquam fortunam vocare consueverunt.

17   Tertiam vero philosophiae partem de disserendo oriri e sensibus volebant, tamen verum iudicium veri a falso dignoscendi habere mentem eique soli esse credendum quod simplicitatem in rebus sola posset cernere (hanc illi vocabant ideam) et scientiam quidem in mente esse. Nam quae orirentur a sensibus opinabilia omnia voluerunt. Itaque ad inveniendum quod verum esset tum diffinitionibus, tum vi vocabuli quam etymologiam vocant, tum argumentis utebantur, necnon etiam orationem nonnunquam perpetuam adhibebant more paene oratorio.

18   Zeno autem, ut iam dicam de Stoicis, verum iudicium petendum dixit a sensibus, quibus quod comprehensum esset (hoc enim verbo utebatur), si divelli ratione non posset, appellabat scientiam,

They saw the second branch of philosophical study, nature, as   16
twofold. For they divided it into power and matter, each being
present in the other: for no matter can be conceived of at all
without some sort of power, and no power without matter. The
bodies which are formed by these two they called "qualities,"
which is how Cicero translated the Greek word *poiotetai*.[24] There
are primary qualities, and secondary ones deriving from the first.
They said the primary ones were fire, air, water, and earth, which
are uniform and act consistently. From these spring animate things
and the rest of what we see produced on earth. Of the primary qualities, fire and air have a power of acting, while water and
earth are naturally receptive and passive. They also posited a certain fifth essence, which Aristotle called an entelechy, of which
they thought minds and stars consisted, and this they thought
to be quite separate from everything composite and material,
which we have called quality. They thought the world was made
by a certain divine power which they say is the same as the
World Soul and a god, and they say it governs the world and is
sempiternal. They used to call this power sometimes necessity,
sometimes fate, and occasionally fortune.

The third part of philosophy they thought arose from discourse   17
and the senses, but that the judgment that distinguishes truth
from falsehood belonged to the mind. It alone was to be trusted
because it alone could discern the simple essence of things (which
they called its idea), and knowledge is in the mind. They considered conjectural all the knowledge gained from the senses. So to
find the truth they relied now on definitions, now on the meaning
of words (which they called etymology), and now on arguments;
and sometimes even used long speeches almost in the manner of
orators.

To turn now to the Stoics, Zeno said that true judgment must   18
rely on the senses. If what is "grasped" (that is the word he used)
cannot be separated from the senses by reason, he call this knowl-

sin divelli et labefactari posset ratione, inscientiam, ex qua fieret opinio cum falso et incognito communis. Medium inter scientiam atque inscientiam esse dixit καταληψιν, id est comprehensionem quandam, quae fit a sensibus in quibus a natura nobis principia essent data cognoscendi et in animis postea notiones imprimendi. Removit penitus ab omni errore sapientem. De moribus autem hic in sola virtute summum bonum ponit nec praeter virtutem quicquam esse bonum. Reliqua vero genera, tum contra, tum secundum naturam, tum interiecta et media appellat. Quae secundum naturam essent digna esse aliqua existimatione; contraque contraria; media vero momenti habere in sese nihil. Rursus quae aliqua dignarentur existimatione, aut pluris esse aut minoris; quae pluris praeposita, quae minoris reiecta appellabat. Aegritudines animi, quas Graeci appellant τὰ πάθη, Cicero perturbationes, nonnulli passiones, non natura inesse animis putavit ut superiores, sed earum omnium immoderatam quandam cupiditatem esse causam. Ab his igitur omnibus longe abesse sapientem. De natura autem (id enim reliquum est), ad quatuor illa principia nihil addebat. Ignem putabat esse ex quo omnia orirentur atque eundem deum. Nam praeter id quod videri sensibus posset nihil esse contendit. Quaecunque efficerentur sine corpore effici non posse. Qua de re commotum Archesilam contra omnia disputasse supra diximus principemque mediae extitisse Academiae.

19   Haec sunt quae breviter ex probatissimis decerpta auctoribus de sectis habui quae dicerem. Quae si dicta tibi videbuntur obscurius, partim rebus ipsis, partim brevitati, cui imprimis consului ne modum excederet epistola, assignabis.

edge; but if reason can so separate and undermine the sensible impression, he called it non-knowledge, whence comes opinion, something akin to falsehood and ignorance. The mean between knowledge and non-knowledge he called [by the Greek word] *katalepsis*, that is, a kind of grasping, which is done by the senses, in which are the principles given us by nature of knowing and of afterwards imprinting notions on our minds.[25] He denied utterly that the wise man is subject to error. As for ethics, he placed the highest good in virtue alone, and said there is no good besides virtue. All other kinds of good he called either unnatural or natural, or something between the two and in the middle. Natural goods he thought worthy of consideration, but not the unnatural ones; as for the intermediate goods, he thought they had no intrinsic value. Again, those which deserve some esteem are either of greater or of lesser value; the former he called *praeposita* or "preferences," the latter *reiecta* or "things to be rejected."[26] The disturbances of mind—which the Greeks called *ta pathe*, and Cicero called "perturbations," and some other people call "passions"—he did not believe to be naturally present in minds, but rather caused by uncontrolled desire.[27] Hence the wise man keeps himself well apart from all these. As for the last part of philosophy, nature, Zeno added nothing to the four elements posited by others. He thought that all things arise from fire, and that it was God. And he maintained that nothing exists except what appears to the senses. No effects take place apart from bodies. As we have said, Arcesilaus was moved by this to argue against it all and so to found the Middle Academy.

These, then, in brief are the ideas I have excerpted as promised 19 from the best authors concerning the schools of philosophy. If these remarks seem to you rather obscure, ascribe it to the subject matter itself or to the brevity I imposed on myself as appropriate to a letter.

20   Nunc vero tandem id est reliquum, ut in quam me familiam philosophando contulerim quibusque maxime adhaeserim ad te rescribam. Non possum non admirari omnibus in rebus antiquorum inventa philosophorum, eorumque maxime qui, magistro Platone, quem semideum appellavit Labeo, tanta tamque abscondita de divinis humanisque rebus nobis scripta reliquerunt. Sed tamen cum sint nonnulla quae reprobat Christiana veritas, necesse est ab illis nonnunquam recedere ac Christo optimo maximo, qui vera sapientia est, ita coniungi ut, cunctis antiquorum deletis erroribus, veri simus in ipso sapientes. Nam qui aliter philosophari volet, obrutus sententiarum infinitissima diversitate vel certe falsis quibusdam maximisque imbutus rebus, cum se scire maxime putaverit, erit insipiens maxime, dicetque in corde suo, Non est Deus.

21   Multa sunt profecto inter praeclarissimas Platonis sententias quae ne dicam puerilia, certe tanta caeterarum quae ab eo scripta sunt rerum maiestate videntur indigna, de mundo, de anima, de diis. Ut enim omittam cetera, quis non explodat audiens de hominis anima in alias pecudes ridiculas transmigrationes? Quis risum contineat qui audiat purgatissimam iam animam rursus in hanc corporis labem turpissimumque carcerem velle redire? Unde nec immerito mirantem facit Aeneam Virgilius, cum illam de Anchise patre sententiam accepisset. Inquit enim:

> O pater, anne aliquas ad caelum hinc ire putandum est
> sublimes animas iterumque ad tarda reverti
> corpora? Quae lucis miseris tam dira cupido?

Quam opinionem non Christiani solum improbarunt, sed ex ipsis Platonicis Porphyrius non ignobilis, qui et animas eorum qui recte honesteque vixissent perpetuis illis itionibus reditionibusque liberavit, et caeterorum qui vitiis animam inquinavissent in alia homi-

Now what remains is to tell you which family of philosophers I   20
am most inclined to follow and stick to the most. I cannot help
admiring the views of the ancient philosophers about all topics,
and especially those who, following their master Plato (whom
Labeo[28] called semi-divine), left us so many profound and recon-
dite writings about matters divine and human. Since, however,
some of these writings reject Christian truth, we must sometimes
turn away from these and adhere to Christ, the best and greatest,
who is true wisdom, so that condemning all the errors of the ancients, we may be truly wise in Him. For anyone who wishes to
philosophize otherwise will be confounded by the infinite diversity
of views and will surely absorb some very false ones, since he will
come to think himself supremely wise, being in fact supremely
foolish, and will say in his heart, "There is no God."[29]

Indeed, there are many among Plato's brilliant thoughts about   21
the world, the soul, and the gods which, if not exactly puerile, certainly seem unworthy to stand beside the majesty of other things
he has written. To leave aside other examples, who would not condemn the ridiculous idea of transmigration, of human souls entering into beasts? Who can keep from laughing when he hears that
the now-purified soul wishes to return again into this corrupt and
shameful prison that is the body? That is why Virgil's Aeneas
quite rightly marvels when he hears the opinion of his father
Anchises. For he says:

> O father! Can it be that souls sublime
> Return to visit our terrestrial clime;
> And that the generous mind, released by death,
> Can covet lazy limbs, and mortal breath?[30]

This is an idea rejected not only by Christians, but even by the
Platonists themselves, like the noble Porphyry, who frees the souls
of those who live rightly and honorably from these repeated com-
ings and goings, and maintains that the rest, who have stained

num corpora, non quarumque etiam pecudum, ut Plato migrare voluit.

22   De paenis quoque aberrarunt Platonici, quas dixerunt esse omnes ad tempus et, ut ita dicam, purgatorias, cum sint, ut Christiani verissime testantur, multae sempiternae, ut ait divus Augustinus in libro undevigesimo *De civitate Dei,* etsi memini me legisse in *Phaedone* apud Platonem in Tartarum ita deici nonnullos ob scelerum in vita perpetratorum magnitudinem ut inde nunquam egrediantur. Et Virgilius illud quoque e Platonis sententia dixisse videtur:

> sedet aeternumque sedebit
> infelix Theseus.

Verum inter hos diiudicare non huius est temporis neque disputationis. Nos in praesentiarum, ne qua in re labamur, Augustino adhaerescimus.

23   Aberrant etiam cum animam a summo Deo, corpus autem a diis, quos Plato appellat secundos, factum esse profitentur. Scriptum est enim: 'fecit hominem ad imaginem et similitudinem suam'; neque homo sine corpore, cum ex animo constet et corpore, a Deo creatus esse potuit. Aberrant etiam neque sibi videntur constare cum asserunt animas corpore liberatas ab omni esse perturbatione longe alienas — corporea enim sublata contagione defaecatas penitus evolare dicunt — et audent deinde addere rursus sic purgatas appetere coniunctionem corporum. Quo enim pacto appetant et vacent omni perturbatione intelligi non potest.

24   Quae cum ita sint, sequor Christianos, quorum est omnibus de rebus sententia divinior. Neque tamen is sum qui antiquorum scripta philosophorum negligenda putem, sed imitandae mihi videntur apes, ut ait Basilius, quae in adeundis floribus et delectum habent florum et ex singulis id assumunt quod melli faciundo aptum vident. Sunt enim multa a Platone, ab Aristotele, a Zenone,

their souls with vices, return to other human bodies—not, as Plato taught, to those of various beasts.

The Platonists also erred on the subject of punishments. They 22 said that all punishments are temporary and are purgatorial, as it were. But as Christians testify with utter truth, many are eternal, as St. Augustine says in the nineteenth book of the *City of God*— although I remember reading in Plato's *Phaedo* that some souls, because of the great crimes they committed in life, are cast down into Tartarus in such a way that they are never able to escape it.[31] And Virgil seems to agree with Plato's opinion:

Unhappy Theseus doomed for ever, there
Is fixed by Fate, on his eternal chair.[32]

But this is not the time or the place for us to sort these things out. For the present, I stick to St. Augustine, lest I lapse into error.

They also go astray who avow that the highest God made our 23 souls, but that our bodies were made by what Plato calls secondary gods. For it is written, "He made man after his image and likeness;"[33] and man cannot been made by God without a body, since man consists of both body and soul. They all are mistaken and inconsistent when they claim that souls freed from the body are unaffected by all perturbation—for they say the soul flies away from the body free of all contamination and filth—and then dare to add that, so cleansed, it longs to return once more to union with the body. How the soul could long for this and also be free of all perturbation it is impossible to understand.

In consequence I follow the Christians, whose thinking on all 24 these mattters is the more divine. Not that I am the sort of person who thinks the ancient philosophical writings should be set aside; my view is that we should imitate the bees, as Basil says, who as they go from flower to flower, make a choice and take from each flower what seems most suitable to making honey.[34] There are many really divine sentiments to be found in Plato, Aristotle,

ab Archesila, a Carneade, nonnulla etiam ab Epicuro scripta sane divinitus. Aberrarunt etiam in multis; ego vero neque propter errata arbitror etiam optima esse illorum praecepta deserenda, neque rursum ob ea quae ab illis scripta sunt praeclare, tanquam hamo pisces, ita nos committere ut improvidi et incauti, falsa pro veris admittentes, mortem obsorbeamus sempiternam. Igitur plane Christianus ita per prata gradior gentilium philosophorum ut continuo existimem letalem in herba et floribus latitantem anguem pedibus pressum nudis in me posse concitari.

Bene et diu vale. Ex Florentia octavo kalendas Maias MCCCCLVIII.

Finis.

Zeno, Arcesilaus, Carneades, and even in Epicurus. They too err in many of their ideas, but I do not think that their errors should cause us to leave behind their best teachings. On the other hand, like fish who swallow bait, we should not, because of the brilliant things they have written, unwisely and incautiously accept falsehoods as truths, and feed on eternal death. Clearly, then, as a Christian, I should walk in the meadows of the pagan philosophers in such a way that I am continuously aware that a deadly snake may be hiding amid the leaves and flowers, which could attack me if I tread on it with bare feet.

May you prosper and live long. From Florence, 24 April 1458.

The End.

Ducendane sit uxor sapienti

1 Petro Medici salutem.

Ducendane sit uxor sapienti video omnes paene mortales velle cognoscere. Omnes enim ita cupiunt esse sapientes, ut hi quoque, qui stultissimi et sunt et habentur, vehementer sapientiae laude delectentur, etsi falluntur saepissime opinione ut, dum se maxime putant esse sapientes, ea faciant quibus nihil stultius excogitari possit. Sed quoniam volumus omnes esse sapientes, ducendane sit uxor sapienti nullus profecto est qui velit ignorare.

2 Qua quidem de re, siquis quid sentias te roget, profecto penitus desipiat. Etenim quam haberes de ducenda uxore opinionem, facto potius ipso quam verbo declarasti. Quod quoniam video mihi contra tuam hanc sententiam esse disputandum, tardiorem paulo me reddidit ad scribendum, quamvis existimo me ea esse dicturum quae non multum, ac fortasse nihil, ab eo quod tu sentis iamque confirmasti opere abhorrebunt.

3 Tu velim attento animo sis nihilque existimes scribenti mihi accidere posse gratius quam ea efferre quae neque speculanti tibi a veritate videantur aliena et legentem non sine voluptate paulum occupatum teneant. Principio, ne vagans nutare nostra videatur oratio, diffiniendum mihi esse videtur quid constituamus esse sapientem. Cum vero considero et Milesium Thaletem et Pittacum Mitylenaeum et ceteros qui septem appellantur apud Graecos sapientum nomen fuisse adeptos, cogor ita diffinire sapientem ut qui investigandis naturae causis, quod illi fecerunt, moribus paulo ceteris melioribus sit deditus, is dignus hoc nomine esse censeatur. Nullus enim ante Socratem, qui fuit Archelai discipulus, qui ab Thalete quintus Ionicae philosophiae principe extitit, nisi de natura rerum disputavit; Socrates primus de moribus. Quis igitur? Putabimusne esse sapientes qui naturae indagant causas? An po-

Whether a Wise Man Should Marry

Greetings to Piero de' Medici.[1]   1

Almost all mortal men would like to know, I think, whether a wise man should marry. For all wish to be wise, so much so that even those who are quite stupid and are generally viewed as such would love to be praised for wisdom — although they are very often deceived in that belief, because while they think themselves wise they do the stupidest things imaginable. Since we all want to be wise, however, there is no one who would not care to know whether a wise man should marry.

If someone asks *you* your opinion on this, he is certainly a fool.   2 For what you think about marrying you have shown by deed rather than by word. But seeing that I must argue against your opinion on this matter, I have been a little slow to write, although what I have to say, I think, will contrast very little, if at all, from what you think and have now confirmed in practice.

I want you to pay close attention and to reckon that I could not   3 be more pleased if you as a thinker find my words consonant with the truth, and if you as a reader find they keep you pleasurably occupied for a time. But first, to keep my discourse from wandering about incoherently, I had better define what we mean by a wise man. When I think of Thales of Miletus and Pittacus of Mitylene and the rest of those the Greeks honored as the Seven Sages, I am compelled to define the wise man as one who, like these men, searches out nature's causes but whose concern for morality is little more than that of other men. For no one before Socrates, who was a disciple of Archelaus (the fifth in succession after Thales, the founder of Ionian philosophy), discussed anything but natural philosophy; Socrates for the first time took up the question of how to live.[2] Who then is the wise man? Shall we think those who

tius adhaerebimus Pythagorae Samio, qui negavit hominem esse posse sapientem, quoniam hoc quidem in solo Deo reperiretur? Proindeque qui inveniendi veri studio flagrarent, non *sophos* sed *philosophos,* id est sapientiae studiosos, ut Cicero interpretatur, nuncupari primus voluit. Quod si placet nobis haec Pythagorae sententia, quae ab eo quod est in sacris isdemque verissimis litteris non abhorret, ubi legitur sapientiam huius mundi a Deo stultam esse factam, procul dubio omnis de capienda uxore sapienti est sublata controversia. Quomodo enim ducet uxorem sapiens si nullus est praeter Deum sapiens? Verum tamen cum dicitur ducendane est sapienti uxor, non de illa intelligi puto sapientia quae in Deo tantummodo reperitur, sed de communi quadam quam homines quoque studio amoreque veri inveniendi consequuntur. Si vero hoc modo intelligimus, citare iam incipiam Epicurum, qui, quoniam in voluptate summum bonum ponit, non debet parvam hac in re habere auctoritatem.

4   Sapiens enim is, de quo loquimur, nihil magis omni studio conquirit quam quietem animi atque tranquillitatem, quam si voluptatem appellasset Epicurus, nihil omnino differet ab his philosophis quos laudamus omnes atque admiramur. Dicit igitur uxores esse in bonorum malorumque confinio; et quoniam non debet unquam in dubium venire sapiens, numquam ducenda uxor erit sapienti. Quod si quis negarit in confinio bonorum malorumque positas uxores, de eo iam nihil disputamus. Non enim video quomodo possit sapere qui hoc negarit.

5   An dicet fortasse quispiam non dubium esse quin omnes sint malae? Aberrabit longe si quis hoc dicet. Quemadmodum enim paulo post ostendam, etiam laudatissimae feminae repertae sunt hodieque reperiuntur. An dicet potius omnes bonas? Multos habebit suae sententiae insectatores atque expugnatores si quis id asserit. Quo enim ore contra dicturum esse putas Agamemnonem, Graecorum regem, quem a Troiano redeuntem incendio Clytem-

explore nature are wise? Or shall we perhaps follow Pythagoras of Samos, who denied that man can be wise at all, since wisdom is found in God alone? He was the first who wished to be called not *sophos* [wise man] but *philosophos* — which Cicero translates as "lovers of wisdom" — a man burning with the desire to find out the truth.[3] If we accept the opinion of Pythagoras, which is not far from the most true and holy Scriptures — where we read that the wisdom of this world is made foolishness by God[4] — doubtless this whole question of a wise man marrying falls away. If no one is wise except God, how can a wise man take a wife? In truth, when I discuss whether a wise man should take a wife, I do not refer to that wisdom which is found only in God, but to the common kind that men attain in their zeal and devotion to find the truth. Understanding the matter thus, I may start with Epicurus, who, since he considered pleasure the supreme good, should possess no small authority on this subject.

The wise man of whom we speak pursues nothing more diligently than peace of mind and tranquillity, and if this is what Epicurus meant by pleasure, he was not much different from the philosophers we all praise and admire. He then says that wives are on the borderline between good and bad, and since the wise man should always avoid actions admitting of doubt, the wise man will never marry.[5] If anyone denies that wives are on the border between good and bad, we will not even argue with him. For I do not see how anyone who denies this can be wise. 4

Perhaps someone will put the question: aren't they clearly all bad? Anyone who says this will be far from right. I shall show in a little while that one can find in history women worthy of the highest praise, and they are still found today. Or will someone assert that they are all good? There will be plenty of people to contradict that opinion and challenge him outright. Do you think, someone would dare counter the example of Agamemnon, the king of the Greeks? When he returned from the burning of Troy, 5

nestra uxor, quod Aegistum illi sacerdotem in amore praeferret, dolo aggressa, adiutore adultero sacerdote, interfecit? Quo ore Amphiaraum vatem, qui cum se abscondisset ne ad Thebanum proficisceretur bellum (noverat enim in eo se, si ivisset, esse peritu-rum) eamque rem omnes celasset mortales praeter Eriphilem uxo-rem, post longam tandem perquisitionem, corrupta Eriphile mo-nili illo, quod Statius ait per longam successionem omnibus qui illud habuerunt male evenisse, virum manifestavit? Ex quo cum necesse illi esset ad bellum proficisci, paulo post, dehiscente terra, vivus absorptus est. Et, ut recedam a fabulis, Actoria Paula, humili loco nata, Catone censorio coniugi superba esse potuit. Utrum laudabit Actoriae superbiam Cato dicetque non in confinio esse, ut ait Epicurus, uxores, sed esse omnes bonas? Profecto non dicet. Philippum quoque Macedonum,[1] Alexandri eius patrem, cui ob res gestas Magno fuit cognomen, dicunt aliquando ad uxorem in-troeuntem ab irata fuisse exclusum, atque illum nihil dixisse, sed versu tragico hanc iniuriam fuisse persecutum. Iratam dicet uxo-rem bonam Philippus, qui tot populorum iras dominavit?

6   Non opus esse arbitror ut plura exempla accumulem. Sentio enim non multum te adhibere fidei Epicuro, neque immerito, si in suavibus titillationibus corporis summum bonum, ut omnes fere dicunt, ponit. Nulla enim vox potuit esse abiectior et, ut mihi quidem videtur, effeminatior, ac magis coquo et pistore, nedum philosopho, digna sententia. At eodem non poteris pacto effugisse Theophrastum, nobilissimum Aristotelis discipulum Peripateti-cumque et doctum, et quod illius quoque nomen testatur, elegan-tem. Is igitur in libro quem scripsit *De nuptiis*, sapienti nunquam ducendam putat uxorem nisi cum pulchra est, cum bene morata, cum honestis orta parentibus, cum tandem sapiens qui ducturus

his wife Clytemnestra, who preferred her lover Aegisthus, ambushed and slew her husband with the help of that adulterous priest. How would one dare counter the case of Amphiaraus the seer? Knowing that if he went to the Theban War he would perish, he hid himself and kept his secret from all mortals except his wife, Eriphile; but after a long search, she finally betrayed him, having been bribed with a necklace — which Statius says passed through many hands, bringing disaster to all who possessed it.[6] As a result, when Amphiarus had to go to war a little later, the earth opened up and swallowed him. But let me leave mythology. Actoria Paula, born in a humble station, was able to become the over-proud wife of Cato the Censor. Will someone praise Actoria's haughtiness and say to Cato that wives are not on the border between good and bad, as Epicurus declared, but all good?[7] No, indeed. They say Philip of Macedon, too — father of Alexander, who for his deeds is called the Great — was once locked out by his angry wife, but said nothing of it but sought to requite the injury with a verse from a tragedy.[8] Will someone say that the angry wife of Philip, a man who restrained the fury of so many peoples, was good?

I don't think I need to pile on more examples. I feel, moreover, 6 that you do not put much faith in Epicurus, and you are right not to, if, as almost all accept, he placed the highest good in pleasant titillations of the body. No statement could be more degraded and, in my view, effeminate; the opinion is more suited to a cook or a baker than to a philosopher.[9] But you cannot escape in the same way Theophrastus, the noblest disciple of Aristotle, a learned Peripatetic and, as his very name indicates,[10] an elegant writer. In the treatise he wrote *On Marriage*, he says that a wise man should never take a wife unless she is beautiful, of good character, and sprung from honorable parents, while the wise man who plans to marry should be of excellent and sturdy health.[11] But it is

sit valetudine sit optima ac confirmatissima. At haec raro reperiuntur simul omnia. Raro igitur concludit sapienti ineunda coniugia.

7   Raro, inquis, Theophraste? Quid si nunquam reperiri quattuor illa simul possunt? Ut enim omittam pulchritudinem – quae et ipsa, si morbos aufugerit, tamen, ut corrumpatur aetate necesse est, sicque vivendum sapienti, etsi duxerit pulchram uxorem, cum deformi – morum profecto nulla potest esse certa vestigatio. Ad hoc enim, quod quotidie, in iuvenculis praesertim, immutantur, merito conqueritur idem Theophrastus ceterarum omnium fere rerum faciliorem nobis esse perscrutationem. Asinum, bovem, equum, agrum, domum et cetera huius generis si emere velimus, omni diligentia adhibita vitia prius virtutesque rimamur, idque etiam hominum consuetudine ita probatur ut dignos laude existimemus cautosque, quod dolos caveant, appellamus, si qui in eiuscemodi rebus decipi se non sinant. Solas uxores prius habere oportet quam quicquam tibi ostendatur, sive corporis praeter faciem – quam etiam nescio an unquam apertam ac non potius fucatam inviscatamque conspicias (unde inquit Iuvenalis, 'Et miseri viscantur labra mariti') – sive ingenii, quo nihil est occultius.

8   Illis enim, vel docentibus matribus vel nutricibus instituentibus vel ipsis per se natura ad fallendum aptissimis, nihil est ex omnibus rebus simulatius ut ne lacrimae quidem desint si necesse sit. Sed nolim in his rebus esse longus, quae et in promptu sunt omnibus et ab doctissimis viris et Latina et nostra lingua decantata. Quod si tibi impudicis sit uxor moribus, ut videtur Iuvenalis omnes fere impudicas asserere, cum inquit:

> Tarpeium limen adora
> Pronus et auratam Iunoni caede iuvencam
> Si tibi contigerit capitis matrona pudici!

rare for all these conditions to be fulfilled. He concluded, therefore, that a wise man should rarely enter into marriage.

Rarely, do you say, Theophrastus? What if these four condi- 7 tions can never be found together? Let me leave out beauty, for even if it escapes illness, it is necessarily eroded by age, so that even the wise man who marries a beautiful woman must eventually live with an ugly one. As for her character, there is no sure way to find it out. In this respect people change every day, especially the young, so that Theophrastus rightly complains that almost anything else would be easier to find out. If we want to buy an ass, moreover, or a cow, a horse, a field, a house, and other things like this, we make every effort first to examine its faults as well as its virtues, and this is sanctioned by custom so that men praise such buyers as wary (*cauti*) because they beware (*caveant*) of deceptions and don't let themselves be cheated about things like this. Only in the case of a wife is one expected to take her without being shown anything of her first, either of her body, beyond her face, or her mind, than which nothing is more hidden. Even in the case of her face I don't know whether you ever see a woman really uncovered rather than painted and sticky with makeup, whence Juvenal says, "And the poor husband's lips get stuck."[12]

For whether women are taught by mothers or nurses or by their 8 own natural talent for deceit, nothing in the world dissembles more than they, and even their tears will appear as needed. I do not wish to dwell on these things, however, which are well known to everyone and have been often repeated by learned men in Latin and in our language. Yet what if your wife behaves unchastely? Juvenal seems to assert that nearly all of them do, when he says:

You should worship at the Tarpeian threshold,
And kill a heifer with gilt horns for Juno
If you happen to get a chaste wife![13]

41

Si erit, inquam, impudica, quas pariet viro voluptates, id est quas aegritudines, quas curas! Sin id eo nesciente, ut plurimum accidit, quae ludibria excitantur, qui moventur risus! Metella, L. Sullae coniunx, palam erat impudica, quod, cum decantaretur Athenis, solus Romae ignorabat. Postremi enim, ut ait divus Hieronymus, ex quo magna ex parte haec excerpsimus, de malis nostris certiores simus. Infinita paene impudicitiae exempla de industria praetereo, tum quod notissimum vitium est ac vulgatissimum, tum quod vix sine rubore huiuscemodi vitia vel ipse referre vel audire ab aliis possum.

9   Honestatis autem parentum valitudinisque ipsius, qui uxorem sit ducturus, etsi diversa ratio est, quoniam non sit difficile id cognoscere et singula ipsa per se non rarissime reperiuntur, tamen ut haec cum illis pariter congreges, non parva et prudentia opus est atque fortuna, ut merito colligi omnibus ex his rebus possit. Non raro, quod inquit Theophrastus, verum nunquam, quoniam non possint omnia concurrere, si pulchritudo ad tempus necessario aufertur, vel saltem quod prius quam experiamur quaedam esse cognita non possunt, ut disputavimus de moribus, ducendam esse uxorem sapienti. Quid est enim ab eo, qui hoc nomine dignus esse velit, alienius quam temere, ut ita dixerim, ei coniungi feminae quae animi quietudinem non tantum possit interturbare, sed auferre penitus miserrimumque efficere?

10   Sed iam video quibusdam mihi esse respondendum qui uxorum commoda in medium adducunt. Imprimisque occurrit illa ratio, quam usurpare omnes solent: propter liberos procreandos coniugia esse admittenda. Hoc vero sapiens nihil existimabit. Quid si etiam refugiat, ne qua in incommoda incidendum sit? Si enim boni erunt, metuendum, ne amittantur,[2] erit. Qui si amittentur,

If she is unchaste, what delight, I declare, she will offer her husband — I mean what anguish, what anxiety! And if the husband, as usually happens, is ignorant of her conduct, what a joke, what a laughing-stock he will be! Metella, the wife of Sulla, was openly unchaste, and yet, while the rumor ran all through Athens, he alone in Rome was unaware of the fact. We only learn of our misfortunes afterwards, as St. Jerome says, from whom I have cited most of these instances.[14] I intentionally omit the almost infinite number of examples of unchastity, however, both because this vice is widely known and practiced, and because I cannot talk or hear about such misbehavior without blushing.

The case is different with the respectability of the parents and 9 the health of the man who is going to marry, since this is not hard to know and individual instances are not in themselves extremely rare. Nevertheless, when you put these things together with the others on an equal basis, there is need for no small amount of prudence and good fortune to be able to unite all these things as they should be. The wise man should marry, not rarely, as Theophrastus writes, but never, since all these things cannot coincide if beauty necessarily fades with time, or at least if certain qualities cannot not be known beforehand, as we have observed about her character.[15] Now what is more alien to a man who wishes to be worthy of the name of a wise man than to live in fear, as it were, that the woman he marries will not merely disturb his peace of mind, but may almost completely destroy it and make him utterly miserable?

But I see that now I must respond to those who would bring up 10 the advantages of marriage. The first thing that comes to mind is the reason that everyone usually cites: marriages are permitted for the procreation of children. But to the wise man this will be nothing. What does it matter if he even flees it to avoid disadvantages? For if indeed his offspring are good, he must fear that he will lose them. If he loses them, the wise man will surely suffer. They say

43

dolendum erit profecto sapienti. Nam quod de Torquato ferunt, iussisse securi percuti filium quod contra ipsius imperium pugnasset in hostes, neque id sine ipsius lacrimis factum fuisse reor, sed iustitiae gloria, sed patriae mores coegerunt. An existimamus M. Pulvillum, quod victus gloria fortiter respondit, cum ei aedem Iovi et Iunoni et Minervae aedificanti falsus de morte filii afferretur nuntius, ut, ipso dolore perculso, eius aedificii laudem collega usurparet (inquit enim 'vel insepultus proiiciatur'), falso etiam nuntio (quod tamen sibi erat incognitum) non fuisse commotum? Immanitas ac feritas quaedam esset ista, non fortitudo. Sin malos contingat ut habeas filios, quid poterit esse miserius?

11   At referent filii post mortem patris nomen. Hoc vero nihil ad sapientem; et innumerabiles profecto sunt qui eodem appellentur nomine. Suave tamen credo est domi nutrire heredem senectutisque malorum levamen ac solatium. Sed nulli meliores ac suaviores esse possunt heredes quam amici, quos eligas, non quos velis nolis habere cogaris. Moses quoque ac Samuel filiis suis alios praetulerunt, nec habuerunt pro liberis quos ingratos esse Deo animadverterunt. Solatia vero cum exoptantur senectutis, frequentissime odio sumus, mortuosque magis gauderent quam vivos consolare⟨n⟩tur. Nolo persequi omnes filiorum incommoditates, ne sim longior et librum potius componere quam epistolam scribere ad te videar, praesertim cum multa restent ad quae festinat oratio.

12   Nam de vindicanda ab solitudine vita multa cum dicunt, frustra videntur verba effutire. Ut enim de Scipione scripsisse Catonem Cicero affirmat, nunquam minus solus est sapiens quam cum solus est. Num vitae iucunditati est consulendum? Maxima scilicet est

that Torquatus ordered the beheading of his own son because he had attacked the enemy against his father's orders. But I think he did this not without tears, and only because the glory of justice and the customs of his country demanded it.[16] And what about Marcus Pulvillus? While he was building a temple to Jove and Juno and Minerva, he was sent a false report of the death of his son, so that while he was stricken with grief his colleague might usurp credit for the building. Overcome by thirst for glory his courageous response was "Let him be cast out unburied, if you like." But do we think Pulvillus was unmoved by that false report (which he did not know was false)? That would have been brutality and savagery, not bravery.[17] And if you happen to have bad sons, what could be more miserable?

But the son will carry on the name of the father after death. 11 But this is nothing to a wise man; surely there are countless men with the same name. I believe, however, that it sweet to nurture an heir at home as a comfort and solace for the evils of old age. Yet heirs can be no better or more comforting than friends, whom you choose and are not forced to accept whether you like them or not. Moses and Samuel, indeed, preferred others to their own sons, and did not even consider as their children those whom they found unpleasing to God. Though we hope for solace in old age, most often we inspire hatred, and they rejoice at our death more than they console us alive. I do not wish to review all the disadvantages of sons, lest I become too long-winded and appear to write you a book rather than a letter, especially since many topics remain, towards which my discourse hastens.

As to the idea that is often expressed about marriage saving us 12 from solitude, it seems a waste of words to reply. According to Cicero, Cato wrote of Scipio that the wise man is never less alone than when he is alone.[18] So should we not consider the pleasures of life? Right: there is enormous pleasure to be had, of course, if

45

iucunditas, si tibi morosa obvenerit, semper in litibus atque iurgiis vitam degere! Ac fortasse verum est quod ait Iuvenalis,

> Semper habet lites alternaque iurgia lectus
> In quo nupta iacet; minimum dormitur in illo

et quae sequuntur. Xanthippe certe ac Miro, Aristidis neptis, Socratis uxores, difficillimae illi extiterunt, ut multis in locis legimus. Et Gorgiam illum Leontinum, cum librum de concordia Graecis tunc inter se dissidentibus recitaret Olympiae, audivisse in iurgio ferunt a Melantho eius inimico: 'En qui tres in una domo, se, uxorem, et ancilla concordare non potuit, vobis praecipit de concordia;' uxor quippe eius ancillulae aemulabatur. Tandem vel matre tibi carendum est, dulcissima vitae socia, vel ab uxore abstinendum. Verissimum enim illud reperitur, quod ait idem satyricus:

> Desperanda tibi est salva concordia socru,

ita ut in Lepti, semibarbara civitate, mos fuisse legatur, ut socrus altera die ollam a nuru mutuo petat, illa consulto deneget; ut sit illud quoque verum Terentii. Quid hoc est? 'Omnes socrus oderunt nurus.'

13 Quid? Si amor impellit, nonne ducere debebit sapiens uxorem? Nihil minus. Nam si in sapientem perturbatio non cadit (quod omnes fere dicunt philosophi ac maxime Stoici, quos appellant masculos), quomodo amor cadet, manifestissima insania? Sed de amore scripta sunt multa a multis, et ipsa aliquando plura; nunc agamus quod instat. Quis est enim vel amore ipso caecior, qui non videat hanc dementiam esse cum sapientia nullo pacto posse? Si enim, ut in libro de amore dicit Seneca, 'Formae amor rationis

you happen to get a quarrelsome mate and spend your life in everlasting bickering and disputes! Perhaps Juvenal is right:

> Arguments and insults abound in bed,
> where your wife lies and you get little sleep,

and what follows.[19] Indeed, Xanthippe and Myrto (who was the
granddaughter of Aristides) became Socrates' wives, and proved
difficult for him, as we read in many places.[20] When Gorgias of
Leontini read his book about concord at Olympia (the Greeks being then in conflict), it is said that his enemy Melanthus reproached him, saying: "He wants to teach you concord when he
cannot get peace in his own house among three people — himself,
his wife, and his maid," his wife being jealous of his maid.[21] In the
end, you must give up your mother, your kindest companion in
life, or abstain from marriage. It has been found to be very true
what the same satirist says:

> It is hopeless to keep peace with a mother-in-law.[22]

Thus in Leptis, a half-barbarian city, we read that it was customary on the day after the wedding for the mother-in-law to ask to
borrow a pot from her daughter-in-law, who would deliberately refuse.[23] So the saying of Terence is true as well. What saying is
that? "All mothers-in-law hate their daughters-in-law."[24]

What then? If love drives him to do it, shouldn't the wise man   13
take a wife? Worse and worse! For if the wise man does not suffer
emotional disturbance (as we learn from almost all philosophers,
and especially from the Stoics, who are called the manly ones),
how can he fall in love, which is obviously utter insanity? There are
many writings about love by many authors, sometimes too many,
but let us now address the issue at hand. For you would have to be
blinder than love itself not to see that this madness is perfectly in-
compatible with wisdom. If indeed, as Seneca says in his book
about love, "Love is a forgetting of the form of reason and is a

oblivio est et insaniae proximus,' si 'turbat consilia,' si 'altos ac ge-
nerosos spiritus frangit,' si 'a magnis cogitationibus ad humillimas
detrahit,' si 'querulos, iracundos, temerarios,' si 'dure imperiosos,
serviliter blandos atque omnibus efficit inutiles,' sapiens procul dubio simul atque amator esse non poterit. Quid quod sunt impedimenta ad philosophandum? Etsi nonnulli id negent, M. tamen
Tullius, repudiata uxore Terentia, rogatus ab Hirtio ut sororem
suam duceret, omnino facere supersedit, affirmans se non posse et
philosophiae et uxori pariter operam dare.

14   Quod si philosophia sapientem facit, quod multo certe commodius facit quam ceterae artes, non erunt philosopho, nedum sapienti, utilia matrimonia. Denique M. Cato, quod vir refert et
doctus et elegans A. Gellius, cur essent uxores ducendae verissime
elegantissimeque expressit in ea oratione quam habuit ad Romanos, cum de ea re consilium iniretur: 'Si sine uxore,' inquit, 'esse
possemus, Quirites, omnes ea molestia careremus, sed quoniam
natura sic nos instituit ut nec commode cum illis, nec sine illis ullo
modo esse possimus, perpetuae saluti potius quam brevi voluptati
est consulendum.' Nonne apertissime significavit molestas esse
uxores quandoquidem inquit: 'Si sine ‹uxore› esse possemus, omnes ea molestia careremus'? Voluptatem contra sine uxoribus vivere, quoniam dixit perpetuae saluti potius quam brevi voluptati
est consulendum? Nam quod hortatur ad coniugia, non id loqui-
tur ad sapientes, quorum est semper numerus quam minimus, sed
ad Quirites, sed ad Romanam plebem, ne proles deficeret. At id ad
sapientem nihil pertinet. Illud ad sapientem potius pertinet, vel
qui iam est vel qui esse cupit, ut ea undecunque conquirat quae
beatum, quoad fieri in hac vita potest, efficiunt, omni cura, omni
aegritudine, omni denique omnino molestia carentem. Id vero, si

close neighbor to madness," and if "it clouds judgment," if "it breaks the highest and most generous spirits," if "it drags the mind from great thoughts to the lowest," if "it makes men querulous, irritable, overbold," and "harshly controlling, sweet in a servile manner, and useless for anything," there can be no doubt that one cannot be simultaneously wise and a lover.[25] And what about the fact that wives are impediments to philosophy? Though some deny this, Cicero, after divorcing his wife Terentia, was asked by Hirtius if he would marry his sister; and he scorned the proposal, affirming that he could not give his attention equally to philosophy and to a wife.[26]

Now if philosophy makes a man wise, and it clearly does 14 this more easily than the other arts, then matrimony is not useful to the philosopher, not to mention the wise man. According to Aulus Gellius, a man both learned and elegant, Marcus Cato expressed most truly and well in a deliberative speech to the Romans why there should be marriage: "If we could live without a wife, Quirites, we would avoid all those troubles; but since nature has created us such that we cannot well manage to live with them or without them, we should provide for our permanent well-being rather than our brief pleasure."[27] Doesn't he clearly indicate that he considers wives a burden when he says "if we could live without wives, we would avoid all those troubles?" And that to live without wives is a pleasure, since he says we should provide for our permanent well-being rather than our brief pleasure?" For his commendation of marriage is not addressed to wise men, whose number is always very small, but to the Quirites, to the Roman plebs, lest they lack children. It has nothing to do with the wise. Rather, this is what concerns the wise man, whether he is one already or wishes to be so: he must seek out, from whatever source, the things that make him as blessed as it is possible to become in this life, free from all care, all illness, and indeed from every sort of trouble altogether. If this indeed is the purpose and *scopos* [target],

est sapientis propositum et tanquam *scopos*, ut appellant Graeci, quod profecto aliud esse non potest, non veniat in dubium suae tranquillitatis perturbandae, quod monet Epicurus.

15   Non facile putet illa Theophrasti quattuor posse concurrere. Non desideret filios quos habeat heredes et odium potius quam solatium senectutis. Non putet fore se sine uxore solum, cum certissimo moneamur proverbio etiam solitudinem societati malae esse praeferendam. Fugiat eam iucunditatem quae innumeras sibi difficultates allatura sit. Amori minime assentiatur, recta semper ac sana consilia aspernanti. Impedimenta sibi non comparet ad philosophandum, quo quidem studio nihil est ad bene beateque vivendum accommodatius. Catonem audiat, qui uxorum molestia carituros omnes dicit, non solum sapientes, si sine illis esse possemus ullo modo. Vitam denique deorum ducat in terris castam, ab omnique libidine alienam, quod genus Latini appellarunt caelibes, quod verbum a nonnullis ita interpretatur ut dicantur caelibes, quasi caelestium deorum vitam traducentes.

16   Satis iam superque intulisse bellum videor uxoribus, ut verear ne Iuppiter ille, quem Graeci Gamelium, id est nuptialem, vocant, quod praesit nuptiis, mihi ob eam rem sit iratus, quod fuerim insectatus nuptias, de quo ridicule tamen Chrysippus ait ideo admittendas nuptias esse ne Gamelius offendatur. Sed hunc Graecum deum non tantum timeo quantum nostros Latinos: Domiducum, quem ducendis domum uxoribus praeposuerunt antiqui; Domitium, quem ut domi esset, Manturnam, quam ut maneret, coluerunt; Iugatinum, quem praefecerunt iungendis coniugibus; Virginensem, Subigum patrem; Premam; Pertundam; Venerem tandem ipsam, quam ideo etiam appellatam Varro dicit, quod sine vi virgo esse non desinat. Hos, inquam, Latinos vereor deos ne offenderim, qui matrimoniis, quibus ipsi praesunt, nulla voluerim esse commercia cum sapientibus.

as the Greeks call it, of the wise man — and surely it cannot be anything else — let him, as Epicurus advises, avoid putting his peace of mind in jeopardy.

Let him not think it easy to obtain all together the four condi- 15 tions set by Theophrastus. Let him not desire sons as heirs to bring hatred rather than solace to his old age. Let him not think himself alone without a wife, for, as we are warned by an indisputable maxim, even solitude is better than evil company. Let him flee the kind of pleasure that will bring him countless troubles. Let him not give way to love, which always spurns righteous and sound counsels. Let him eschew obstacles to philosophizing, which is the pursuit most suited to living well and blessedly. Let him listen to Cato who says that everyone, not just the wise, would do without the trouble of having a wife if they could live without them. Finally, let him live the chaste life of the gods on earth, a life free of all lust, the type of life the Latins call celibate [*caelebs*], a word interpreted by some to mean "living the life of the celestial gods."

I seem to have waged enough and more than enough war against 16 wives, so that I am worried that the Jupiter whom the Greeks called Gamelius — the god of nuptials who presided over weddings — may be angry with me, as Chrysippus joked that one had to allow marriage for fear of offending Gamelius.[28] But I fear this Greek god less than our Roman ones. The Romans worshipped Domiducus, whom they put in charge of bringing the bride to her new home; Domitius, for keeping her in the home; Manturna, for her staying there; Jugatinus, whose job was to join spouses; Virginensis; Father Subigus; Prema; Pertunda; and Venus herself, who was so called, Varro says, because a virgin doesn't cease to be one without violence [*vis*].[29] These Roman gods, I say, I am fearful of offending — I who would wish the wise man to have no truck with matrimony.

17   Quamobrem necesse mihi forsan est facere quod fecit Plato in libello *De amore*, qui cum fuisset in deum acriter invectus offendisseque se illum comperisset, *palinodiam* (quam Graeci vocant), id est recantationem, aggressus est, quod et prius Stesichorum fecisse scribit. Cum enim Helenam vituperasset ob eamque causam luminibus fuisset captus, recantatis quibusdam carminibus, quorum est principium Latine, ut traduxit Leonardus noster Aretinus:

> Non verus sermo ille fuit, nec navibus altis
> Existi fugiens, nec adisti Pergama Troiae,

visum recuperavit. Idem dicit Plato sibi faciendum esse in Amorem. Quod ille igitur propter unum deum fecit, nonne mihi faciendum est propter tot tantorumque deorum turbam, quos me offendisse haud incerto sentio superiore oratione? Dicam igitur et ipse cum Stesichoro, non verus sermo ille fuit, neque est sapientis hominis uxores insectari tanquam rem noxiam iniucundamque et vitae beatae, quam omnes, non tantum sapientes, volunt, perturbatricem.

18   Nam quae tandem est ista sapientia repugnare naturae generique humano inimicum esse eiusdemque desertorem? Si enim natura nos sic instituit ut inesset imprimis procreandi appetitus curaque eorum quaedam quae procreata sunt, ut Cicero in primo libro disputat *De officiis,* naturae profecto repugnat qui uxores exagitat. Quod si nunquam aberrat qui naturam optimam vivendi ducem sequitur, quemadmodum idem Cicero in eodem libro testis est, is profecto aberrabit qui repugnabit naturae, neque erit sapiens, quoniam errorem a sapiente longissime esse necesse est. Qui vero nihil ad se humanae societatis conservationem pertinere arbitrabitur, is mihi non solum insipiens repugnansque naturae, sed brutis quoque et quidem efferatissimis videbitur inferior. Videre enim licet leones, tigres, ursos, lupos, quibus vix quicquam excogitari potest truculentius, ad sui generis conservationem ita esse pro-

Perhaps because of this I must do as Plato did in his book *On* 17
Love [*Phaedrus*]. Having furiously attacked the god of love, he
knew that he had offended him and launched into a palinode,
as the Greeks called it, that is, a recantation, as he wrote that
Stesichorus had done before him. For that poet had defamed
Helen and was blinded for it, but he regained his sight when he
wrote some recantatory verses, which have been translated into
Latin by our own Leonardo Bruni of Arezzo:

That tale is not true; you never left
A fugitive in the tall ships sailing,
Nor did you come to the citadel of Troy.[30]

Plato says that he has to do the same in the case of the god of
Love. If he did this for one god, won't I have to do it for the whole
crowd of gods whom I have no doubt offended in the earlier part
of my discourse? Let me say then, with Stesichorus, that my tale
was untrue, and a wise man should not vilify wives as harmful,
unpleasant disturbers of the happy life, which not only the wise,
but all men, want.

For after all, what sort of wisdom is this that rejects nature and 18
makes itself the enemy of mankind and a deserter from it? If nature indeed gave us a basic desire to procreate and to care for our
offspring, as Cicero says in the first book of *On Duties*,[31] then to attack marriage is to fight against nature. And if someone who follows nature as the best guide to living never goes wrong, as Cicero
bears witness in the same book,[32] anyone who fights against nature
is surely in error, nor is he wise, since error is necessarily the very
opposite of wisdom. If a man decides that the preservation of
mankind is of no concern to him, in my view he not only foolishly
fights against nature but seems to fall below the beasts, indeed, the
most savage of them. For one sees that lions, tigers, bears, wolves,
than which one can scarely imagine anything more ferocious, are
so inclined to the preservation of their kind that they are never

pensos ut nunquam efferatiores sint quam cum est pro his quos genuerunt repugnandum. Neque solum id fieri in his animosis, ut ita dixerim, feris quotidie videmus, sed mansuetissima quaeque animalia atque abiectissima irritari saepe efferarique, ut eorum, quos ex se ad sui generis conservationem procrearunt, vitam salutemque defendant; quodque magis mirum est, sapientes, qui futurorum curam ad se nihil asserunt pertinere, non advertisse arbores, plantas, omne tandem genus eorum quae aliquo modo vivunt, ad se ipsa conservanda niti, quantum natura omnium instituit atque compellit. Quarum quae sine seminibus nascuntur, ut lauri, corili, ulmi et quaedam, ne omnia persequar, eodem modo in plantis mirum in modum pullulant ab radicibus. Quae vero egent seminibus primo quam vim producunt seminis? Deinde quam facile etiam sine nostra opera in terram veniens nascitur! Crescit quod natum est semenque adeo multiplicat ut unicum frumenti granum—hoc enim exemplum pro omnibus sat erit—plus quam mille unica messe produxerit. Et audebunt dicere ad sapientes curam nihil pertinere conservandae humanae societatis!

19   At non vult Epicurus in dubium venire sapientem, propterque id abhorrere ab nuptiis, quod in confinio sint bonorum et malorum. Non persuasit id Metrodoro eius discipulo, qui duxit uxorem Leontiam. Et nobis poterit persuadere? 'Sed nunquam veniet in dubium sapiens.' Nam in quodnam dubium venire potest? An ne in impudicam, ne in morosam, ne in avaram, ne in superbam incidat uxorem erit dubium, de quibus incommodis supra est a nobis disputatum? At haec omnia nil movent sapientem, qui tanquam ex arce quadam longe ab se habet omnes perturbationes. Neque putaverim aut Xanthippen Socrati aut Paulam Catoni, etsi essent morosissimae ac difficillimae, ne hilum quidem, ut aiunt, mentis illorum tranquillitatem turbare potuisse. In quod ergo dubium?

fiercer than when fighting for their offspring. Nor is this something we can observe only in these fiercely spirited wild animals, as
I may call them; we also daily observe that the gentlest and most
timid animals grow fierce and savage when they defend the life and
safety of their offspring in order to preserve their kind. And what
is even more amazing, the sages who assert that future beings are
of no concern to them have overlooked how trees, plants, and all
that sort of living thing struggle to preserve themselves, insofar as
the nature of all these forms of life instructs and drives them.
Plants that come into existence without seeds, like laurels, hazel
bushes, elms and the like (not to list them all), sprout in the same
fashion from roots to plant in a wonderful way. But do these need
seeds before producing the power of a seed? How easily, then,
even without our help, living things come forth from the earth!
What comes into being grows and multiplies its seed so much that
a single grain of wheat — let this one example stand for all — produces more than a thousand grains in one harvest! Yet they dare to
say that concern for the preservation of human society is no business of the wise!

But Epicurus holds that the wise man should not take a chance, 19
and for this reason he should stay away from marriage, since it lies
on the border between good and bad. This did not persuade his
disciple Metrodorus, who married Leontia.[33] And will it persuade
us? "But the wise man will never enter upon something doubtful"
[you will say]. Well then, what is the doubtful thing, if you please,
that he can be entering upon? Is he going to be in doubt about the
misfortunes alluded to above, i.e., taking a wife who is unchaste,
hard to please, greedy or proud? But these things will not move
the wise man at all, who keeps all such troubling concerns far
from the citadel of his soul. I should not have thought that Xanthippe was able to disturb the peace of mind of Socrates, or Paula
that of Cato, not a bit, though these wives were miserably difficult.
Wherein, then, will his doubt reside? For my part I don't see

Profecto non video; nec quid Epicurus dicat satis attendit. Nam si omne dubium vitare debet, fugiendum est e vita sapienti, in qua nihil fere nisi dubiorum periculorumque plenissimum reperiri potest. Quod quam absurdum sit vel bruta testantur, quae vitam omnibus tuentur viribus conservantque. De ceteris quoque incommodis quae Theophrastus exequitur, de quibusque pauca dicta sunt a nobis, idem videtur dicendum. Nulla enim incommoda sunt quae non superet sapiens, qui mortem etiam mortisque dolores contemnendos putat.

20   Quid si sunt in nuptiis multa etiam probatissima ac desideratissima? Ut enim cetera omittam, quas nanciscitur voluptates is qui pudicam virique amantem, qui fortem, qui omni genere virtutis ornatam sortitus sit uxorem? Negabunt inveniri, in promptuque habebunt illud sacrum, 'Mulierem fortem quis inveniet?' atque illud satyricum,

Rara avis in terris nigroque simillima cygno.

At ego, ni penitus fallor, ni omnis negligenda est historia, et pudicas multas et fortes fuisse feminas, et ex nostris et ex barbaris, quanto potero brevius dilucidiusque ostendam. Atque ut prius de pudicitia amoreque in viros dicam incipiamque ab extraneis, nonne Demogenis, Areopagitarum principis, filia, cum audisset Leosthenem maritum, qui bellum Lamiacum concitarat, fuisse interfectum, ipsa superstes esse nolui‹t›, asserens quod Leostheni mente nupsisset (nondum enim duxerat sed desponderat), alteri nubere nunquam velle. 'Verum non mirum in una hoc reperiri posse femina.' Certe non mirum, quando quinquaginta etiam virgines Lacedaemoniorum, ne a Messeniis vim paterentur, mortem sibi sponte conscivere. Cum enim esset Spartiatis diuturna cum Messeniis amicitia, consueverunt quibusdam in sacris virgines

where; Epicurus wasn't paying attention to what he was saying. For if the sage is to avoid all doubt, he would have to flee from life itself, for in life there is almost nothing one can find that is not re-plete with doubts and dangers. The absurdity of this is clear even from the evidence of the brute animals, who use all their strength to protect and preserve life. And it seems the same applies to the other misfortunes Theophrastus rehearses, which we have briefly described. For there are no misfortunes which the wise man can-not overcome, since even death and the pains of death are despised by his philosophy.

And what of the good and welcome aspects of marriage? To   20 omit others, what joy for a man who happens to be allotted a modest and loving wife, a strong woman adorned with every sort of virtue? They will say such a being cannot be found, they will have at the ready that holy text, "Who has ever found a strong woman?"[34] and the satirist's remark,

She is a rare bird on earth, most like a black swan.[35]

But if I am not entirely mistaken, if history is not entirely set aside, permit me to show briefly and clearly, as best I can, that there have been many strong women, both among us and among the barbarians. Let us begin with examples of modesty and loving devotion towards husbands among non-Latins. There is the daughter of Demotion, a chief of the Areopagites, who, when she heard that her betrothed Leosthenes, who had started the war of Lamia, had been killed, did not wish to outlive him, claiming that she had married Leosthenes in her mind (she was betrothed but not yet married) and never wanted to marry another.[36] "But it's not surprising you can find this in the case of a single woman" [you say]. It's certainly no surprise, since there were also fifty Spar-tan virgins who willingly chose death rather than be raped by the Messenians. During a long period of friendship between the Spar-tans and the Messenians, it became the custom to exchange some

etiam mutuo ad se mittere; quas cum aliquando Messenii vitiare contra foedus amicitiae temptassent illaeque (ut dictum est) morte vim Messeniorum aufugissent, grave inter utrunque populum bellum concitatum est. Et quoniam mihi amor uxorum in maritos probatissima videtur pudicitia, Artemisiam, Cariae reginam, ferunt, Mausolo viro defuncto, ex ipsius cadavere factum cinerem ebibisse in eiusque honorem sepulchrum illud condi curasse, quod inter septem orbis miracula numeraretur; a quo et cetera quoque sumptuosiora monimenta defunctorum Mausolea nuncupantur.

21   Magna haec sunt signa continentiae in virumque amoris. Lex est et apud Indos, qui plures habent uxores, ut carissima cum defuncto marito cremetur. Contendunt itaque inter se de caritate in maritum barbarae uxores; et quae vicerit, in habitu ornatuque pristino iuxta cadaver accubans, amplexando deosculandoque, suppositos quibus exuritur ignes pudicitiae laude contemnit. Sed, ne persequar Penelopen, cuius est multis iam poetis decantata pudicitia, ne Laodomiam, quae mortuo ad Troiam Protesilao viro non potuit supervivere, ne Hypermestram, quae et patris imperium et periculum contemnens, Lino marito sola ex quinquaginta puellis Danai parcere maluit quam cum reliquis dilecti viri sanguine virgineas manus commaculare, ne has, inquam, ac Didonem Sychaei ac Rhodoginem Nicerati, quem triginta tyranni interfecerunt, coniugem persequar, aliquandoque ad nostras veniam, quis est qui Lucretiam non norit, quis qui Biliam, eius Duilii qui primus ex Romanis mari vicit uxorem, non laudarit? Quam cum rogaret maritus cur illi nunquam animae vitium (audierat enim in iurgio male sibi os olere) non dixisset, quo illi medicamentis subveniret, respondit se existimasse omnibus viris ita os olere. Valeriam, Messallarum sororem, ferunt roganti cuidam, cur mortuo viro nulli

sacred virgins, but at one point the Messenians, breaking the com-
pact, tried to violate these women, and they escaped (it is said) the
violence of the Messenians through death, resulting in a great war
between the two peoples. And since in my view the love of wives
towards their husbands is the most excellent form of purity, they
say Artemisia, the queen of Caria, upon the death of Mausolus
her husband drank the ashes of his corpse, and saw to it that the
sepulchre was built which came to be counted among the seven
wonders of the world, whence other sumptuous monuments to
the dead are called Mausoleums.[37]

These were great marks of chastity and love for a spouse.   21
Among the men of India, who have multiple wives, the law re-
quires that the wife who is the most loved be cremated with her
dead husband. These barbarian wives compete among themselves
for that love, and the winner, dressed in antique and elaborate
dress, stretches out beside the corpse, kisses him, and is burned
for the glory of chastity, regarding the flames with contempt. I
will not discuss Penelope, whose chastity has been sung by many
poets; nor Laodameia, who could not survive her husband
Protesilaus who died at Troy; nor Hypermestra, who, despising
both the command of her father and all danger, was the only one
of the fifty maidens who preferred to spare her husband Lino
rather than bloody her virgin hands with the blood of her beloved
husband along with the rest;[38] nor shall I enumerate those others,
Dido, wife of Sychaeus, and Rhodogune, wife of Niceratus, whom
the Thirty Tyrants killed. But coming at long last to our Roman
women, who does not know of Lucretia, who will not praise Bilia,
the wife of Duilius, who was the first Roman to win a maritime
victory? When her husband asked her why she had never said
anything to him about his bad breath (he had heard during a
quarrel that his mouth stank) so that he might remedy it, she replied that she had thought all men's mouths smelled like that.[39]
When, they tell us, Valeria, one of the Messalla sisters, was asked

nuberet, dixisse sibi maritum Servium vivere. Huic simile est illud Martiae, minoris Catonis filiae, a qua cum quaererent matronae post defunctum virum quem diem habitura esset luctus ultimum, quem et vitae respondit.

22   Dies me profecto deficiat si referre cuncta velim quae de feminarum pudicitia laudeque possunt et vera quidem enarrari. Non enim est haec laus legitimarum tantummodo uxorum ac liberarum. Nam de concubinis quoque ancillisque eadem in historiis reperiuntur, ut intelligamus non consuetudine aut alia quapiam causa magis quam natura virtutes has inesse feminis. Alcibiadem illum Socraticum ab Atheniensibus eiectum ad Pharnabazzum fugisse tradiderunt. Is corruptus auro a Lysandro iussit interfici; cumque suffocato caput esset ablatum atque in caedis signum ad Lysandrum missum, cetera vero corporis pars inhumata iacere, sola concubina adversus crudelissimi regis imperium, inter extraneos omnia contemnens, derelicto funeri iusta persolvit. An non satis ostendit quo fuerit amore in Alcibiadem, pro quo etiam mortuo mortis periculum non vitarit? Ancilla praeterea, Tutela sive Philotis (nam de nomine non constat, ut ait Macrobius in libro *De saturnalibus*), ut de fortitudine quaedam aliquando dicamus, post captam urbem Romam, cum nacta occasione finitimi conspirassent creatoque dictatore Postumio Livio Fidenatio per legatos ab senatu ut matres sibi familias virginesque dederentur postulassent, sponte pro matronis virginibusque profecturas ancillas est pollicita; assensumque cum esset, matronarum ornatu ancillae missae sunt ad hostes. Quae non multo post in castris diem festum simulantes, cum vino provocassent complures altiusque dormire coegissent, tandem signo ex caprifico dato Romanos accersivere. Qui

why, since her husband was deceased, she did not marry again, she said that for her, her husband Servius lived still. Similarly Marcia, the younger daughter of Cato, when the matrons asked her what day would end her mourning, replied "the same that ends my life."[40]

The day would surely be over if I told, as I should like to do, all the true stories that could be told of women's modesty and glory. Nor is all this praise confined to legitimate wives and freed women. For the same things are found in stories of concubines and maid servants, so that we may understand that this is not a matter of upbringing or caused by anything other than the virtues that naturally inhere in women. They tell us that Alcibiades, the famous follower of Socrates, was expelled from Athens and fled to Pharnabazum. Because he had been bribed with gold Lysander ordered him killed, and when he had been strangled, the head was cut off and sent to Lysander as a token that he had been killed, while the rest of his body lay unburied; but his concubine alone, against the order of this cruelest of kings, despising her peril amid strangers, performed the due burial ceremonies for the abandoned corpse. Does this not show the love she had for Alcibiades, for whom, even in death, she herself risked death? Beyond this, a maid servant, Tutela or Philotis (for we are not sure of her name, as Macrobius says in his *Saturnalia*) provides a tale of courage — to come finally to this virtue.[41] When the city of Rome was taken, her neighbors took the opportunity to conspire against her. When Postumius Livius of Fidenae had been elected their dictator, they demanded of the Senate via ambassadors that they hand over the matrons and maidens of their families. Philotis thereupon promised that the maid-servants would go in place of the matrons and maidens, and when this was agreed to, the servants dressed up in their ladies' finery and were sent out to the enemy. Shortly thereafter the maids, now in the enemy camp, pretended it was a holiday and aroused many of the enemy with wine, which made them sleep all the more deeply. Finally, the maid gave the signal from a

parta de hostibus victoria domumque reversi ancillas manumise-
runt omnes concesseruntque data illis ex publico dote ut eo semper quo profectae fuerant ornatu uti possent. Feriae quoque sunt
ancillarum Nonis Iuliis, quae ab caprifico ex qua signum datum
est feriae Caprotinae nuncupantur. Quid igitur ais, Theophraste?
Nonne vel ancillae, non tantum honestis ortae parentibus, dignae
coniugio erunt sapientum? Sed de mulierum fortitudine et supra
commemoratum est, cum pudicarum exempla poneremus; con-
iuncta enim sunt adeo in multis ut disiungi nullo pacto possint. Et
dicemus aliqua, nisi iam fortasse prolixiores tibi videmur quam necesse sit.

23   Sed tu velim patienter audias, quandoquidem mihi opus est ut
apud deos illos nuptiales me expurgem. Nondum enim impetra-
tam veniam esse a me sentio; sed impetrabo profecto, si attente me
audieris. Mirantur Catonis, qui Uticae sibi vim attulit ne victorem
sustineret Caesarem, animi magnitudinem fere omnes ac recte quidem admirantur, si fortitudo magis illa fuit quam, ut sentit divus
Augustinus, pusillanimitas mollis quaedam neque omnino virilis.
Verum tamen qui illum admirantur, multo magis admirentur
oportet Stratoris, cuiusdam reguli Sidonis uxorem, de qua ferunt
quod cum vir propter imminentes Persas, quorum foederi Aegyptii regis societatem antetulerat, propria se manu, ne in hostium ve-
niret potestatem, confodere temptaret neque id perficere auderet,
verum pavidus gladium quem arripuerat prospectans hostium ex-
pectaret adventum, illa intrepida acinacem extorsit e manu mari-
toque necato se super illum transverberatam de more composuit.
O mirandam feminae fortitudinem, atque haud scio an ulli ex omnibus viris comparandam!

24   Sunt et aliae infinitae mulierum, sed prae hac mea quidem sententia vulgares fortitudines, nisi etiam Hasdrubalis coniunx huic

wild fig tree, summoning the Romans to attack. The latter, having gained the victory, came home and freed the maids, granting them dowries from the public treasury and allowing them henceforth to make use of their borrowed finery. The seventh of July became the maids' holiday, and in memory of the wild fig tree [*caprificus*] from which the signal was given, it is called Caprotinae. What then do you say to this, Theophrastus? Are these maid servants, born of less than honorable parents, unworthy to marry wise men? We have recalled above the courage of women when giving examples of modest and pure ones; these virtues are so closely connected in many women that they cannot be separated. And we might give some [further] examples, if it didn't seem to us that we had already, perhaps, been more prolix than necesssary.

But please listen patiently, as it is now my task to clear my   23
name before those gods of marriage. For I feel that even now they have not yet granted me the pardon I ask for, but I shall plead properly if you will listen carefully. Nearly everyone marvels at Cato's greatness of soul, and rightly so, the man who took his own life at Utica rather than surrender to victorious Caesar — if that was really courage rather than, as the divine Augustine thought, a soft and not altogether manly cowardice.[42] Nevertheless, those who admire him ought to admire much more the wife of Strato, ruler of Sidon, of whom we are told that, when her husband saw the Persians coming, to federation with whom he had preferred an alliance with Egypt, he tried to evade capture by impaling himself. Yet he dared not carry out the deed, but stood waiting for the enemy's arrival, gazing at the sword in his hand. She, his intrepid wife, wrenched the gleaming sword out of her husband's hand and killed him, then laid herself upon him, piercing herself likewise by the sword.[43] Oh marvellous feminine courage, I hardly know with what man to compare her!

There are indeed a multitude of more common examples of   24
female courage, but in my view perhaps only the consort of

63

aequanda est quae, capta et incensa Carthagine, cum se Romanos fugere posse non cerneret, apprehensis ab utroque latere parvulis filiis in subiectum se suae domus incendium praecipitem deiecit. Neque vero Stymphalidem tacitus virginem praeterierim, quam cum amaret Aristocles, Orchomeni tyrannus, obque eam potiundam patrem occidisset, illa vero ad Dianae templum confugisset et simulacrum eius ita teneret ut ne vi quidem avelli posset, in eodem loco confossa est. Eius autem necem ulta est omnis Arcadia publico consensu. Neque praeterierim septem Milesias, quae nequid impudicum paterentur in corpus, Gallorum impetu cuncta vastante, morte id periculum vitavere. Neque praeterierim duas Thebanas quarum altera, subversis Thebis, ne Nicanoris amantis vim experiretur, semet ipsam interemit. Alteram ferunt Graeci scriptores, cum illam hostis Macedo violasset, paululum dissimulato dolore suum aggressam corruptorem ferro superasse. Neque praeterierim Phidonis Atheniensis filias, quem cum triginta tyranni in convivio necassent, illas autem nudas supra patris cadaver saltare iussissent, post aliquandiu dissimulatam indignationem, tandem quasi ad necessaria egredientes naturae, se ipsas complexae praecipitarunt in puteum ut virginitatis bonum morte conservarent. Sed cum impetrasse veniam me videam, Scedasi omittam filias in Leuctris, Panthiam Abradotis, de qua scribit Xenophon in *Cyri infantia*, Rodogynen, Darii filiam, aliasque innumerabiles.

25   Nihil dicam non solum non esse impedimento philosophiae feminas, quod omnes fere sapientes qui habiti sunt facto comprobarunt, neque gentiles tantum, sed apud Hebraeas, quorum maxima est in fama sapientia, sacerdotes, principes, prophetae, re-

Hasdrubal is comparable to Strato's wife. It was the wife of
Hasdrubal who, when Carthage had been captured and was
aflame, saw that she could not escape the Romans, and taking
her little children, one under each arm, threw herself into the fire
consuming her home. Nor should I pass over in silence the story
of the maiden of Stymphalus, whom Aristocides, the tyrant of
Orchomenos, loved; when he killed her father to gain possession
of her, she fled to the temple of Diana and clung to the image so
that not even force could remove her, and was run through on that
very spot. All Arcadia avenged her death by popular consent.[44]
Nor should I pass over the seven virgins of Miletus who, when the
Gauls were sacking and destroying everything, avoided the peril
of physical violation by self-inflicted death. Nor shall I pass over
the two Theban women of whom one, after the fall of Thebes,
killed herself lest she be raped by Nicanor, who was in love
with her. The other, as the Greek writers tell us, after a hostile
Macedonian enemy raped her, hid her sorrow for a while, then attacked with a sword the man who had corrupted her. Nor let me
forget the daughters of Phidon the Athenian, whom the Thirty
Tyrants killed at a banquet. Commanding his daughters to dance
naked over their father's corpse, they gained a little time by hiding
their outraged feelings and at length, pretending to go out to answer a call of nature, embraced each other and threw themselves
into a well, to preserve the treasure of their virginity through
death.[45] Since I think now I have begged enough for pardon, I
may omit the daughters of Scedasus in Leuctra and Panthea, wife
of Abradotes, of whom Xenophon writes in the *Cyropaedia*,[46] and
Rhodogune, daughter of Darius, and countless others.

I need hardly say anything to show that women are no impedi-
ment to philosophy, which almost all those who are known as
wise have established by their actions, not only Gentiles, but also
the Hebrews, whose great wisdom is famous. For their priests,
princes, prophets, kings and judges had wives, and there were even

ges, iudices uxores habuerunt, sed ex ipsis quoque feminis fuisse complures sapientes atque in omni doctrinarum genere claruisse. Hoc quoque loco tacebo Sibyllas, prophetas, vates, poetas, infinitas paene mulieres; et quod fortasse expectas, de corporum laudibus omnia praeteribo silentio, nullamque tibi Camillam, nullam Penthesileam, nullas Amazones, nullam Atalantam Calydoniam, nullam Harpalicem, nullam tandem Dianam, de qua tam multa in fabulis, memorabo. Nam de pulchritudine quidem haberem multo plura quae dicerem sed nulla est corporis laus quam non huic putem esse praeponendam.

26   Quae cum ita sint, quis est qui non debeat omni studio, cura et industria, noctes sudando ac dies, nullos labores recusando, ut sit sapiens dare operam, cui non modo uxores suaves sint voluptati, sed quem neque difficillimae quidem morosissimaeque e quietissima animi sede dimovere quicquam possint? Ut intelligas, quando nocere sapienti nihil potest uxor, voluptati esse potest, saltem ne naturae repugnetur neve societas deseratur humana, non esse sapienti feminarum coniugia fugienda.

Vale. Ex Trebbio Mediceo Mugellano IIII Kalendas ianuarias.

among these women who shone for their own wisdom and for
learning of every kind. I shall say nothing here of the Sibyls, the
female prophets and seers and poets, almost an infinite number
of women.[47] And because you may perhaps be expecting it, I
shall pass over in silence all that could be said of their physical
beauty, so I shall record nothing about Camilla, nothing about
Penthesilea, nothing about Amazons, nothing about Atalanta of
Calydonia, nothing of Harpalyce, nothing finally of Diana, of
whom so much is said in the myths. For I have much more that I
might say of her beauty, but there is no praise of beauty which
could, I think, surpass hers.

Given all this, who would not exert himself to become wise   26
with zeal, care, and diligence, working day and night, sparing no
effort? To such a man not only may wives give pleasure, but even
wives who are utterly difficult and hard to please will not be able
to budge him from the quiet repose of the mind. As you will understand, while a wife can do nothing to hurt the wise man, she
can be a source of pleasure to him, and in any case the wise man
should not flee marriage, so that he is not at odds with nature, and
so human society is not left to perish.

Farewell. From the Medici castle of Trebbio in the Mugello, 29
December.

Dialogus de consolatione

1 Investiganti mihi diligenter atque ad consolandum leniendumque summum dolorem meum, quem ex acerbissimo Iohannis Medicis, Cosmi filii, obitu suscepissem, animum huc atque illuc versanti, nihil penitus veniebat in mentem quod non augere magis quam levare dolorem videretur. Quis enim durissimis vel roboribus vel lapidibus, ut Graeci fabulantur, natus tam adversum casum tamque toti etiam civitati deplorandam sortem siccis, ut ita dicam, oculis atque animo non perturbatissimo possit conspicere? Mihi quidem ita visum est, qui potuit animo non vehementissime commoveri deosque atque astra crudelia non appellare, ut ait poeta, hominem illum omnino non fuisse, aut certe omnem penitus humanam ac mortalem naturam exuisse. Tanta enim virtus, tanta humanitas, tanta et publice et privatim tamque miranda agendis in rebus prudentia repentina et immatura morte amissa est ut valde dolendum sit amicis, quibus erat certissimo praesidio, ingemiscendum suis, quos et ornabat et augebat miris laudibus; bonis omnibus et civitati debitis piisque lacrimis eius sit funus prosequendum, patrono suo atque suorum consiliorum amisso auctore. Quae ego cum vere et omnium sententia cogitarem, accedebat quasi squalor quidam et aspectus, in quemcunque oculi inciderent, maestus admodum atque miserabilis. Voces praeterea lamentationesque passim audiebantur, quae roboribus quoque et silicibus, non tantum ex his natis hominibus, lacrimas valeant extorquere. Occurrebat etiam animo quanto essem patrocinio orbatus, qui talem tantumque virum amicumque praestantissimum amisissem.

: 3 :

Dialogue of Consolation

While diligently investigating ways to console myself and to heal ⟨I⟩
my deep sorrow at the premature death of Giovanni de' Medici,
the son of Cosimo,[1] I turned from one thought to another but
nothing came to me that did not exacerbate rather than reduce my
pain. Who is so unfeeling by nature — or "born from stone" as the
Greeks put it — that he could behold such a blow of fate and view
the pitiful lot of the whole city with dry eyes and an untroubled
spirit? I felt that anyone who could look on calmly and did not, as
the poet says, rage at the cruelty of gods and stars, was not really
human or had entirely shed his nature as a mortal man.[2] That
such virtue, such compassion, such wisdom in both public and
private life was suddenly and prematurely lost to death brings sorrow to his friends, of whom he was the surest defense; draws tears
from his clan, of which he was an ornament and a new source of
wondrous praise; and makes all good men as well as the city itself
attend his funeral rites with due and reverent tears, as they have
lost their patron and the author of their counsels. While I was
meditating on the truth and universality of these sentiments, a
kind of mournful squalor came to me and on whomever my
eyes fell, there lay a wretched and gloomy mien. Everywhere you
heard exclamations and lamentations which might have wrung
tears from wood and stone, not only from human kind. I realized
the greatness of the patron of whom I had been bereaved, what a
fine and excellent man I had lost.

2   Illud vero me in primis angebat noctesque et dies quietum esse
non sinebat, quod oculis continuo obversabatur venerandissima et
sanctissima senectute Cosmus pater, quem etsi fortissimum virum
quantumque semper fortuna‹tum› cognovissem, tanto tamen
tamque alto ac paene letali vulnere esse duraturum vix sperabam.
Quinto enim et septuagesimo iam anno (nam eum agebat), gravis
diuturnoque podagrae morbo vexatus et debilis, quonam pacto
tantum ferre dolorem posset non videbam. Quod si quid in
Cosmo quoque adversi accidisset, causam omnem cur aliquando
laetari amplius possemus sublatam esse iudicabam. Itaque vehementer anxius memet ad Cosmum ipsum frequentissime confere-
bam; neque me hercule consolandi eius gratia, quippe qui con-
solatione ipse maxime indigerem, sed id agebam ut praesentia mea
ab solitudine hominem vindicarem, dabamque operam nunc hoc,
nunc illo sermone, etsi ineptus mihi esse videbar plerunque, ut a
silentio ac muta cogitatione animum eius avocarem. Accidit enim
ut quasi delectetur solitudine qui maiore aliqua aerumna afflicta-
tur, validioresque contra animi robur vires tacita praesentium
contemplatione malorum nanciscatur dolor, ut non inscite Homerus de Bellerophonte cecinerit, cum a Proeto regno esset privatus,
vestigia etiam hominum ob dolorem vitavisse; et Nioben in silicem
conversam ob perpetuum silentium existimat M. Tullius, turma,
ut poetae tradunt, filiorum ob laesum numen amissa.

3   Igitur cum sederet ille aliquando medio fere cubiculi, ut solebat,
compluresque ad eum, id est omnis fere civitas, consolandi causa
venirent, ego astabam, qui omnia eius dicta factaque ita diligentissime observarem ut ne emissiones quidem spiritus aut retractiones
praetermitterem. Quem cum viderem praeter omnium opinionem
praeterque mortalium naturam tam aequo ferre animo tantam calamitatem, eaque et dicentem et respondentem quae supra vires
hominum communemque sapientiam essent animadverterem, nefas esse duxi tantae rei memoriam divinaeque penitus et fortitudinis et sapientiae adeo rarum mirandumque exemplar, quod

At first my anguish gave me no peace night or day, for to my 2 eyes there kept appearing his father Cosimo in his venerable and holy old age, and though I had known him as a courageous man and always as a fortunate one, still, I hardly expected now that he would survive the great and almost lethal wound he had sustained. Aged seventy-five, frail, and in daily pain from gout, I did not see how he could bear such suffering. Yet if something happened to Cosimo, I thought all further cause of joy would be taken from us. Thus I was very worried and often called on Cosimo himself, not to console him, by Hercules, since I utterly lacked consolation myself, but so that my presence might recall him from solitude, and I made an effort with various lines of conversation, ineffective for the most part as it seemed to me, to summon back his spirit from silence and mute cogitation. It does happen that a man afflicted with some great sorrow almost enjoys solitude, and that suffering lights upon stronger powers to fight stolidity through the silent contemplation of present evils. Hence Homer had the insight to sing of Bellerophon who, after King Proetus had robbed him of his kingdom, avoided the footsteps of men because of his suffering; and likewise Cicero thought that Niobe was turned into stone because of her perpetual silence, having lost her troop of children because of the injury she had done the goddess.[3]

Thus when he was sitting one day, as he used to, in the middle 3 of his chamber, and many people, indeed almost the whole city, were coming to offer him condolences, I was standing by and watching carefully all that he said, so much so that I didn't miss even the inhalation and exhalation of his breath. I saw that he maintained an equanimity in his great suffering beyond what anyone expected, even beyond ordinary human nature, and I noted the things he said and the responses he gave, which were beyond the strength and wisdom of ordinary men. All this made me feel it would be wrong not to put into writing, as well as I could, a record of so great an episode, that rare and marvelous exemplar of

maxima cum utilitate posteri cognoscerent, quemadmodum quidem possem, non mandare litteris. Etsi enim vix me idoneum, qui ea audirem quae ab eo de rebus humanis arcanisque naturae dicerentur plane divinitus, existimarem, satius tamen me facturum utiliusque posteritati consulturum putavi si ita curarem ut, si non possent pro rerum maiestate auctorisque ipsius dignitate, saltem quocunque modo scriberentur.

4   Cosmum autem ipsum feci loquentem mihique nonnunquam interroganti materiamque disputationis obiectanti respondentem, non solum ut, cum res geri videretur, legentium animi facilius attentionem praeberent, verum etiam quia putavi fore ut eius ipsius persona quam ageremus non nihil esset auctoritatis orationi nostrae allatura, si vel audientibus vel lectitantibus nobis legere vel audire Cosmum ipsum putaretur. Sermo autem inter nos ita fere exortus est. Nam cum aliquando nactus essem solum tacitumque et imo de pectore trahentem suspiria sentirem, coniectaremque de morte illum atque amisso filio cogitare, ne esset in ea commentatione diutius, ita visum est ut hominem excitarem.

5   'Quam multa, igitur,' inquam 'et quam praeclarissima sunt profecto, Cosme, deorum immortalium in humanum genus beneficia. Neque assentiendum mihi videtur poetis, cum aiunt Prometheum nescio quem, sive Iapeti genus fuerit, sive quid aliud—sunt enim modestiores, ut arbitror, nonnulli qui subtilius interpretantur—sed tamen non assentiendum, cum hominem de luto primum, quanvis 'ad effigiem moderantum cuncta deorum,' ut ait Naso, finxisse fabulantur, Pandoramque, opitulante Minerva et facula de solis corpore rapta, flamma inertem prius frigidamque statuam, anima deinde immissa, vivam rationeque utentem reddidisse. Illud etiam multo absurdius mihi videri solet de Pyrrhae nos Deucalionisque lapidibus esse generatos. Nam robora quidem et truncos procreasse homines minime putarim poetas quoque ipsos id existi-

almost divine courage and sagacity, which could be of the greatest use to posterity. And though I hardly thought myself worthy of hearing the things he was saying, with an inspiration that was clearly divine, about human life and the mysteries of nature, I decided it would be better for me to do so, and that I would be better consulting the interests of posterity if I should be careful to write them down after some fashion at least, even if not in a way consonant with the dignity of the subject matter and the speaker.

I have presented Cosimo himself speaking to me, responding to   4 my questions, and sometimes to my objections, not only so that the conversation might seem lifelike and more easily hold the reader's attention, but also because I thought that using his persona in the action would lend authority to our discourse, especially if those who heard or read us believed themselves to be hearing or reading Cosimo himself. Our discussion arose in approximately the following manner. Once when I found him alone and silent and heard him sighing deeply, and I guessed he was thinking about death and the loss of his son, it seemed a good thing to stir him up to keep him from further brooding.

"How many and how wonderful," I said, "are the gifts of the   5 immortal gods to humanity, Cosimo. I think we should not accept what the poets say when they say some Prometheus or other, whether of Iapetus's kind or some other — I think the men who interpret this in a more subtle way are too restrained — we should not accept, I say, the story that he first made man of mud, although he 'fashioned him according to the image of the gods who rule all things,' as Ovid says,[4] and that Pandora with Minerva's help placed a stolen spark from the sun into a cold, inert statue, introducing a flame which would become the soul, making it a living thing that uses reason. Even more absurd, I've always thought, is the idea that we were born from the rocks thrown by Pyrrha and Deucalion. I doubt that the poets themselves believed that we were born from oaks and tree-trunks, but I think they meant that

masse, sed incultam olim eorum vitam sine lare, sine domo, per silvas passim significare voluisse. Ita cum e truncis, quos pro tectis contra vim et intemperiem uterentur aeris, nudi aliquando et horridi egrederentur, causam dedisse Graecis scriptoribus confingendi fabulas. Aegyptii quoque, etsi illi quidem multa sibi arrogant, nihil mihi probant qui naturam ipsam quemadmodum cetera ex corruptione humorum protulisse, ex terra hominem quoque putaverunt; neque magis in hominibus elaborasse naturam aut maiorem adhibuisse diligentiam quam in muribus aut stellionibus procreandis.

6   "'Animal enim hoc,' ut elegantissime Cicero inquit in libris *De legibus*, 'providum, sagax, multiplex, acutum, memor, plenum rationis et consilii, quem vocamus hominem, praeclara quadam condicione generatum esse a supremo deo. Solum est enim ex tot animantium generibus ac naturis particeps rationis, cum cetera sint omnia expertia.' Atque ita sine dubitatione verum arbitror in creandis rebus atque animantibus praecipuam fuisse deorum curam ut quos ad sui similitudinem formarent, exactiore atque excellentiore artificio, etsi nullo penitus labore ut cetera — nam ipse dixit et facta sunt — homines effingerentur. Quare et loquimur et ratione ad veri contemplationem deorumque ipsorum naturam maiestatemque soli ex omnibus perducimur, tantumque ceteris praestare animantibus videmur ut difficile sit, si non divinam ob corpoream et terrenam labem, at certe non mortalem omnino naturam esse humani generis non existimare ac pro certo habere. Quod eorum munus, etsi omnibus aequissimi dii aeque impertiti sunt, fit tamen nescio quo modo ut, iacentibus ac fere naturam humanam plerisque depravantibus, adeo sese efferant nonnulli ut quanta inter bruta rationeque carentia atque homines differentia est, tantum hi videantur ceteris omni genere laudis vitaeque ornamentis antecellere. Quod si omnia quidem debet humanum genus propter tot tantaque diis immortalibus beneficia, quid de te,

men were at first rough and uncouth, scattered about in the
woods, without culture, without shrines, without a settled home.
They used tree trunks to shelter from the force and turbulence of
winds, and they came forth as naked and shaggy creatures, which
led the Greek writers to create these myths. The Egyptians, on the
other hand, though they made such great claims for themselves,
do not satisfy me at all, for they trace nature itself and all that belongs to it from the corruption of the earth's humors, and have
man spring from the earth; and they say that nature worked no
harder to produce man than to to make mice or lizards.

"As Cicero says elegantly in his books *On Laws,* 'This animal we   6
call man, who has foresight, wisdom, many-sidedness, wit, memory, and abundance of reason and counsels, was made by the supreme god to enjoy a kind of preëminent position. He is the only
one among all the kinds of living things who takes part in nature's
rationality, from which all others are excluded.'[5] And this I think
is without doubt the truth, that the gods in creating the world and
life fashioned men with special care to form something similar to
themselves, applying a more exacting and more excellent art, although, as with the rest, with no effort whatsoever — for he spoke
and they were made.[6] For this reason we alone speak and alone are
led by reason to contemplate truth and the nature and majesty of
the gods, and seem so much superior to other animate beings that
it is difficult not to think and hold for certain that the human race,
if not divine owing to the corruption of its corporeal and earthy
part, is at any rate not altogether mortal. It must be noted, however, that, though the most equitable gods gave their gift to all
equally, still it somehow happens that many are brought very low
and have corrupted their humanity, while some have been so
raised up that they excel the rest of mankind in the embellish-
ments of life and every genus of praise as much as men excel the
brutes. But if the human race owes so much to the generosity of
the immortal gods, what shall we say of you, Cosimo, who easily

Cosme, dicendum est, qui rebus his omnibus quae appellantur
bona facile praestas ceteris, quique virtute ac sapientia tua, quae
sunt deorum munera, exuperasti hominum naturam? Nisi te in-
tuens rubore quodam impedirer, ipse iam ac libentissime quidem
aperirem, quanquam adeo nota felicitas tua est, adeo magna cum
omnium admiratione per universum orbem vulgata sapientia ut
neque mea neque cuiusvis oratio magnopere sit desideranda.'

7   Cum haec ita dixissem pluraque pararem, modestissime Cosmus sic interpellans abrupit, 'Quanquam,' inquit, 'nec me nec
mortalium quenquam fas esse putem cognomine appellari sapientiae quoniam ea stultitia est apud Deum, soleamque saepe
non probare Graecos propter illos septem, contemnere etiam
Apollinis oracula propter unum Socratem, etsi valuerit ille quidem
ingenio, si Platoni credimus; nostros etiam nonnihil mirer, qui et
Sempronium et Atilium primo propter legum eruditionem, deinde
aliam tamen ob causam Laelium sapientes nominarint, tamen
paulo ante mecum tacitus, ipse quoque animo evolvebam eadem
fere quae a te sunt paulo ante narrata de unius immortalis atque
omnium patris et creatoris Dei in homines munificentia, cum
etiam paulum me addubitare coegisti. Nam cum de Deo mentionem faceres, non tanquam unus sit ac solus omnium creator et
rector, sed quemadmodum plures esse putares numero es locutus.
Quid autem est stultius, immo vero puerilius quam turba quadam
omnigenum deorum inanissimisque quibusdam commentationi-
bus confictorum caelum ita oneratum reddidisse ut potuisse
Atlantem diutius sustinere vehementer admirer? Soleoque Varro-
nem legens non mediocriter sive superstitionem sive ignorantiam
accusare antiquorum, qui etsi excellentissimis fuerunt ingeniis, ut
multis rebus manifestissime constat, hac tamen una in re non
modo non ingeniosi mihi videntur, sed tanquam pueri potius aut
certe delirantes senes deridendi. Quis enim non rideat non Ianum
aut Iovem aut Neptunum aut alios, quos appellat selectos viginti

surpass all others in what are called the goods of life, and who by your virtue and wisdom, which are gifts of the gods, surpass human nature? If I were not prevented by seeing your embarrassment, I might expand upon this theme, and with the greatest good will, although your felicity is so well known, your reputation for wisdom is so universally admired throughout the globe, that there is no great need of either my own or anyone else's discourse."

When I had spoken these words and was getting ready to speak 7 more, Cosimo interrupted me with great restraint and said: "It is not fitting" he said, "to call me or any human being by the title 'wise,' since our wisdom is foolishness to God,[7] and I have never approved of the Greeks and their Seven Sages and contemn even the oracle of Apollo for saying that Socrates alone was wise[8] — even though, if we may believe Plato, he was remarkable for his intellect. I also wonder a little at the way our own Latin authors call Sempronius and Atilius wise for their knowledge of the laws, and Laelius wise for another reason.[9] Yet a little while ago, I was turning over silently in my mind almost exactly the same thoughts which you just expressed about the generosity towards mankind of the one immortal God, father and creator of all things, when you began to throw me into some uncertainty. For when you spoke of God, you spoke as though you thought he was not the one and only creator and judge of all things, but rather as though there were a plural number of gods. What is more foolish and indeed more childish than to burden heaven so with gods of every kind, manufactured in certain absurd accounts, that I really wonder Atlas can hold it up any longer? Reading Varro, I used to blame the ancients for their superstition and ignorance, who despite being wonderfully clever, as is clear from many things, on this one subject seem to me not only lacking in intelligence, but even laughable, like children or senile old men. For who would not laugh, if not at Janus and Jove and Neptune and the others whom he calls the twenty highest gods, at the crowds of others he insisted on in

deos, sed quasi gregarios ceteros et paene infinitos, ut ne potare quidem, cui Potonam praefecerint[1] deam, neque edere, cui Educam, appellatione deorum indiguerint? Aesculanum vero et Argentinum, quos propter aes argentumque habendum coluerunt, Seiamque et Segetiam, Nodatum, Volutinam, et cetera rusticorum numina consideranti, ex vitae utilitate et necessitate potius quam aliqua excellenti disciplina religionem sibi constituisse mihi videntur, ut non solum triginta deorum milia quae sunt apud Hesiodum, verum multo etiam plures pro rerum creatarum diversitate confingi potuisse non dubitaverim. Quod etsi te pro tuo Christianae pietatis perpetuo ardentique studio longe ab eo tam futili errore abesse putem, tamen tua illa deorum tam saepe repetita pluralitas, ut ita dicam, me admonuit ut paulum antiqua illa somnia confutarem priusquam ad ea ipsa accederem quae a te de praeclarissima humani generis condicione deque mea felicitate sunt narrata.'

8   'Recte tu quidem,' inquam, 'de me, Cosme, neque praeter naturam tuam opinaris. Neque ego, cum deos dicerem, unum esse et solum non intelligebam. Sed ita loqui mihi licere putavi, recte quidem sentiens, non ad plures tamquam ad diversos referens orationem meam, sed ad tres dumtaxat, qui ita inter se personis tantum distinguntur, ut in trinitate summa unitas et indisseparabilis substantia intelligatur. Veruntamen non me poenitet dedisse tibi aliquam dubitandi causam, quando quidem tanta me voluptate affecit superior tua confutatio ut parum ita dubitasse valde molestum sit. Velim autem, nisi impudens tibi forte videor, ut in hoc quoque sententiam mihi dicas tuam. Existimesne priscos illos omnes, quorum tu quoque paulo ante laudabas industriam, tam ridicula de diis tamque inania, immo vero immania credidisse?'

9   'Ego vero de omnibus,' inquit, 'non existimo. Etsi enim vulgus fortasse tota, ut aiunt, aberravit via, conspicere tamen licet non-

their almost infinite number, so that they couldn't even drink without putting the goddess Potona in charge nor eat without calling on Educa? When I consider Aesculanus and Argentinus, whom they thought to honor for the sake of copper and silver, Seias and Segetia, Nodatus, Volutinas and other peasant deities, it seems that they founded their religion in response to the needs and necessities of life rather than from some excellent teaching, so that I have no doubt that not only the 30,000 gods that Hesiod mentions, but many more could be invented to correspond to all the diversity of created things.[10] But although you, thanks to your long and serious study of Christian piety, are far from falling into so vain an error, I think, still, your frequent allusions to a plurality of gods, if I may put it that way, reminds me that I ought first to refute those ancient delusions a little before I come to the things you said about the noble condition of the human race and of my own happiness."

"You are right about me, Cosimo," I said, "and how like you 8 that is. For when I say 'gods,' I do not fail to understand that there is one God and one alone. But I think it is permissible for me, while knowing the truth, to speak in these terms; my speech does not refer to a plurality of gods as though they were different ones, but merely to three, who are only distinguished amongst themselves as persons in such a way that the highest unity and one inseparable substance is understood to be in the Trinity. Yet I don't regret having given you reason for doubt, for your refutation caused me such pleasure that to have caused too little doubt would have been a nuisance. I should like, if it wouldn't be impertinent, to ask your opinion on this matter too. Do you think those ancients whose application you just praised really believed such laughable nonsense, or rather monstrous nonsense, about the gods?"

"I don't think all of them did," Cosimo said. "Perhaps the com- 9 mon people took, as they say, a completely wrong road,[11] but it is

nullos ex doctis, qui habiti sunt, multo aliter esse opinatos, ut si ex gentilibus quoque quos appellant invenire licet qui non omnino falsa et inania de Deo cogitaverunt; neque Varro ipse vera existimat quae narrat, ut auctor est Aurelius Augustinus: praeclare quidem suismet auctoribus videantur antiquorum errores esse confutati. Orpheus enim non inscite aut irreligiose de Deo cecinisse videtur cum inquit—si Latini hi versus nescio a quo traducti (nam ipse Graece non novi) illum exprimunt:

> Solum illum suscipe mundi
> Ingentem auctorem solum, interituque carentem,
> Quem nos presenti quid sit sermone docemus:
> Unus perfectus Deus est, qui cuncta creavit,
> Cuncta fovens atque ipse ferens super omnia sese,
> Qui capitur mente tantum, qui mente videtur,
> Quique malum nullum mortalibus invehit unquam,
> Quem praeter non est alius.

Quapropter et Protogonum appellat, quod ingenitus ipse principium sit omnium rerum generationis. Item Phaneta, quod antea etiam quam aliquid esset creatum ipse apparuerit, ut audio interpretari.

10   'Mercurius etiam ille, qui leges ac litteras edocuit Aegyptios cuique propter scientiam Maximo fuit cognomen, unum esse dicit Deum sine nomine, sine patre, ingenitum omnia procreantem. Item alio loco Asclepium instituens sic inquit:

> Solus enim Deus et merito: solus ipse est et ab se est et circum se totus est, plenus atque perfectus; eiusque ipsius firma stabilitas est, nec alicuius impulsu loco moveri potest, nisi aliquis audeat dicere ipsius commotionem aeternitatem esse.

apparent that some of the men who are considered learned held quite different views, as among the so-called Gentiles one may find some who did not think in an altogether false and foolish way about God; nor does Varro himself, as we read in Augustine, consider those things true that he describes, for he himself brilliantly refuted, using his very own authorities, what seemed to him to be the errors of the ancients.[12] Orpheus also seems to sing of God in a way that is neither ignorant nor irreligious — if these Latin verses translated by someone (for I myself do not know Greek) express his thought correctly:

> Exalt him alone, of the world
> The great and sole creator, free from death,
> Whose nature by these present words we teach:
> God is one and perfect, who created all things,
> Cherishing all things and holding himself above all,
> Who is understood by mind only and seen by mind,
> Who brings no evil to mortals ever,
> Than whom there is no other.[13]

Therefore he calls him *Protogonus*, being himself uncreated, the principle of generation of all things. So too he calls him *Phaneta*, since he himself appeared before anything was created, as I hear it interpreted.

"Mercury, who gave the Egyptians laws and letters and for his wisdom was called Maximus, says that God is one, without name, fatherless, having generated all things. In another place, he cites Asclepius thus:

> God is alone and rightly so: He alone exists from himself,
> and around himself he is completely full and perfect; and He
> is the unshaken stability of His own self, nor can any other
> being move him from his place, unless someone dares to say
> that his con-motion is eternity. But more, He is also an im-

10

Sed magis et ipsa immobilis aeternitas, in quam omnium temporum agitatio remeat, et ex qua omnium temporum agitatio sumit exordium.

Zoroaster quoque, antiquissimus magus, eadem fere de Deo sentire videtur in libro sacro cum ita scripsit: 'Deus incorruptibilium primus est, sempiternus, ingenitus, expers partium, sibi ipsi simillimus, omnium bonorum auriga, munera non expectans, optimus prudentissimus pater iuris, sine doctrina iustissimus, natura perfectus, sapiens sacrae naturae unicus inventor.' Sibyllas quoque et philosophos nonnullos, atque in primis Platonem, Deum ita prosecutos legimus ut nulli dubium esse possit ab illo deorum vanissimo grege sententia sua longissime abfuisse.

11   'Quamquam de philosophis quoque pauci omnino sunt quos libenter legam, nonnullos etiam audire nolim ac plurimum detestor. Quis enim ferre possit Diagoram Milesium, Theodorum Cyrenaicum, Euemerum Tegeatidem² aut Callimachum Euripidemque, etiam poetas, quos adeo nihil pudet ut omnino Deum esse nullum asseverent? Epicurei quidem et ipsi sunt ridiculi; dum enim quietos deos omnique labore doloreque vacare volunt, quod existimant illi summum bonum, dormientes atque negligentes res humanas inducunt. Et, ut ad summa colligam, perpauci sunt ex omni antiquitate quos non putem esse despiciendos, ut tria illa Scaevolae deorum genera, qui iuris apud Romanos pontificii doctissimus vir est habitus, sive a poetis, sive a philosophis, sive a principibus civitatum illi conficti sint, nulla aut certe quam minima videantur auctoritate esse digna. Nam praeter paucos illos, quos supra memoravi, ex tot et poetarum et philosophorum et principum multitudine vix aliquos invenias qui non pueri aut insani quidam potius videri iure possint.

12   'Quapropter multo etiam plura debent nostri homines, qui unius filii Dei salvatoris humani generis divino praecipuoque munere tot tantisque erroribus liberati sunt ut inter ea quae fuerunt a

mobile eternity itself, into which the movement of times resolves, and from which the movement of times takes it origin.[14]

Zoroaster too, the most ancient of mages, also seems to think almost the same way about God in his sacred book when he wrote: 'God is first among incorruptibles, eternal, unborn, indivisible, always most like to himself, the charioteer of all goods, expecting no gifts, the best and wisest father of law, most just without learning, perfect by nature, the only all-wise creator of sacred nature.'[15] We read too that the sibyls and some philosophers, especially Plato, so pursued God that no one can doubt that their views on the gods were far as possible from being those of the foolish herd.

"Although there are a very few philosophers whom I read gladly, 11 there are some I prefer not to listen to and many that I heartily despise. Who really can bear Diagoras of Melos, Theodore of Cyrene, Euhemerus of Tegea along with Callimachus and Euripides, poets though they were, who were so shameless as to assert that there was no God at all? The Epicureans make themselves ridiculous saying that the gods are tranquil and free of every care and sorrow, which is what they consider the highest good, and inferring that the gods are asleep and indifferent to human affairs. To sum up, there are very few from all antiquity whom I do not think worthy of contempt. As for the three kinds of gods posited by Scaevola, whom the Romans considered their most learned jurist—those invented by poets, those invented by philosophers, and those invented by the leaders of cities—they seem to be of little or no authority. So except for those few I have mentioned above, of all the multitude of poets and philosophers and princes you will hardly find any who do not seem, and rightly so, like children and madmen.

"For this reason our Christian folk are much more God's debt- 12 ors, as we were freed from so many great errors by the special divine gift of the only Son of God and Savior of Mankind, so

te in humanum genus enumerata beneficia, huic quoque non in postremis sit locus. Si enim, ut recte quidem dicebas, tanto artificio hominem Deus—hoc est ad suam et imaginem et similitudinem—creavit, quid fuit convenientius quam auctorem sui et cuius similitudinem in se gereret mortalium natura cognovisse? Cernere enim licet corpus ipsum nostrum tanta tamque incomparabili industria compositum ut si a capite incipias, quod etiam Varro, quod inde cetera initia capiant dictum putat, perque omnia, etiam minima, mente cogitationeque percurras, nihil reperias nisi summa sapientia planeque divina esse constitutum. Ita non solum oculos, qui nominantur sive quod ab ciliis occulantur, ut Varroni videtur, sive ab eius sensus mirabili celeritate, quod mihi magis placet, aut aures, ab vocibus hauriendis denominatas, aut nares, aut ora, quae procul dubio sunt in homine praecipua, summa cum ratione facta esse omnia conspicimus, sed et cartilagines quidem et capillos et ungues non tantum non neglectos, sed exactissima etiam industria fabricatos. Quod si membra ipsa corpusque humanum ita fictum est a summo rerum omnium opifice Deo, nonne multo magis animum ipsum, qui proprie imago Dei est, excultum fuisse oportuit? Quod ab eodem ita curatum extitisse et multis aliis constat rebus, et illud in primis manifestissime declarat, quod auctorem unicum nostrum verum Deum, non quemadmodum prisci illi, quos supra refellere conati sumus, sed ut iam Christiana nos religio edocuit, cognoscimus, eumque ipsum Deum et Dominum nostrum, ut divina praecipitur adnuntiatione, ex toto corde nostro totaque anima nostra diligendum intelligimus. Quam quidem ad rem multum, ut mihi videtur, confert non solum dignitatis humanae contemplatio, quod abs te paulo ante factum est, verum etiam uniuscuiusque de se ipso naturaque seorsum sua accuratis-

that, among the benefits you enumerated as bestowed by God on mankind, this was not the least. If indeed, as you were rightly saying, God made man with great art—that is, after his own image and likeness—what more appropriate than that man should recognize his creator, the one whose likeness our mortal nature carries within itself? For it may be seen that our very body is made with such marvellous skill, that if you begin from the head (*caput*), which Varro thought to be so called because the other parts of the body take (*capiunt*) their origin from it,[16] and you survey everything, even the smallest thing, in mind and thought, you will see nothing that is not the creation of a supreme and manifestly divine wisdom. Consider not only the eyes (*oculi*), which are so called either because they are hidden by eyelids (*ciliis occulantur*), as Varro thought, or for the wondrous speed of their perceptual ability (*ob celeritatem*), which I find preferable. Consider too the ears (*aures*), so named because they imbibe sounds (*ab vocibus hauriendis*), or the nose, or the mouth, which are beyond doubt man's outstanding features: we recognize these as created with highest degree of rationality, and even the sinews and the hair and the nails have not only not been neglected, but made according to the most exacting design. And if the parts of the body and the human body itself are made by God, the high artificer of all things, how much more must the soul, which is, properly speaking, the image of God, be finely fashioned? That he was so concerned in its creation is evident from many proofs, but this one in particular makes it perfectly plain: that we know Him as our unique maker, the true God, not as those ancients did whom we have tried to refute above, but as the Christian religion now teaches us, and we understand Him to be God Himself and our Lord, as taught by divine revelation, Who is to be loved by us with our whole heart and our whole soul. What helps us greatly to do this is not only the contemplation of human dignity which you stressed just now, but also an individual's careful and distinct exploration of himself and of

sima indagatio. Quod etiam Apollo — quem supra contempsimus, in hoc autem minime mihi videtur esse contemnendus — voluisse videtur, dum id praecipit, ut nosmetipsos cognoscamus.

13 'Ego quoque, ut aliquando tandem ad me veniam, iampridem id dabam operam ut me cognoscerem, cumque tantis affluentem me bonis, tantaque utentem felicitate intelligerem, nullamque in me cur huiusmodi me fortunis dignarer causam reperirem, eram in magna quidem felicitate vehementer anxius, illaque Philippi Macedonis bene humana sententia veniebat in mentem. Cum enim uno eodemque die esset nuntiatum et Alexandrum sibi filium natum esse et se Olympia quadrigis vicisse et Dardanos hostes a Parmenione praefecto suo fuisse superatos, non est, vir fortunae assuetus ludo, tam laetis nuntiis aliquid elatus, sed oculos ad caelum tollens, mediocrem pro tantis bonis calamitatem deprecatus est. Idem fere de Furio Camillo fertur, Veiis captis, ut tum res erant, potentissima civitate et opulentissima. Ego quoque minime tam blandienti fortunae confidendum ratus, magni continuo mihi aliquid mali impendere cogitabam. Itaque etsi videri tibi aut cuivis felix poteram, tantum tamen amaroris ob formidinem inerat ut nesciam an miseria potius quam felicitas illa mea nuncupanda fuerit. En tandem vides quantum mihi vulneris fortuna inflixerit, eo amisso filio qui et senectutis erat et totius familiae ac dignitatis meae magnum columen ac paene necessarium. Quid enim ego hoc aetatis hocque valitudinis? Quid alter filius ita debilis, itaque podagrae hereditario gentis nostrae morbo confectus? Quid, inquam, in vita agemus, qui simus et nobis ipsis et ceteris qui a nobis aliquam fortasse expectant opem penitus inutiles? Is vero, qui et nobis et amicis magno et ornamento et adiumento erat, cur e vita migravit? Profecto aut caeci omnino sumus nec quid bonum in vita sit vide-

his own nature. This even Apollo seems to mean — of whom I spoke above with contempt, though I think in this matter he is not at all to be contemned — when he teaches that we must know ourselves.[17]

"Coming now to my own case, I too have long sought to know 13 myself, and when I understood that I enjoyed affluence and happiness and I could find no reason within myself why I should be worthy of such good fortune, I became anxious amid my great good fortune, and that fine humane sentiment of Philip of Macedon used to come into my mind. For when on one and the same day he was told that his son Alexander had been born and that his chariot had won at Olympia and that the army of the Dardanians had been beaten by his general, Parmenio, this man, accustomed as he was to the mockery of fortune, was not in the least elated by the good news, but raising his eyes to heaven, asked for some middling calamity to offset so much success.[18] Almost the same thing is reported of Furius Camillus when he had taken the city of Veii, a most powerful and wealthy city by the standards of the day.[19] I too reckoned that one could hardly count on the flattery of fortune, but imagined all the time that some great evil was bound to strike me. Thus, though I might seem happy to you and to anyone else, my fear brought me so much bitterness that I don't know whether my condition should not have been called misery rather than happiness. Now you see the wounds fortune did in the end inflict on me, through the loss of that son who was the great and almost indispensable support of my old age, of my whole family, and of my position in life. What am I to do at my age and in my state of ill health? What can my other son do, who is so weak and suffers so from the gout which is hereditary in our family? How can we go on, being useless to ourselves and to those who perhaps expect some help from us? He who was truly a great ornament and support to ourselves and to our friends, why has he departed this life? Surely either we are totally blind and do not see what is

mus, aut certe misera admodum hominum vita est, quae tot fluctibus procellisque iactetur nec stationem unquam in qua vel paululum modo conquiescat nanciscatur.'

14 Haec cum dixisset protulissetque ad posterum magno cum suspirio carmina illa ex Hecuba:

> Quicunque regno fidit et magna potens
> Dominatur aula nec leves metuit deos
> Animumque rebus credulum laetis dedit,
> Me videat et te, Troia,

tandem postea, vultu in terram inclinato oculisque occlausis, conticuit.

15 At ego in meo instituto perseverans, 'Etsi,' inquam, 'Cosme, fas vix esse puto aliqua in re a tua opinione dissentire, tamen illud tibi minime concesserim, non posse te, modo velis, vel senectute vel morbo impeditum, utilitati eorum qui a te expectant opem non vel multo, etiam melius quam iun‹i›ore aetate ac robustiore pulcherrime consulere. Languent membra vetustate; infirma sunt ob morbum. At mens ipsa tua divinissima ratioque quae tot tantaque domique et foris et tanta cum gloria ac felicitate gessit, nonne viget? Nonne in dies maior etiam admirabiliorque existit? Illud profecto verum est, quod non velocitate aut viribus corporis res magnae geruntur, sed consilio atque auctoritate. An quem pontifices, quem imperatores, quem reges, quem duces, quem populi etiam barbari rebus suis dubiis consultum adhibent, non poterit suis opem expectantibus succurrere et dare consilium? Petrum vero, alterum filium, gentili podagrae morbo et, ut tu dixisti, hereditario ita confectum, cui vel ex nostris vel ex antiquis magis praeclaris viris non merito comparabimus? Quem ita iam et omnis nostra civitas et tota Italia admiratur, ut vere Cosmi filium omnes existiment ac

good in life, or life is indeed terribly hard, exposing us to floods and storms and never offering solid ground where we might find some safety."

After saying this, he sighed deeply and recited these lines of 14 Hecuba:

Whoever trusts in kingship and rules mightily
Over palace and fears not the fickle lesser gods
And naively puts faith in happy things,
Let him look at me and at you, Troy.[20]

Whereupon he looked down, closed his eyes, and fell silent.

But persevering in my purpose, I said, "Though I think it is 15 hardly right for me to contradict you in any way, Cosimo, still, I would not concede for a moment that you cannot, if only you wish to, serve beautifully the interests of those who hope for some support from you, however constrained you might be by age and infirmity. Indeed, you can do so even better than a younger and more robust man. Your limbs are weighed down by old age and weakened by illness, but that utterly divine mind of yours and that reasoning ability which you have exercised with so much renown and success at home and abroad, are these not vigorous still? Are they not even greater and more admirable every day? The truth is that great things are done, not by physical speed and strength, but by wise counsel and authority. Cannot the man whom pontiffs, emperors, kings, commanders, whom even barbarous peoples consult in doubtful matters, can he not give succor and counsel to his own clientele? Take Piero, your second son, afflicted with the gout though he is, which is, as you say, a hereditary ailment.[21] To whom among the best men of our own time or among the great and celebrated men of antiquity can we not fairly compare him? He is so much admired now by our whole city and by all Italy that everyone reckons him truly the son of Cosimo and considers him the inheritor, not only of your illness, but also of your wis-

praedicent, neque morbi tantum, sed et sapientiae et dignitatis tuae certissimum successorem meritissimumque heredem autument.

16   'Sed haec arbitror te pro perpetua tua et constantissima humanitate fuisse locutum. Illud autem ex te sine admiratione quadam audire non potui, quod qui paulo ante humanam visus sis condicionem etiam complecti laudibus, tam cito mutatis verbis caecos homines aut certe admodum miseros edixeris. Age vero, quid est quod te vel mutavit, vel id certe effecit, ut tuis ego te verbis mutatum suspicarer? Nam etsi, ut dicis, graviter a fortuna percussus es, non tamen eum te esse certo scio qui ex fortuna pendeas quique in alio potius quam in te ipso tibi felicitatem positam esse arbitreris. Id enim esset et a tua sapientia longe alienum et perverse admodum natura comparatum ut tanto in nobis virtutis atque honestatis innato ardore laboriosissima quaeque et periculosissima etiam libentissime ob virtutem subeamus, si nihilominus ea vis est aut doloris aut cuiuspiam alius perturbationis ut de sede sua ac tranquillitate animum, tanquam vallo fossaque virtutibus munitum, deiicere valeat atque prosternere. Quid enim valerent virtutes? Aut quid eas tanto studio, laboribus etiam quibusque periculisque posthabitis, compararemus? Quid Decii tandem, quid Curius, quid fortissimi Bruti, quid trecenti Fabii, quid alii innumerabiles, qui pro patria vel fortiter depugnavere vel gloriosissime interiere? Nonne illi quidem ridiculi fuissent atque contemnendi, quos nihilominus immortalitate ob egregiam virtutem donatos videmus, ut non solum Romani, quibus illi laborarunt, sed et Graeci et barbari homines, si modo paulo humaniores sint, nunquam de eorum memoria et magna quidem cum laude conticescant?

17   'Tu quoque, Cosme, qui tantum evigilasti in vita, quid tot tantasque curas laboresque et discrimina pro amicis, pro patria adivisti, quid te semper privasti omni voluptate nisi quae ex recte factorum conscientia manaret? Quid ambitiosissimis olim civibus, ne

dom and position in life, to which he is the surest successor and the most deserving heir.

"But I think you spoke as you did out of your invariable and 16 unfailing humanity. Still, I cannot help marvelling at what I hear from you, for a moment ago you seemed to view the human condition as crowned with glory, and now you suddenly declare that men are blind and undeniably wretched in the extreme. Tell me, what is it that has changed you, or at least has made me think you have changed in what you say? For although, as you point out, you have been dealt heavy blows by fortune, I know for certain that you are not the kind of person to depend on fortune, and you have always believed that your happiness depended on yourself, not on anything external. It seems unlike your wisdom and even perversely arranged by nature that we would willingly accept hard toil and great danger for virtue's sake, driven by our innate love of virtue and honor, if nonetheless the power of pain or any other mental disturbance can cast our soul down from its tranquil seat and knock it flat, fortified by the virtues though it be, as if by trench and fosse? What good then are the virtues? Why should we secure them with such zeal, despising the effort and peril they cost us? What of the Decii then, of Curius, of the brave Bruti, of the three hundred Fabii and countless others who fought valiantly for their country or died for it gloriously? Would they not have been ridiculous and worthy of contempt, these heroes — whom nevertheless we see blessed with immortality for their amazing virtue, so that not only the Romans for whom they labored, but Greeks too and even the barbarians (provided they have some degree of culture) never cease to extol their memory and sing their praises?

"And what of you, Cosimo, who all your life were watchful of 17 your conduct, why did you take up so many great cares, toils and crises on behalf of your friends and your country, why did you always deprive yourself of all pleasure except the kind that flows from the consciousness of deeds well done? Why did you long

patriam hanc nostram pulcherrimam et florentissimam insanissimo furore suo perditi homines conculcarent, tanta prudentia tantaque animi moderatione occurristi ut ne inimici quidem, minime quieti homines aut boni cives, si non laudare te, qui tanquam ex voracissimis ferarum faucibus de eorum manibus extorsisti patriam et rempublicam confirmasti, tamen, tantus est virtutis honestatisque decor, vituperare te, inquam, inimici ipsi tui, id est reipublicae hostes, iam non audeant? Quid terribilissimis regibus et ducibus fortissimis, quid superbissimis populis et nationibus patriam infestantibus adeo fortiter obstitisti pacatosque tandem et quodam modo superatos nobis reddidisti? Quid, ut ad ea veniam quae propria magis sunt et tua, philosophiae studiis tantopere insudasti? Quid tandem neque terra neque caelo, ut aiunt, intactum aliquid aut incognitum reliquisti si eam casus vim habet, si id est fortunae imperium ut ita constitutum animum itaque partam nobis felicitatem temeritate sua possit pervertere, deque virtute ipsa, quae regina est et vitae beatae domina, tanquam de devicto captivoque hoste gloriosissime triumphare?'

18   Haec ego cum dixissem illeque tandem vultum substulisset, 'Si,' inquit, 'negarem adeo acerbum, adeo insperatum vulnus non sensisse, ferreum me profecto aut lapideum, non de infirmissima carne, esse profiterer. Neque enim, ut ait Iob, illud unicum patientiae et fortitudinis in sacris litteris documentum: 'Fortitudo lapidum fortitudo mei est, nec caro mea aenea? Ecce non est auxilium mihi in me necessariique mei recesserunt a me.' Quod et dissimile illius poetae non est:

> mollissima corda
> Humano generi dare se natura fatetur
> Quae lacrimas dedit.

Neque ego is sum qui datas esse mihi a naturam negem lacrimas et dolorem sentiendi mollitudinem. Sentio etenim tantoque me

ago oppose those excessively ambitious citizens to prevent those wretches from grinding underfoot with their insane fury this most lovely and flourishing country of ours? Such was your prudence and moderation of spirit that not even your enemies, restless men and bad citizens and enemies of the republic though they were, dared criticize you (even if they didn't praise you) — such was the aura of virtue and honor with which you snatched our country from their hands, as though from the voracious jaws of wild beasts, and placed the republic on a sound footing. Why did you stand up so bravely to the terrible kings and powerful generals, the proud peoples and nations filled with hatred of your country that you in the end pacified and somehow overcame on our behalf? And, to come now to those things which more properly belong to you, why did you toil so mightily in the study of philosophy? Why, finally, did you leave nothing unknown or untouched, as they say, on earth or heaven, if chance has this power, if the sway of fortune can pervert with its rashness a mind so constituted, a happiness so created, if it can triumph in glory over Virtue herself, the queen and mistress of the blessed life, like a defeated and captive enemy?"

After I had said this, he finally raised his head and said, "If I 18 denied I felt this bitter and unexpected blow, I should have to call myself a man of stone or iron, not a creature of weak flesh. For is it not as Job said — that unique Biblical example of patience and fortitude? 'Is my strength the strength of stones? or is my flesh of brass? In truth I have no help in me and any resource is driven from me.'[22] And the thought of the poet is not dissimilar:

> softest heart
> to humanity Nature confesses she gave,
> who gave us tears.[23]

I am not one who would deny that nature has given me tears and the softness to feel sorrow. I grieve very deeply indeed for the good

bono privatum esse vehementer doleo. Neque probare possum
Stoicos tuos, quos aut nequaquam recte interpretantur, aut certe
videntur praeter verum praeterque humanam sortem de dolore
disputare. Dum enim tantum tribuunt virtuti, dumque tantum
animi fortitudinem magnifica quadam verborum supellectile ita
exornant, corporis mihi omnino videntur oblivisci. Quod etsi servire animo imperanti debet, tamen id efficere animus nunquam
poterit si torqueatur corpus, si uratur, si secetur, ut non sentiat, ut
non doleat; neque id praecipienti obtemperabit quemadmodum
neque domino servus, ut sine pennis volet aut sub aquis vel unam
tantam horam ut enatet edicenti. Quis enim non videt id repugnare naturae, neque doctorum vel potius humanorum philosophorum mereri assensionem, neque Deus ipse auctor et rector
mortalium id procul dubio voluit, qui adeo imbecille nostrum genus tantisque et morbis et omniformium malorum casibus ita obnoxium effecit ut ignobilissimi etiam vermiculi afferre levissimo
quoque attactu pestem possint?

19   'Aliter profecto, aliter quam Stoici, qui etiam, propterea quod
dolere videri nolunt, se appellant masculos; aliter, inquam, de dolore, si recte, ut supra dixi, interpretantur, sentiendum est. Afferunt enim praeclaram duntaxat quandam magnificisque ornatam
verbis orationem, rem autem ipsam ac naturam deserere oblivis-
cique videntur. Quapropter et Dionysius ille Heracleotes optime
illos arguit. Cum enim fuisset Zenonis discipulus Stoicorumque
disciplinam imbibisset, tandem vero renum vexaretur doloribus,
falsa illa esse omnino quae in Porticu didicisset asserebat, astante
etiam atque acclamante condiscipulo eius Cleanthe Zenonemque
ipsum tragico versu ab inferis excitante:

I have lost. Nor can I approve of your Stoics, who are either incorrectly interpreted or at any rate seem to defend views on sorrow in a way that is opposed to truth and to the human lot. While they pay so much tribute to virtue, while they adorn fortitude of spirit with a magnificent furniture of words, it seems to me they entirely forget the body. Although it is meant to serve at the command of the mind, the mind is not able to achieve control when the body is racked with pain, when it burns, when it is cut; and it cannot help feeling and suffering. Nor will it obey the mind when it gives precepts, like a slave who will not obey its master, any more than it will fly without wings or swim under water for an hour on command. Who does not see that this demand for control is contrary to nature, and does not merit the assent of the learned, or rather of humane philosophers? Nor, undoubtedly, does God himself, the author and guide of mortal men, wish it, for did he not make human kind so liable to numerous illnesses and to all sorts of misfortunes that even the slightest contact with the vilest of worms can infect us with plague?

"We ought to think differently, quite differently from the Stoics, 19 who call themselves manly just because they were unwilling to show pain. We must, I say, think differently from them about pain—assuming I have understood them correctly, as I said above. For fine as their discourse is, however magnificent its ornate eloquence, they seem to have forgotten the thing itself and to have left nature behind. For this reason Dionysius of Heraclea rightly refuted the Stoics. At one time he was a disciple of Zeno, and absorbed the Stoics' teaching, But later, when he experienced pain in his kidneys, he said that everything taught in the Stoa was altogether false. Present was his fellow student, Cleanthes, who cried out and summoned Zeno from the underworld with this tragic line:

Audisne haec sub terra, Amphiaraë abdite?

Nonne videtur nobilissimus hic transfuga, multo illa dici melius
quam re fieri posse, dilucide ostendisse? Ea enim est verborum, ea
subtilium argumentationum vis ac natura ut facile capere indocto-
rum possint animos atque extorquere assensionem, praesertim si
paulo accuratius tractentur: neque prius animadvertatur verum
quam cum tandem aliquo modo contigerit ut experimento ipso
atque usu rerum natura melius nobis innotescat. Est enim illud
humanae mentis proprium veritatis duci quaestione, nec prius de-
sistere quam aliquid, ubi demum consistere possit, invenerit. Si
autem, quoniam, ut Platoni quoque placet, tanquam carcere quodam obscuro clausa est, errantem adhuc et quasi caecutientem nec
verum invenientem declinare a vera semita obtigerit, mirabile dictu
est quam facile corruat. Quod si malus etiam sit additus prae-
monstrator, nil reliqui esse potest quin ita trahatur in praeceps ut
ad eam liberandam vix sufficiant humanae vires, sed omnipotentis
Dei, qui veritas ipse, unicus est veritatis et certissimus auctor,
auxilium implorandum sit.

20   'Unde enim putas tot tantosque errores, et in philosophia et in
religione, iam tum a principio fere conditi orbis aliunde pululasse?
Graecia ipsa profecto, quae semper ob suorum hominum praeclara
ingenia et ad inveniendum exornandumque sollertiam fabulosissima fuit, hinc tantam habuit disciplinarum diversitatem ut ad
sectarum numerum ducentarum et octuaginta octo, ut Augustinus
auctor est in libris *De civitate Dei*, pervenisse iam potuerit; et scien-
tiarum quasi certamen quoddam et confusionem excitarit, ut sive
de summo bono, sive de virtutibus quaeratur, ut maiora illa de religione deliramenta praetermittam, nihil fere ex his quae sunt de
genere aliquo bonorum defensores atque assertores proprios non
invenerit. Nam de dolore quidem aut 'aegritudine' – ita enim aspe-
rum animi motum praesentis alicuius mali opinione appellari

Do you hear this under the earth where you are hidden,
   Amphiaraus?[24]

Has not this noble deserter shown plainly that such doctrines can
be more easily stated than followed? Such is the power and nature
of words and of subtle argumentation that they easily conquer the
minds of the unlearned and compel their assent, especially when
they are carefully set out. But we do not fully appreciate what is
the truth until it happens in some way that nature makes itself
known to us through real experience and application. For it is the
nature of the human mind to be led by the search for truth, and
not to stop until it has found a resting place. But if, as Plato
thinks, our mind is shut in a sort of dark prison, it falls to our lot
to wander here blindly and to leave the right path without encoun-
tering truth, and it is marvelously easy to stumble off it. For if evil
too is given us as a guide, nothing can be left us but to plunge on
ahead, so that human powers hardly suffice to free our mind, but
we must instead beg for help from Almighty God, who himself is
Truth, the only and sure Author of Truth.

   "Where do you think they come from, all those many great er-   20
rors in philosophy and in religion which have sprung up everywhere almost since the creation of the earth? Greece itself, indeed, which was always fabled for its men of genius and their
resourcefulness of invention and elaboration, had such a diversity
of schools of thought that, as Augustine writes in *The City of God,*
the number of sects reached 288 sects;[25] this aroused a kind of
competition and confusion among the sciences, so that whether
the question was about the highest good or the four virtues—to
ignore their even greater delusions about religion—there is practically no opinion about any kind of good that has not found its defenders and proponents. As to pain or 'anguish'—as they prefer to
call these sharp mental motions caused by an opinion that some
evil thing is present, rather than grief or pain[26]—they did notice

malunt quam dolore – etsi similitudinem animi morborum et corporis (et vero quidem) inducant, tamen, sive dolor ille sit sive aegritudo nuncupanda, nihil nobis afferunt praeter contentionem et
quasi digladiationem quandam perpetuis eorum disputationibus,
dum sapientiam nescio quam defendunt atque complectuntur,
quae tanquam ex altissima specula despiciat et quasi ad se nihil
humana pertineant, ambitiose contemnat ac pro nihilo habeat.
Quod bona eorum venia dictum sit, non video quo modo ipsi quidem sint existimandi sapientes.

21   'Ea enim afferre et praecipere hominibus quae humaniter
consequi homines non possint. Quid aliud est quam, nulla ad auctores ipsos redundante utilitate, frustra se iactando atque osten-
tando hominum studia ad se ipsum tandem contemnendum irri-
tare? Afferunt tamen Brutos, Torquatum, Maximum, Paulum,
Catonem, et ex Graecis Telamonem, Anaxagoram, Theseum,
compluresque alios, mulierculas etiam fortissimas, ut hi colligunt
qui consolationes scribere consueverunt. Indolentiam tamen illam
suam sive potius stuporem mihi non persuadent. Etsi enim fortiter
illos tulisse facile crediderim dolorique viriliter repugnavisse, tamen nihil omnino sensisse, si homines illi fuerint, nunquam dede-
rim. Quod neque Crantor, ille nobilissimus Academicus, dandum
putat, qui illud nil dolere affirmat non sine magna mercede evenire
immanitatis in animo et stuporis in corpore—quanvis extraneis
nullis opus sit auctoribus. Unus enim Christus, Dei filius et verus
homo, qui saepenumero nobiscum vivens et doluit et ingemuit,
cum contristata est anima eius usque ad mortem et cum flevit super Lazarum et cum a patre, ut ille ab eo transiret calix, sudore
etiam sanguinolento oravit, quid contra dolorem miseri possent
mortales, exemplo suo, qui errare non potuit, nobis aperuit.

22   'Neque ego existimo, quoniam naturae gemimus imperio, si
quid accidat adversi, ut multis antea et mihi nunc, alienum esse a

correctly a similarity between the suffering of the spirit and of the body, whether one calls it sorrow or illness. Yet from this they offer us nothing in their interminable disputations beyond contention and a kind of gladitorial combat. They defend and embrace a sort of wisdom that looks down as though from a great height on all human concerns, as though they were irrelevent to themselves, pretentiously despising them and dismissing them as worthless. With all due respect, I do not see how philosophers like this can be considered wise.

"They offered and taught things to men that men, being human, could not follow. All this is perfectly useless to the authors themselves and amounts to nothing more than vain boasting, a showing off of their erudition to the point of goading others, in the end, to regard them with contempt. They cite the two Brutuses, Torquatus, Maximus, Paulus, Cato, and among the Greeks, Telamon, Anaxagoras, Theseus and many others, and even courageous little women, cobbling them together like the people who write consolations. They do not persuade me of their indifference to pain, or rather numbness. Even if I might easily believe that they bore things very stoically and fought against pain in a manly way, I shall still never grant, if they were human beings, that they felt nothing at all. Not even Crantor, that noble Academic, thought we should grant that anyone who claimed freedom from all pain achieved that except at the cost of an inhuman hardness of spirit and numbness of body — although we need no pagan authors to know this.[27] Indeed the one Christ, Son of God and true man, lived among us, often suffering and groaning when, with soul afflicted unto death, he wept over Lazarus and called upon his Father in prayer, sweating blood, to let this cup pass from him.[28] Thus He Who cannot err shows us by his own example what we poor mortals can do against pain and grief.

"Since we groan under Nature's power, I do not think, if adversity strikes us, as has happened to many others and is happening

condicione mortalium aut vituperatione aliqua dignum talem dolorem. Qui enim fieri potest ut, cum his privari nos videmus quae
natura quoque ipsa demonstrante bona sunt, non sentiamus, id est
silices simus et non homines? Bona autem ex communi hominum
sententia ea omnia existimanda reor quae ad vitam bene beateque
traducendam conferant. Tantum enim tribuere honestati, quae et
ipsa summa quaedam res est et praeclarissima rerum humanarum,
tantum tamen ei tribuere ut ea sine quibus ne vita quidem ipsa et
honestas esse potest, bona nullo modo appellemus, nihil esse aliud
videtur quam collegisse fortissimum atque ornatissimum exerci-
tum, sed ad id deduxisse angustiarum ut nihil ad eum commeatus
possit deferri.

23   'Vita enim ipsa, quae inter Dei munera una quaedam res de
maximis existit, etsi praeponenda quidem semper honestas est,
ipsa tamen, qua sublata honestatem quoque tolli necesse est, minime profecto negligenda est. Quod si est curanda vita, ea quoque
sine quibus vel omnino non constare illa potest vel certe in miseria
constare, cur ita a generibus exterminamus bonorum? Deus enim,
rerum omnium sapientissimus creator, cum spiritum vitae insuffla-
vit in hominem, ut habent sacrae Hebraeorum litterae, praeposuit
eum omnibus quae crearat, quibus vitae et utilitati suae necessaria
sufficeret. Quae autem crearat, vidit idem opifex et pater Deus
quod erant valde bona. Neque enim qui summe bonus est, immo
vero ipsum bonum, aliquid non bonum creare potuisset. Igitur, si
placet, sit vel summum honestas bonum. Sed neque boni nomine
expertia faciamus cetera, quae vitam honestatemque ipsam, quae
sine vita quid sit non facile dici potest, sustinent. Quod si ea bona
sunt quibus spiritus ille vitae alitur, quem nos tanquam Dei praeclarissimum munus tueri conservareque debemus, quae tandem
hominis vituperatio est, quando haec amiserit, dolere, id est si
quae amiserit, cognoscere? Sed dicet fortasse quispiam neque in
bonis annumerandos filios neque ad agendam aetatem aliquid

to me now, that pain is alien to the human condition or that suffering somehow deserves blame. How is it possible for us not to feel it when we are deprived of those things which Nature herself has taught us are good; how is it possible for us to be stones and not men? Those things should be reckoned goods, I think, that enable us to live our lives well and happily, following the common view of humanity. Honor is the highest and most excellent of all human goods, but to set it at so high a rate that we may not in any way call goods those things without which life itself and honor are impossible—this seems no different than collecting a powerful and handsomely equipped army, then leading it into a narrow defile where it would be impossible to victual it.[29]

"The claims of life itself, which is among God's greatest gifts, 23 must surely not be disregarded, for without it honor is necessarily lost as well, even if honor is always to be placed before life. Now if one must devote one's care to the means of living, why would we place outside the genera of goods those things without which life cannot exist, or can only exist in misery? God, the all-wise creator of all things, when he breathed the spirit of life into man, as the sacred Hebrew scriptures tell us, placed him in charge of all the things he had created, that by them he might have enough for his life and needs. When he had created them, God the Creator and Father saw that they were very good.[30] Nor could he who is the highest good, indeed the Good itself, create anything not good. So if you like, let honor be the highest good. But let us not deny the name "good" to other things that sustain life and honor itself, since it is hard to say what honor there is without life. For if those things are good by which the breath of life is nourished—which we have a duty to protect and conserve as God's excellent gift— why, after all, should a man be blamed for grieving when these are lost, that is, for knowing what he has lost? But perhaps someone will object that our children should not be classed among goods and that they do not contribute to living one's life, since the Evan-

conferre, quoniam 'beatas etiam quae non pepererint' asserat
Evangelium. Non me praebebo acerrimum adversarium, si quis id
dixerit; talem autem amisisse hoc aetatis hocque valitudinis, ut supra dixi, quin sentiam ac doleam, efficere nullo pacto possum. In
eo enim persistere, ut omnino dolor non sit malum, id mihi eorum
videtur esse qui nihil unquam penitus doluerint. Quod et Heracleotes ostendit, qui transfugit cum dolet. Neque plus valet prae-
ceptorum quasi quaedam contra naturam bene instructa acies,
quam naturae veritas.

24   'Sed detur non esse malum dolorem, quod tamen non dabit
Crantor aut Carneades; sed nos demus, qui verum non alicui ad-
dicti sectae, sed liberi inquirimus. Quid tamen erit effectum?
Nunquid propterea in rota, in insulis, ad metallum, in eculeo,[3] in
aere, in exilio, in egestate, in omnium calamitate nihil sentiemus?
Fieri quidem id non potest, ut supra dixi. Neque tamen quod dolor non sit malum non consenserim. Illa enim inter se non pu-
gnant, neque quod dolet statim malum est, immo vero non nunquam etiam bonum. Quemadmodum si quis aut secandam aut
urendam partem aliquam corrupti corporis medico tradiderit ne
reliquum quoque contabescat atque dissolvatur, non erit sine dolore sectio aut ustilatio, id ipsum tamen secari et uri non solum
existimari non malum debet, sed fortassis etiam bonum, quoniam
causam praebet ut reliqua a contagione et morbo liberentur. Quid
est enim aliud bonum quam, cum recta ratione, causa quaedam
qua vita, quam paucioribus fieri potest molestiis, ita traducitur ut
propter vitam vita non defraudemur? Quod si cuipiam videatur
insolens et dura ista diffinitio, erit forte aliud tempus cum de ea re
dicemus prolixius. Non enim inutilis ad vitam aut indigna res est
de qua fieri debeat diligentissima indagatio.

25   'Nunc tamen quod instat peragendum est dandaque opera, si
possumus, quoniam ita tempus postulat, ut quomodo dolendum

gelist says, "Blessed are the women who shall be barren."[31] If someone were to say this, I would not oppose him energetically, yet I cannot help feeling and grieving for the loss of such a son at my age and in my present state of ill health, as I said before. To persist in maintaining that pain is not bad at all seems to me the view of persons who have never experienced it. This is what the story of Dionysius of Heraclea shows, who deserted [Stoic philosophy] when he experienced pain. No teachings arrayed against nature like a line of battle are more effective than the truth of nature.

"But let it be granted that pain is no evil, which however 24 Crantor and Carneades will not grant;[32] but we shall grant this, since we inquire into the truth as free men and not as persons bound to a single sect. What will be the outcome? Shall we on this account feel nothing when being broken on the wheel, in exile, in the mines, on the rack, burned in a copper caldron,[33] in exile, in destitution, in utter disaster? It is impossible, as I have said above. Yet I wouldn't disagree that pain is not an evil. This is not a contradiction, for what causes pain is not automatically an evil; indeed, it is sometimes a good. For example, someone might sacrifice part of his sick body to a doctor to be cut or burned away to prevent the rest being infected and destroyed, but even though this cutting and burning will not be painless, one still thinks of it not only as no evil thing, but perhaps even as a good, since it is the cause whereby the rest of the body may be freed from contagion and illness. For what is a good but that whereby, rationally speaking, life is conducted with as few difficulties as possible, so that we are not cheated of life for the sake of life? This might seem to some an unusual and difficult definition, but if so, we shall have to speak of it more fully, perhaps, at some other time. Such a discussion would not indeed be irrelevant to our lives and would be worth an extremely careful investigation.

"Now, however, we should finish our discussion and exert our- 25 selves to find out, if we can—since this is the question of the mo-

sit et quatenus progredi dolor debeat inveniamus. Nam nec pauci sunt inducti errores a Graecis philosophis, qui, ut arbitror, gloriae ac contentionis avidi, dum unusquisque nova se invenisse gloriari cupit, multis veritatem involucris implicaverunt. Nam et Epicurei, qui etsi mihi penitus improbandi videntur, tamen audio a quibusdam non omnino contemni, dum voluptati faventes, dolorem dicunt non solum malum sed etiam summum, minus etiam quam Stoici tolerabilia videntur afferre. Qui enim ita dicit, idem dicat necesse est ab iustitia, ab fortitudine, ab omni fere honestate frequentissime, ne in dolorem incidant, esse recedendum. Quid autem est minus tolerandum in publicis et privatis actionibus ea voce, quae deserendam praecipiat honestatem quaeque ceteris omnibus et amicorum et parentum et patriae utilitatibus commodisque ne quid doleat anteponat? Utrum tandem, Epicure, ut dolorem fugias, incendes patriam sacrasque aedes et templa Dei profanabis? Etsi enim scio confidentius agere te cum diis, utrum tamen divina humanaque, ne te culex figat aut pulex, omnia pervertes? Non facies, arbitror. Virum enim etiam te bonum praedicant, multoque aliter quam vixeris locutum. Nam morientem in maximis doloribus, qui summum malum putat dolorem, scripsisse aiunt et illum diem ultimum fortunatissimum appellasse. Non poterat, ut mihi videtur, qui voluptati omnia tribuisset, de dolore aliter ac fecerit praecipere. Quod autem avocat a contemplatione rerum humanarum praemeditationemque tollit ne quid ob metum voluptatem perturbemus, id mihi nullo modo probari potest, neque gravitate videtur philosophi, sed mulierculae cuiusdam potius inanitate digna sententia. Multoque melius, ut videtur, Epicureorum voluptati erit consultum, quandoquidem sine omni penitus incommoditate tota non traduci vita potest, si quam citius fieri

ment—in what way we ought to suffer and how far suffering should go. For not a few errors have been introduced by the Greek philosophers who, I think, often wrapped the truth in many layers of obscurity in their eagerness to achieve glory and to compete, each wanting to win the glory of having found something new. And even though the Epicureans seem to me to merit utter rejection I hear that some do not altogether despise them. As defenders of pleasure, they say that sorrow and pain not only are bad, but are actually the worst of things, and seem to regard them as even less tolerable than the Stoics did. If you say this, you must necessarily say that we should regularly step back from justice, fortitude, and every sort of honor so as to avoid pain and sorrow. What could be less acceptable in public and private life than such a point of view, urging men to desert honor and all other things, and not serve the interests of friends and parents and country lest they themselves get hurt? Would you, Epicurus, in order to escape suffering, set fire to your country and profane the sacred chambers and temples of God? Although I know that you treat the gods with great freedom, would you pervert all things human and divine to avoid being stung by a gnat or a flea? I don't think you would. They tell us that you were a good man, and that your way of talking was very different from the way you lived your life. Indeed, they say that as you lay dying in great pain, the man who believed that pain was the ultimate evil called that last day his most fortunate.[34] It seems to me that the man who made pleasure the supreme principle could not act otherwise than he taught. But when he dissuades us from contemplating human affairs and forbids us to contemplate the future lest some fear disturb our pleasure, I can in no way approve a view that seems unworthy of a philosopher's seriousness, but more like the vacuous opinion of some little woman. It would much better suit Epicurean pleasure I think—since we cannot go through life with no experience at all of suffering—if throughout life we see and recognize as quickly as

per aetatem poterit, ea perspecta et cognita necessitate, iam tum ceperimus contra ea quae ventura sunt arma et ad resistendum repugnandumque pro viribus humanis nosmet ipsos paraverimus.

26 'Si enim praemeditatos etiam praeparatosque et quantumvis munitos excitari, saltem dolore superveniente, necesse est et aliquo modo commoveri, quid fieri putamus si improvisos atque inermes nos offenderit? Cum igitur remedia sibi videntur contra dolorem attulisse — de aegritudine enim propter similitudinem in hoc sermone nostro idem semper dicendum esse intelligi volo — non solum id non efficiunt quod volunt sed, tanquam mali medici consueverunt, vires adaugent aegritudinis; ad idque videntur perducere, ut aut nihil unquam doleamus, quod natura fieri non potest, aut postea quam dolore inceperimus, intelligentes nos in summo esse malorum omnium, nullam admittere consolationem possimus. Quid enim afferri solacii ei poterit qui ita sibi persuaserit accidere sibi peius nihil posse quam acciderit et, voluptate amissa, id est summo bono, extrema se in miseria collocatum putarit? Ita igitur victum, ita prostratum, quid poterit a miseria liberare? Putabit enim eo duntaxat minus se miserum quo eiulabit, quo suspiriis lamentationibusque omnia complebit? Videtur enim sic affectos huiusmodi recreari insania et quasi quandam animi relaxationem nuncupare. Et ita tunc dicunt, ut Hecuba apud Senecam:

> Lamenta cessant? turba, captivae, mea,
> Ferite palmis pectora et planctus date.
> [. . .] — iamdudum sonet
> fatalis Ide, iudicis diri domus.

Et paulo post utiles esse existimans eiulationes:

> Fidae casus nostri comites,
> Solvite crinem, per colla fluant

possible the sufferings that are to come and if we start to take up arms now against them, preparing ourselves to resist them and fight back as well as human strength allows.

"If we must necessarily experience emotion in some manner   26 even when we have been forewarned, forearmed and ready to resist the coming of pain, what do we think will happen if we are caught unawares and unarmed? Although they think they offer us remedies for suffering—and I want it understood that I mean [the technical term] "anguish" [or mental pain] in this discourse for the sake of consistency—not only do they not achieve what they wish but, like bad doctors, they make the illness worse. They seem to bring us to the conclusion either that we never suffer anything—which is impossible by nature—or that after we begin to be in pain, we understand that we are subject to the worst of all evils, and we cannot allow of any consolation. For what sort of solace can there be for one who has convinced himself that the worst has happened, that having lost pleasure, i.e. the highest good, he thinks he has fallen into the extreme of misery? Thus defeated, thus prostrate, what can free him from misery? Will he think himself the less miserable if he wails and fills the air with sighs and lamentations? For it seems that people so affected relieve themselves by such madness, which they call a sort of easing of the mind. Thus may they lament, like Hecuba in Seneca:

> Do your wailings falter?
> O throng of mine, captive as I am,
> smite breasts with palms, make loud laments.
> Long since 'twere time for fatal Ida to resound
> Home of the ill-omened judge.[35]

And a little later, thinking the wailings are useful:

> Trusty comrades of my fate, unbind your locks;
> over your sorrowing shoulders let them flow,

107

> Maesta capilli tepido Troiae
> Pulvere turpes. [. . .]
> Paret exertos turba lacertos

Demumque, cum eas veluti ad pugnam aliquam rebus omnibus instruxerit, concludit iterum:

> iterum luctus redeant veteres,
> solitum flendi vincite morem.
> Hectora flemus.

Cur non ipsa tantum flet, sed ceteras invitat ad luctum? Cur illa tandem vertitur in canem a poetis nisi quia, amissa ob nimium dolorem ratione et mente alienata, etsi hominis figura restaret, animus tamen in bruti abierant naturam?

27   'Quamobrem ita dolendum minime existimo, neque putandum nos statim, si quid accidat incommodi, propterea esse miseros, quoniam ita nati sumus ut quam plurimis fortunae telis obnoxia sit vita nostra. Etsi enim ea vim habet dominatumque fortuna ut necesse aliquando sit sentire ferientem, non tamen animus ratioque fortiter resistere repugnareque non potest. Ita fit ut causa adlata dolendi, quod plerunque accidit, non possimus funditus non dolere, quod velle videntur nonnulli, id est duros nos lapides et non mollem humum putare. Neque rursus manus dedere debeamus dolori eoque prosterni, tanquam qui in maximo constituti malorum, nihil cur non miserrimi simus videre valeamus.'

28   'Audire mihi visum sum, Cosme,' inquam, 'dicente te, naturam ipsam tuo sese nobis ore aperientem. Et mirabile dictu est quantum Graecos philosophos prae te contempserim, qui impetu quodam verborum subtiliumque dumtaxat argumentationum, quasi

defiled with Troy's warm dust.
Let the band their bared arms make ready.[36]

And finally, when she has instructed them in all things as if for some battle, she concludes again:

Repeat once more your old lamentations;
exceed your wonted manner of weeping;
'tis for Hector we weep.[37]

Why does she not only weep herself, but invite others to loud mourning? Why is she eventually turned by the poets into a dog?[38] Isn't it because, having lost her reason and her sanity through excess of grief, she retains a human form, but her soul has descended to the condition of a brute animal?

"For this reason I reject the idea that one should give way to grief in this fashion, but I also do not think that, if something unfortunate happens, we should on that account automatically be made wretched, since we are born in such a way that our lives are subject to numerous darts of ill fortune. And though Fortune has such power and dominion that one necessarily at times feels her blows, one is still able to resist and fight back bravely with one's mind and powers of reason. This means that when there is cause to sorrow, which happens often, we cannot avoid all suffering whatever, as it seems some people would like us to, thinking us hard as rock and not soft clay. On the other hand, we ought not to surrender to grief and be prostrated by it, as though, being beset with the worst evils, we were unable to see any reason why we should not be at an extremity of misery." 27

"As you spoke, Cosimo," I said, "it seemed to me I heard your very essence opening itself to us. And it is amazing how much I have come to despise the Greek philosophers in comparison with you. Although they assailed you with words and subtle-sounding arguments, as though deploying siege weapons, and seemed to be 28

machinis tormentisque quibusdam admotis, non assentiri animum, quod tu egregie fecisti superiore oratione tua, sed oppugnare potius captivumque non ducere, sed trahere videntur. Illam enim, ut ita dixerim, Stoicitatem, quam tu nunc primum fecisti ut non probem, etsi antea sum sectatus, magis mehercule Epicureos et voluptatem callidam quidem et blandam vitae nostrae insidiatricem fugiens, quam, quod illi mihi omnino satisfacerent, iam non possum non despicere, eaque, quae soleo splendore ductus virtutis atque honestatis laude magnopere admirari, nunc demum, postea quam audivi te, falsa etiam apparere occeperunt.[4] Ea enim concludunt semper quae, etsi sunt auditu gratissima, quod liberant ab omni morbo, ut pollicentur, et sapientem nulla re unquam indigere aut perturbari posse asseverant, tamen, quoniam de his quae fieri nequeunt natura, ut est a te clarissime disputatum, omnis est eorum oratio, merito videntur nunc tandem, non dolore urgente, ut de Dionysio supra dictum est, sed natura ipsa et ratione tua demonstrante, deserenda.

29   'Quid enim agunt, cum ita dicunt? Iuvat enim referre. Quemadmodum membra non probe affecta non possunt implere suum munus, ut lippitudine impediti oculi aut surditate aures, ita et animus aliquo modo perturbatus suum exequi officium non potest. Est autem proprium animi munus a vero nihil aberrare, et sapiens quidem numquam aberrabit. Igitur nec unquam erit perturbatus. Qui enim perturbatur, etiam ducatur errore necesse est. At aegritudo sive dolor — es enim in hac disputatione indifferenter his usus — vel maxima est omnium perturbationum. Non cadet igitur in sapientem dolor. Item si aegritudo est opinio praesentis mali, ut eam diffiniunt, necesse est ut qui praesentibus commovetur incommodis, timeat etiam futura; ita in quem cadet dolor, cadet et timor. Est autem fortitudini timor contrarius. Ita dolore affectus

attacking you and dragging you (not leading you) captive,[39] you did not assent to their thinking in the brilliant oration you just gave. Indeed, you have convinced me for the first time to reject Stoicism, if I may call it by that name, though I used to be a follower of that school; and you have made me flee more than ever, by Hercules, from the Epicureans with their seductive pleasure and soft insidious effect on our life. The Stoics had entirely convinced me of this but now I cannot but despise them. And finally, after hearing you, those Stoic teachings that I used to admire greatly — moved by the splendor of virtue and the praise of honor — now finally have begun to appear false. Their conclusions are always just such as to please the hearer, seeming to promise us freedom from every ill and claiming that the wise man will never have need for or be affected by anything. But since, as you have clearly argued, their whole discourse is about things that are by nature impossible, it looks like all their arguments must be rejected, and deservedly so, not only when pain is pressing on us, as you noted in the case of Dionysius, but as Nature herself and your reasoning demonstrate.

"Then what are they doing when they talk this way? It may 29 help to recall what they say. As our bodily members cannot fulfil their tasks when impaired [they would say], as our eyes cannot see when clouded over, and deaf ears cannot hear, similarly the mind, when somehow disturbed, cannot perform its office. The mind's proper task is not to deviate from the truth, and the wise man will never deviate from it. So he will never be disturbed. Yet anyone who is disturbed must necessarily be led into error. But anguish or pain — you used these terms interchangably in your discourse — are the greatest of all such disturbances. So suffering does not befall the wise man. Likewise if anguish, as they define it, is belief that an evil is present, necessarily someone who is agitated by present troubles may fear future ones as well; thus if pain befalls someone, fear does as well. But fear is the opposite of fortitude. So the man

non erit fortis. At omnis sapiens est fortis. Nullus igitur sapiens afficitur dolore.

30 'Afferunt huiusmodi compluria, quae, quoniam prae se speciem ferunt quandam potius quam dilucidi aliquid veri in se contineant, praetermissa sunt a te et disputationis tuae lumine confutata, ut nunc tandem aliquid de philosophia cognovisse existimem, nihilque vero simile iam nunc putem, nisi quod sit naturae consentaneum. Quid enim ad communem affert vivendi utilitatem pompa illa verborum atque ostentatio, quibus tam multa de sapientia, tam multa de honestate, quasi ambitione quadam turgidi, in multitudinem rerum imperitam credulamque effundunt, quandoquidem, ut de reliquis fere virtutibus et de fortitudine in primis, ea dicunt quae praeter naturam sint mortalium? Sapientiam vero eam complectuntur verbis quam si quis sit nactus, in numerum erit divorum et non amplius hominum referendus. Verum sunt haec abs te omnia perhumaniter quidem et graviter et dilucide disputata. Illud vero quod de hominis miseria dixisti, quem paulo ante tantopere laudaras, nisi aperias, male me habet. Quanquam non mediocris me formido tenet, ne quem etiam felicem a Deo factum hominem putaram, tu nunc miserum ostendas, quod sentire paulo ante mihi visus es, vel fallor?'

31 'Non falleris,' inquit, 'sed re vera miseri omnes sumus. Quamvis non facile persuadebuntur hi qui florente aetate, affluentibus et honoribus et divitiis, valitudine etiam nihil impediente, adeo sibi ipsis placent ut etiam felices se existimare audeant. Tamen non erit absurdum, quoniam ita vis, neque alienum ab hoc sermone nostro, aliquid de nostra natura diligentius dispicere. Nihil enim reperio quod tantam vim habeat ad consolandum quantam humanarum rerum contemplatio, quae efficere etiam, modo recta ratio non desit, potest ut quae ferme omnes tanquam extrema malorum fugienda putant, apertis, ut ita dicam, oculis et amotis errorum quibus omnis humana vita ducitur tenebris, sectanda fortasse potius quam fugienda valeant discernere. Paupertatem dico, morbos,

of fortitude will not be stricken by suffering. But every wise man is brave. Therefore no suffering affects the wise man.

"They proffer many arguments like that one. But since these 30 offer only a semblance of truth, rather than containing some clear truth in themselves, you omitted them and they stand refuted in light of your discussion, so that now indeed I think I understand something about philosophy; and I now think nothing possesses verisimilitude unless it conforms to nature. What practical benefit does the public gain from their verbal ostentation and display — when, as if swollen with pretension, they spout at length about wisdom and honor, playing on the ignorance and credulity of the many? What they say about the other virtues, and fortitude in particular, is clearly beyond the nature of mortal men. They describe wisdom in such words that anyone who achieved it would be counted among the gods, and not among men. Your whole speech, however, was argued with great humanity, weight and clarity. But what you said about man's misery — after previously praising his condition so highly — perplexes me unless you clarify it. Though I am rather afraid that the creature I thought God had made to be happy you may now show to be a wretched creature. That was my impression of how you felt, or was I mistaken?"

"You are not mistaken," he said; "in reality we *are* all unhappy.[40] 31 It is not easy for those in the prime of life, possessing honors and wealth in abundance and in good health, to believe this, and they are pleased with themselves to such a point that they dare think themselves happy. It won't be absurd therefore, nor irrelevant to our discussion, since you wish it, to look more closely at some aspects of our nature. I know of nothing that has so much power to console as the contemplation of human affairs. For if right reason is not absent, it lets us see with open eyes, so to speak, and remove the dark errors which overcloud human life, till we are able to see that the things almost all think must be shunned as extreme evils may be worth seeking out instead. I mean poverty, illness, humili-

abiectionem, repulsas, relegationes, exilia, orbitates, mortem, et quae sunt eiusdem generis, quae plerique, ut devitent, pericula etiam quaecunque putant esse subeunda.

32 'Sed plerunque aberrant mortalis de more infirmitatis. Quis enim non videt divitias saepenumero obfuisse compluribus et ob eas etiam male amissam vitam? — quanvis soleo divitiarum incommoda detrimentaque considerans multo illa maiora existimare, quod inertes atque otiosos soleant efficere earum possessores, et omnium generum libidinibus intentos. 'Est enim hominum genus a labore proclive ad libidinem,'⁵ ut ait Terentius. Qui igitur affluunt divitiis sectatores effecti propter otium voluptatis, minimam virtutis atque honestatis curam retinebunt. Ita fit ut bona quoque animi propter divitias amittantur, Chilone etiam teste, qui asserit virtutem simul et divitias esse non posse; et Diogenes ille canis Graecis scribens sic inquit: 'et indigentes plerunque adspexi ob paupertatem sanos esse, opulentos autem ob miseri ventris incontinentiam insanos.' Qua quidem nulla maior excogitari iactura potest, si quidem etiam ab futurae vitae gaudiis ob divitias excluduntur. Non enim inscite scriptum est a sacris auctoribus difficillime civitatis aeternae portas divitibus reserari. Mihi quidem, quem nostri homines divitiis abundare putaverunt, multo plura sunt semper incommoda quam utilitates per divitias importata, ut sine dubitatione aliqua audeam affirmare quibusque paupertatem divitiis anteferendam esse. Caret enim invidia paupertas, quae cum ceteris omnibus in rebus, tum in administrationibus civitatum magnas habet vires, ut etiam bonis saepenumero vehementer noceat, et proscriptiones et exilia, dira quoque nonnunquam supplicia et mala indignissima, qui sunt de patria optime meriti, pati ab invidia compellantur.

33 'Neque vero possunt aliquae opes vel animi vel corporis mederi morbis, immo vero animum plerunque aegrotum reddunt. Corpori autem quantum prodesse possint elegantissimis versibus ex-

ation, rejection, banishment, exile, bereavement, death and many other things of that sort, which most people think it worth running any risks to avoid.

"Most, however, go wrong from the usual human weakness. 32 Who has not seen riches bring harm to people and even make them lose their lives? — Though, considering the disadvantages and drawbacks inherent in wealth, by far the greatest is that riches make their possessors lazy and idle and bent on the satisfaction of all kinds of lust. 'For mankind is inclined to turn away from labor and towards lust,' as Terence says.[41] The affluent become seekers of pleasure thanks to the leisure they enjoy, keeping only a minimal concern for virtue and honor. Thus the goods of the mind are lost through material wealth. Chilon tells us this when he declares that virtue and wealth cannot exist together. And Diogenes the Cynic, addressing the Greeks, speaks as follows: 'I see many people without money who are healthy because of their poverty, and wealthy men who are unhealthy because of the unrestrained wants of their wretched belly.'[42] One cannot imagine a greater downfall for the rich, however, than to be excluded from the joys of the future life. The sacred authors knew what they were saying when they wrote that for the rich the gates of the eternal city are opened with difficulty.[43] As for me, whom my fellow citizens think to be overflowing with riches, there have always been more drawbacks than advantages from wealth, so that without hesitation I would dare to affirm that poverty is better for anyone than riches. For poverty is free from envy, which has great power everywhere, and plays a major role in the governance of cities, as in everything else, so that it often even harms the good, those most deserving of their country's gratitude, who are forced by envy to endure proscription and exile, and sometimes also torture and undeserved suffering.

"Nor can riches cure the diseases of mind and body; rather, 33 they very often make the soul sick. How helpful wealth is to the body is expressed by Lucretius in highly elegant verses in his

pressit Lucretius in his libris quos *De natura rerum* scripsit, magna, quantum ego intelligo, copia dignitateque praestantes:

> Nec calidae — inquit — citius decedunt corpore febres
> Textilibus si in picturis ostroque rubenti
> Iacteris quam si in plebeia veste cubandum est.

Illa vero Dionysii supra Damoclis caput eius felicitatem admirantis equina saeta ensem ruenti similem sustinens, et potestatem et divitias quantis essent refertae curis sollicitudinibusque declarat. Neque minus eiusdem Lucretii versus:

> Re veraque metus hominum curaeque sequaces
> Nec metuunt sonitus armorum nec fera tela
> Audacterque inter reges rerumque potentis
> Versantur, nec fulgorem reverentur ab auro,
> Nec clarum vestis splendorem purpureai.

34   'Ego quoque, cui satis est amplum a maioribus meis relictum patrimonium, quodque ex Dei munificentia non conservavi solum, sed fortasse etiam non nihil auxi, nihil unquam opis vel contra hunc et ipsum haereditarium podagrae morbum invenire potui, neque in exilio meo olim, neque in praesentia, quicquam dolenti pecunia opitulata est. Aliunde profecto, aliunde medicina petenda est. Quae si quo in loco inveniri potest, ea omnis, ut mihi videtur et supra dixi, in rebus contemplandis nostris et qua condicione nati simus intelligendo reperietur. Quae res mihi videri solet omnium difficillima. Quis enim non sibi ipsi placet? Quis membris non etiam gloriatur suis, modo mancus non sit aut debilis? Quis, ubi multo maior invenitur error, prudentiae consiliisque suis non applaudet, ut haec ipsa non minima sit mortalis naturae calamitas,

books *On the Nature of Things*, books distinguished, to my mind, by their great eloquence and dignity:

> Nor yet the quicker will hot fevers go,
> If on a pictured tapestry thou toss,
> Or purple robe, than if 'tis thine to lie
> Upon the poor man's bedding.[44]

The horse-hair of Dionysius that suspended the sword over Damocles' head when the latter marvelled at Dionysius' happiness just demonstrates how both power and wealth, however great, come to be a source of care and worry.[45] And this verse of that same Lucretius says no less:

> And of a truth man's dread, with cares at heels,
> Dreads not the sounds of arms, the savage swords
> But among kings and lords of all the world
> Mingles undaunted, nor is overawed
> By gleam of gold nor by the splendor bright
> Of purple robe.[46]

"Having an ample legacy left me by my ancestors, I have been 34
able, thanks to God's munificence, not only to preserve it but even perhaps to increase it somewhat. But I have never been able to use this wealth against the equally hereditary disease of gout, nor has money been helpful in reducing the pain of my past exile nor any of my present troubles. Surely one must seek medicine from another source, yes, another! If that medicine can be found anywhere, it is to be found entirely, as I have said, in the contemplation of our estate and in understanding the condition into which we are born. And that, as it has always seemed to me, is the most difficult thing of all to do. For who does not like himself? Who does not pride himself on his limbs, provided he is not crippled or weak? Who (and this is a much greater error) does not applaud his own prudence and his own counsels, so that not least of hu-

quod pauci omnino se esse calamitosos queant dignoscere? Nos autem de miseria nostra aliquid detrahamus si possumus, quod forsan non incommode faciemus, si qualia sunt quae excellentiora putantur ab hominibus breviter et pro viribus nostris tanquam lance quadam expendemus.

35   'Igitur qui vivendi se magistros profitentur quique in praecepta quaedam vitam nostram redegerunt, triplicem afferre de his rebus disputationem solent, ut eorum, quae ad vitam conferunt beatam, aliqua corporis nostri, aliqua vero animi respiciant naturam, interiectis etiam quibusdam tertiis, quae appellant propterea externa, quod a corpore animoque separata, magna tamen sint adminicula ad degendam vitam. Et in his quae sunt corporis enumerant in primis valitudinem, vires, formam, pernicitatem, dexteritatem, et quae sunt huius generis. Quae quidem qualia sint non est multum difficile cognoscere, quanquam ex omni numero perpaucos invenias, quibus vel magna ex parte vel omnia simul non desint. Sed fac adesse omnia. Quid tandem qui huiusmodi fuerit erit consecutus? Saepius enim offuerunt eis qui illa in se haberent, quam profuerint. Milonem Crotoniatem nudae manus ictu bovem aiunt interfecisse. Eundem in vestigio cum constitisset, dimovere nemo poterat. Malum tenenti digito nemo eripiebat. Quid tamen invenit in viribus Milo, propter quod minus se fortem malle non debuerit? Quid Lygdamus Syracusanus, quem etiam sine ossium medullis fuisse tradunt in pancratii corona? Quid Tritannus Samnites gladiator fortissimus? Quid eius filius, Cn. Pompeii miles, qui ipse inermis armatum devicit hostem detulitque in castra? Quid M. Sicinius Dentatus, quid Fufius, quid Athanatus, quem se vidisse Plinius confirmat quinquagenario thorace plumbeo indutum et quinquagenariis coturnis calceatum per scaenam incessisse? Quid inquam omnes ex fortitudine commodi et non magis detrimenti importaverunt? Pulchritudo autem, quae etiam solet ad

man disasters is the general inability to see how disastrous we ourselves have been? If we could, we would all subtract something from our misery, and perhaps it will be to our advantage if we briefly examine the things men think more excellent, weighing them as best we can, as though in a kind of balance.

"Now those who claim to teach us how to live, who sum up our   35
life in a few points, customarily debate three things. Of the goods that make life happy and blessed, some have to do with the nature of the body, some of the soul, and a kind of third class of goods is also thrown in which they call "external" goods because they are distinct from bodily or psychic goods but nevertheless minister greatly to the conduct of life.[47] Among the body's goods they count, first of all, health, then strength, beauty, agility, dexterity, and things like that. It is not hard to recognize the sort of things they are, although you'll find few men who are not missing a good many on the list, or even all of them simultaneously. But let's imagine someone possesses them all. What in the end will be the consequences of this for him? Very often these goods do their possessors more harm than good. They say that Milo of Croton killed a bull with a blow from his bare fist; that he could not be budged by anyone when he stood firm; and that he could hold an apple with one finger so that no one could wrest it away. What did Milo gain from his strength that he should not have preferred to be less strong?[48] What about Lygdamus the Syracusan, who they say lacked bone marrow but still won first place in the pancratium?[49] What about Tritanus the powerful gladiator in Samnite armor? And what of his son, a soldier of Pompey, who, unarmed, defeated an armed foe and dragged him back to camp?[50] What of Marcus Sicinius Dentatus, and Fufius, and Athanatus? Of the last, Pliny says that he saw him onstage wearing a leaden cuirass and boots both weighing fifty pounds.[51] What advantage, please, did they all gain from their strength? Wasn't it actually a disadvantage? And beauty, which predominantly tends to produce vanity and mad-

vanitatem et insaniam perducere, orationem meam non desiderat.
Si quidem non illi solum qui ea excellit saepenumero nocuit, sed
et totas plerunque civitates nationesque subvertit. De velocitate
item velim mihi Polymnestor dicat Milesius, quem etiam leporem
consecutum fuisse tradunt; aut Ladas, qui super harenas currens
vestigium non relinquebat; aut Anystus aut Philonides, Alexandri
Magni celebratissimi cursores, aut Virgiliana illa

> Volsca de gente Camilla
> [. . .] assueta [. . .] proelia virgo
> dura pati cursuque pedum praevertere ventos

aut noster Papirius, de quo tam multa Livius commemorat, aut alii
infiniti. Quid ex pernicitate sua ad aetatem bene agendam opis ret-
tulerunt praeter anhelitum, sudorem, laborem, dolorem? Idem de
ceteris quoque corporis attributis sine cunctatione videtur dicendum. Valitudo enim, quae in primis ideo desideratur quod ut plurimum non adest, nonne saepius invitat ad crapulam, nonne mentem nostram et rationem perturbat? Qua de re et Plato non
salubri in loco de industria constituit Academiam, philosophiae
studiis officere valitudinem arbitratus.

36   'Ita vere, ne omnia persequar, concludi potest nullam esse nostri
corporis dotem cui vel paululum modo confidere possimus, aut a
qua, nisi Deus (qui solus pericula potest avertere) adiumento fuerit, discrimina potius ac pestem non expectare debeamus. De externis vero in primis habent divitias, adeo ut ex nobilissimis philosophis finem eas administrandae rei familiaris ausi sint dicere.
Nihilominus quid hae in se contineant boni, satis, ut arbitror, supra est explicatum. Et qui his abundant, cum nihil auxilii in illis
contra morbos vel dolorem inveniant sed edacissimis potius plenas

ness, does not require any discussion from me. Not only does it often hurt those who are outstanding for their beauty, but it has even brought about the total ruin of many cities and nations. As for speed, then, do you want me to speak of Polymnestor the Milesian, who they say was able to overtake a hare; or Ladas, who left no footprints when he ran over sand, or Anystus or Philonides, famous racers recognized by Alexander the Great,[52] or Virgil's

Camilla of Volscian race,
a warrior-maid hardy
to bear the battle brunt
and in speed of foot to outstrip the winds.[53]

or our Papirius, whom Livy commemorates at such length,[54] or countless others. What did Papirius get for his agility, what reward for the right conduct of life except panting, sweat, hard work, and pain? The same, to be brief, seems to apply to the other bodily attributes. Even health, which is all the more desired because it is so often lacking—does not it too often entice us to drunkeness, does it not disturb our mind and reason? This is why Plato deliberately established the Academy in an insalubrious place, judging that health was an obstacle to philosophical studies.[55]

"Truly, without going into every detail, we can conclude that there is no physical endowment we can in the least rely on, or which we ought not rather to expect to become a danger or a plague, unless God helps us, for he alone can ward off dangers. Of external gifts, wealth is most respected, so some of the noblest philosophers have dared to claim that it is the goal of managing family resources.[56] Nonetheless I have sufficiently made clear above what I think of the real value of riches. And the rich, since they find no help in them against disease or sorrow, but rather find them full of voracious cares, know this better than those who are

36

curis, multo noverunt melius quam qui in omnium sunt rerum egestate, qui beatos divites existimare solent, communi quodam humano errore, quo efficitur ut nostris permoti malis, eos semper admiremur quos ab his ipsis quibus angimur incommodis, quam longissime conspicimus. Tamen, si recte volemus iudicare, "tollemus[6] querelas," ut ait Horatius.

> Pauper enim non est cui rerum suppetit usus.
> Si ventri bene, si lateri est pedibusque tuis, nil
> Divitiae poterunt regales addere maius.

Quae autem est paupertatis quies cum insano illo divitiarum tumultu comparanda? Adde quod misera est magni custodia census:

> Ut[7] vigilare metu exanimem, noctesque diesque
> Formidare malos fures, incendia, servos,
> Ne te compilent fugientes.

Recte Flaccus "horum" se "pauperrimum bonorum" semper optarit. Verum iam plura fortasse de divitiis quam necesse sit. Quando autem me ob eas forsitan nonnulli putant minus miserum, plerique etiam beatum, non est visum ab re verbosius de his talia disputavisse. Restant autem praecipua inter externa, honores atque imperia, quorum tanta insania est ut qui aliquo modo miserrima ambitione non laboret vix inveniatur. Insita est enim in animis nostris laudis ac gloriae cupiditas, quae tantam vim habet ut etiam in contemnenda gloria nonnulli sibi gloriam quaesitaverint. Quod ideo desiderium inesse nobis puto ut, intelligentes ex Deo omnem esse gloriam, in eo esse nos gloriosos contenderemus, quamvis natura et consuetudine depravata ex fortuna magis quam ex Deo gloria petatur. Quo merito accidit ut, cum ad culmen etiam laudis pervenisse sibi videri possunt, saepe superbiente ac saeviente for-

utterly needy and who are wont to reckon the rich to be happy. This common human error causes us, struggling with our own misfortunes, to always be astonished that men whom we see from a great distance can be troubled by the very same misfortunes that trouble us. If we wish our judgment to be accurate, however, 'We shall banish complaints,' as Horace says.

> To use at pleasure, who shall call you poor?
> Sides, stomach, feet, if these are all in health,
> What more could man procure with princely wealth?[57]

How can one compare the tranquility of poverty to the mad chaos of riches? Moreover, having the care of a great fortune is a cause of misery:

> But to go mad with watching, nights and days
> To stand in dread of thieves, fires, runaways
> Who filch and fly [. . .].[58]

Horace was right to wish always to be 'the poorest in goods like these.'[59] But I've already said more than was necessary about wealth. Considering, however, that some people think me less miserable because of my wealth, and many even think me happy, it does not seem inappropriate that I have discoursed about it at some length. But there remains the most important of the external goods, honors and power, about which men are so insane that you may scarcely find a single person who does not in some way labor under this most wretched of ambitions. For I think the desire for praise and glory is innate in our souls, running so strong that some seek to attain glory for themselves even in the very act of despising it. I think that this desire is in us so that, understanding that all glory is God's, we may compete to gain glory in him. Despite this, because we are corrupted both in nature and our habits, we look for glory from Fortune more than from God. So it is only right that, when some persons seem to themselves to have arrived

tuna, quantum ab vero aberrarint facile recognoscant. Exemplorum plena sunt omnia, ut in his tempus terere minime videatur
necessarium.'

37 'Minime,' inquam, 'Cosme. Sed perge, quaeso. Ita enim afficior,
dicente te, ut vel libentissime fiam miser.'

'Si quis igitur,' inquit, 'tamen ea requirat, non in libris dumtaxat
sacris abundantissime poterit reperire, sed et Latinos omnes ac
Graecos codices, non historiarum modo sed et philosophiae et
oratoriae et poeticae facultatis refertissimos comperiet. Tanta
enim copia est ac semper fuit omnibus aetatibus atque omnibus
nationibus eorum qui fortunae secuti auram, miseranda hominibus spectacula praebuerunt ut uberior sive paratior nulla possit
esse materia rerum scriptoribus. Atque ego quoque nunc iam trahi
in exemplum possum, ut qui paulo ante pientissimi filii umeris im-
becillus ac fere exsanguis senex gestarer, repente eo subtracto cor-
ruerim, nec a quo erigar invenire possim.

38 'Ex quo etiam addubitare cogor quod et supra dixi, utrum
conferant filii ad degendam vitam. Qui locus, etsi difficilius peri-
culosiusque tractetur et propter naturae vim et generis necessitatem, tamen est id omnibus fere in promptu: nullam esse in vita
maiorem curam quam liberorum aut alendorum aut instituendo-
rum. Qui enim in Pythagorae bivio non aberrent, vel corrupto vivendi more vel male ducentibus praemonstratoribus, vix e multis
milibus paucos reperias. Sed finge altos rectamque vivendi ingres-
sos viam, ut amicis, parentibus, patriae suis meritis cari esse possint. Quis eos a morte poterit liberare? Ita evenit ut cum his
quibus assueti sumus privari nos commodis videamus, quantum
fuerat voluptatis cum illis frueremur, tantum ex eorum amissione
maeroris relinquatur necesse sit.

at the peak of renown, Fortune often disdains them and rages against them, and they quickly come to realize how far they have strayed from the truth. The world is full of examples which we hardly need to waste time on."

"Not at all, Cosimo, please continue. I am so affected by your 37 words that I shall become perfectly willing to become wretched."

"If anyone needs examples," said he, "they can find them abundantly, and not only in holy books. Indeed he will find all the Latin and Greek books filled with them, not only the histories, but also the philosophical, rhetorical and poetical subjects. There is, and has always been, such a large number of men of all ages and nations who follow Fortune's favor, and so offer a pitiful spectacle to mankind, that authors have had no richer and readier subject-matter. And now I too can be cited as an example, for a short time ago, though a weak and almost bloodless old man, I was carried on the shoulders of the most pious of sons,[60] but now am suddenly deprived of him and am falling down to earth, nor can I find someone to raise me up.

"Hence I am driven to doubt what I said earlier, about whether 38 children improve our lives. The topic is rather difficult and a dangerous one to treat, both because of natural inclination and family necessities, yet it is obvious to almost everyone that nothing in life involves a heavier burden of responsibility than the raising and educating children. You will find but a few among many thousands of offspring who do not go wrong at the crossroads of Pythagoras,[61] either by engaging in a bad sort of life or led astray by bad leaders. Yet imagine the noble ones embarked on the straight path of righteousness, who are able to be dear to their friends, parents, and country for their merits. Who will save them from death? Thus it happens that when we look at those for whom we were accustomed to sacrifice our own convenience, the more we have enjoyed their company, the more grief it is for us to lose them.

39   'Quid alii sentiant nescio. Ipse certe ea sententia sum, ut existimem sapientissimum humani generis auctorem et conditorem Deum nihil concessisse mortalibus quod, si statera expendatur, non multo plus in se aloes continere cernatur quam mellis. Quod si quis aliter fortasse aliquando putarit, arbitror fore ut, si ad hos se annos senectutemque perduxerit, non sit tandem ita se rem habere infitias iturus. Quid igitur habet fortuna quod expetendum sit? Quid non magis propter eius ipsius temeritatem insanamque libidinem etiam fugiendum? Est autem, ut mihi videtur, ista vel maxima hominum miseria, ut quorum illis insita cupido est quaeque tanto studio curaque conquirunt et necessaria etiam ad vitam et felicitatem opinantur, in potestate omnia sint illius dominae quae ea vertere et pro temeritatis suae arbitrio miscere iocum et risum putet, ut exclamare cum Lucretio libeat:

> O miseras hominum mentes, o pectora caeca:
> Qualibus in tenebris vitae quantisque periclis
> Degitur hoc aevi quodcunque est!

Et ita est profecto. Si enim, ut iam ostendimus, quae homines habent in primis huiusmodi sunt ut saepius afferre possint ea habentibus detrimentum, quid non ingenue iam fateamur nos miseros blandirique admodum nobis ipsis amplius desinamus?'

40   'Ita faciendum,' inquam, 'Cosme. Sed iam id dudum me Porticus edocuit, quae a te enumerata sunt corporea et externa non esse de numero bonorum, quamvis te paulo ante disputantem contra meminerim.'

'Meministi,' inquit, 'et re vera sic est. Quae Deus fecit, omnia bona sunt, etsi multo aliter nobis saepenumero videri possit. Ea enim est natura bonorum ut videantur plerunque non bona his qui, quod sit vere bonum, exactissime non comprehenderint.'

41   'Desidero,' inquam, 'a te aliquando quid de bono sentias cognoscere, ut et supra pollicitus, quamquam quae ad hunc pertinent

"I don't know how others feel. I certainly am of the opinion that God, the supremely wise author and founder of the humankind, has granted mortals nothing which, if you weigh it in the balance, does not contain much more of bitter aloe than of honey.[62] If perchance someone thinks otherwise, I think that he is not in the end going to deny it if he survives to my advanced age. What has Fortune to offer that makes it worth pursuing? What is more to be shunned than the recklessness and insane lust she excites? It seems to me that the very greatest source of human misery is the inborn lust for these things which men pursue with such zeal and devotion, thinking them necessary, even, to life and happiness, all of which are in the power of Lady Fortuna, who thinks it a great joke to overturn and arbitrarily reshuffle the deck, so that one wants to exclaim with Lucretius:

O wretched minds of men! O blinded hearts!
In how great perils, in what darks of life
Are spent the human years, however brief![63]

That is just how it is. For if, as we have now shown, the things of this kind that men most esteem are such as often bring harm to their possessors, why don't we frankly admit that we are wretches and stop flattering ourselves any more?"

"So we should, Cosimo," I said. "But some time ago the Stoa taught me that those corporeal and external goods you listed should not be counted among goods, although I remember your arguing to the contrary a short while ago."

"You remember well," he said, "and what you say is true. For all that God made is good, though it often seems very much otherwise to us. It is in the nature of good things that they often do not seem good to those who lack a very precise idea of what the true good is."

"I would like," I said, "to learn from you some time your views on the good, as promised earlier, though I know well enough what

locum satis intelligo, et divine sane mihi dicere videris, ut cetera. Veruntamen tertium quoddam bonorum genus, cui quidem Stoici omnia tribuenda censent, nunc restat, quod ego te existimo propter excellentissimam mentem tuam non esse non etiam elaturum laudibus. Animus enim, vera creatoris sui imago, quem tu ita excoluisti ut ad imaginis ipsius veritatem propinquissime te accessisse cuncti fateantur, nonne res quaedam praeclarissima est, nonne etiam maior quam dici verbis aut comprehendi cogitatione possit? In eo igitur nonne potest etiam gloriosa putari humana natura et de miseria multum auferre?'

42 'Multum,' inquit, 'neque aliquo pacto commodius quam si vera esse quae supra diximus animus cognoverit, eaque se condicione corpori coniunctum ut donec unde demissus a Deo est redierit, nihil omnino sit inventurus quod nisi umbram quandam veri solidique boni prae se ferat. Quod etsi difficillimum sit propter innatam vivendi maximam cupiditatem, quam sapientissimus Deus summa cum sapientia constituit, tamen ea tandem vera philosophia est, ut Platoni quoque placet, quae mortis habet commentationem. Solent enim et quidem non absurde, ut mihi videtur, qui sapientiores sunt habiti, etsi vita excellentissimi loco muneris a Deo nobis data est, vitae quoque ipsi mortem saepenumero anteponere. Cum enim quae in vita sunt ante oculos, unusquisque sibi praeponet recteque de illis volet iudicare, nihil, ut arbitror, inveniet propter quod discessus hic noster et e vita migratio multum lamentanda esse videatur. Incipias licet ab nascente homine perque progressus omnes actionesque percurras, plena omnia laborum dolorumque invenies. Est enim et vero quidem scriptum in sacris litteris quod "militia est hominis vita super terram et sicut mercennarii dies eius."

43 'Saepe ego, ut fere fit, mecum loquens de natura nostra et ab incunabulis, cum in hanc lucem primum demittimur, considerans deinde reliquam omnem aetatem mente ac cogitatione persecutus,

pertains to this topic, and you seem to me to have spoken divinely on this as on other topics. But there remains still the third kind of good, which the Stoics consider the only real good, and I think, in view of the excellence of your own mind, that you will not avoid singing its praises. The mind is the true image of the the Creator, which you have so cultivated that all confess you have approached very close to the truth of that image. Is not then the mind something of supreme value, is it not great beyond what can be said of it in words or understood in thought? Is it not possible to think human nature truly glorious in this respect, and that the mind is able to free us from much misery?"

"Much indeed," said he, "and in no way more suitably than if 42 the rational soul recognizes that what we have said above is true, that its condition is to be joined to the body until released by God for its return, and until then it will not encounter anything but the shadow of a true and real good. Yet this is difficult because of our great innate desire to live, which God's supreme wisdom has given us, while true philosophy is in the end, as Plato thought, a meditation on death.[64] And therefore those who are thought very wise seem to me not absurd (even though life is given us to use as an excellent gift of God), when they prefer death to life, as they often do. For although every individual will place before himself the things under his eyes and will wish to judge correctly of them, he will yet find nothing, as I believe, to make it seem that we should mourn our departure hence and our going to another place. You may begin with man's birth and run through his all his development and his activities, and you will find them all to be full of labor and suffering. It is true indeed what is written in the Sacred Scriptures that 'the life of man on earth is like service in war, and his days as those of a mercenary.'[65]

"When I meditate inwardly upon human nature, as often hap- 43 pens, and pursue in thought how we are sent forth from the womb and placed in the light of day, and how we go through our various

lacrimas etiam saepenumero non contineo. Nam cum infantium vagitum, qui et ipse, etiam si parum illa aetas sentiat, tamen eos aliquid pati non iucundum declarat; cum puerorum gemitum, qui facile propter aetatis teneritudinem a frigore, aestu, ceterisque infinitis paene rebus quibus illa nova caro et recens humus offenditur, moventur, contemplor; cum eorum ipsorum horrores et delusiones, quae ne punctum quidem dormientes etiam quietos permittunt, cumque iam adultioris aetatis libidinum incendia, totque et tam varias rerum vel turpium vel periculosarum, quibus dies noctesque miserrime vexantur, appetitiones atque ob quas in morbos alii, alii in egestates, alii in manifestissima pericula et calamitates mortesque inciderunt; cum provectiorum iam studia, labores et vanissimas omnino et inquietissimas curas; cum negotiationes, peregrinationes, navigationes, militias, gubernationes, scriptiones, lectiones, sermones, disputationes, digladiationes, quibus omnis omnium vita implicata est; cum tandem, si quis ex magnis innumerabilibusque quieti nostrae insidiantibus periculis animam ad senectutis hanc miseriam usque protraxerit, taedia, languores, et, ut uno verbo multa complectar incommoda, ipsum proprie senium, quo ego nihil puto natura esse posse molestius; cum haec, inquam, omnia considero, cogor non solum putare non malum mortem, sed malorum etiam humanorum omnium perfugium, eique saepius habendam esse gratiam quam deflendam duco.

44   'Quapropter et antiquissimum rhetorem Alcidamum soleo etiam admirari, qui, cum laudationem mortis litteris mandaverit, tantum abfuit ut eam inter mala enumerari voluerit. Carissima profecto vita est eiusque ipsius omnibus innatum animantibus ardentissimum desiderium; tantum tamen ratio nonnunquam potest ut etiam despiciatur. Hegesias quidem Cyrenaicus librum scripsit

ages, I often cannot restrain my tears. For I think of the crying of babies who, though that young age has little feeling, appear to be suffering from something unpleasant; and then the crying of children, easily upset at their tender age by cold, heat, and the pain of an infinite number of things which hurt that new flesh and that but-lately-turned soil. And then I think of these same children's horrors and delusions which give them not a moment's rest, even when asleep in bed. And then I think of the burning lust of the next age, troubled by so much and so many sorts of things, by appetites and diseases that bring shame or danger and trouble them sorely night and day. Then I think of how some people fall into addictions and the diseases they lead to, while others fall into want, and still others into manifest dangers, calamities and death. I think of all the pursuits of more advanced age, the labors, the futile and restless anxieties, all the business, travel, sea voyages, military expeditions, and political offices; the writing, reading, sermonizing, disputing, and violent struggles — all of them part of everyone's life. I think, finally, how if someone survives the great and innumerable dangers that undermine our tranquility and reaches this misery of old age, its weariness, torpor and — to summarize its many disadvantages in a single word — its senility, which personally I think is the worst thing nature can give us — when, I say, I think of all this, I am forced not only to believe that death is not an evil, but even to consider it a refuge from all the evils of human life, and regard it more often as something to give thanks for rather than to mourn.

"For this reason, I've always wondered at the ancient rhetori- 44 cian Alcidamus, who, in composing a speech in praise of death, could not bring himself to list it among evils.[66] Life is indeed very dear to us, and the desire for it, innate in all living things, is very powerful, yet an argument can sometimes become so strong as to reduce life to an object of contempt. Hegesias of Cyrene wrote a book about the disadvantages of human life, and discussed the

de humanis incommodis, cumque de his in scolis quoque copiosissime disputaret, tam multis taedium iniciebat vitae ut ab Ptolemaeo id agere sit prohibitus. Operae pretium est in his divum ut audiamus Hieronymum. Ille igitur paulo antequam moreretur ait:

> O vita—inquit—mundi non vita, sed mors; vita fallax, vita onusta tristitiis, imbecillis et umbratica, vita mendax. Nunc flores, statim arescis. Vita privans vita cui inhaerens, vita fragilis, vita momentanea et caduca, quae quanto magis crescis, [tanto magis] decrescis, cum plus procedis, plus ad mortem propinquas. O vita plena laqueis, quot in mundo illaqueas, quot per te iam sustinent tormenta infernalia! Quam beatus, qui tuas cognoscit fallacias! Quam beatior qui de tuis non curat blanditiis! O quam beatissimus, qui de te bene privatus est. Melior est negotiatio eius argento, et auro purissimo fructus eius.

45 'Enumerare quoque licet ex his quos antiquitas etiam admirata est, qui vel bonum mortem vel certe non malum re ipsa iudicaverunt. Etsi ob id ipsum non laudandi sed vituperatione digni sunt, quod non fugiendum est e vita sed abeundum, cum quasi receptui canere iubet imperator omnium Deus, qui nos huc tanquam ad pugnam aliquam milites propterea demisit ut, non deserto loco neque tergis versis, victores tandem perpetua et quiete et gloria quasi triumphantes frueremur; tamen declarant illi quidem mortem non tantopere extimescendam esse, neque si quis ex hac quae verius mors est ad illam sit vitam revocatus, ideo dolendum quod bona reliquerit, sed potius quod nos relicti sumus ingemiscendum. Est enim opinione mea multo eorum sors melior, quibus, quasi laboriosissimo quodam vivendi munere completo et decurso spatio, unde discesserint in caelum revolare contigerit, quando qui-

topic at great length in the schools. In the end, he made so many weary of life that he was forbidden by Ptolemy to continue.[67] It is worthwhile to listen to St. Jerome on this matter. Shortly before he died, he said:

> O life (he said), the life of the world is not life but death; deceitful life, life burdened with sadness, weakness and darkness, life the liar! First you flourish, then you wither. Life, destroying life in anyone it inhabits, fragile life, life fleeting and frail. The more you grow, the more you diminish, the more you go forward, the closer you approach death. O life full of snares, how many do you trap in the world, how many through your agency are afflicted with the torments of hell! How blessed the man who recognizes your deceits! How much more blessed the man who cares nothing for your flattery! O how utterly blessed is the man who is well rid of you! His bargain is better than silver, and the profit thereof is purest gold.[68]

One may list here also those whom the ancients admired, who 45 either reckoned death a good thing or at least not in itself an evil. They should not be praised but blamed, since we must not flee this life, but retire from it when God, the commander of us all, sounds the retreat. For he sent us here as soldiers to do battle, so that, neither deserting our post nor turning our backs in retreat, we may in the end triumph as victors and enjoy peace and glory. Still, those ancients declared that death is not greatly to be feared, and that if someone is recalled from this life, which is truly death, to that true life, we should not grieve because he left behind the goods of life, but should weep rather that we ourselves have been left behind. In my opinion, the better lot belongs to those who have accomplished the hard task of living and completed their course, so that now they fly back to heaven whence they descended. For the wisest man among the Jews, King Solomon, in

dem et sapiens ille Hebraeorum rex Salomon, in eo libello in quo calamitatem deflet humanae condicionis, magis laudavit mortuos quam viventes et feliciorem utroque iudicavit qui nondum natus esset. Iob autem de vulva se eductum queritur: "Utinam," inquit, "consumptus essem ne oculus[8] me videret." Quibus illud Sileni simile videtur ad Midam pro manumissionis mercede, quo regem edocuit, "Esse quidem homini optimum non nasci, proximum quamprimum mori." Fabulosissima quidem semper fuit antiquitas; tamen nescio quo pacto illae quoque me fabulae nonnunquam delectant, et ad vitam videtur quarundam cognitio non inutilis. Cleobis quidem et Bito, ob pietatem cum a dea praemium ‹peterunt›, referunt mortem; Trophonius item atque Agamedes post tertium diem, adaedificato[9] in Delphis Apollini templo, mercedem petentes mortui reperti. Nonne id nos instruere videntur ut mortem etiam divino testimonio anteponamus vitae? Sed haec quidem ornatius, ut opinor, a Graecis. Nos audiamus spectemusque nostros atque a fabulis recedamus. Paulus enim, is qui raptus in caelum arcana Dei viderat, vitae taedium habet et dissolvi cupit et esse cum Christo.

46 Idem de quo paulo ante mentionem fecimus, divinissimus Hieronymus, quibus verbis quoque animo e vita egreditur? Non possum, cum illum lego, non multum damnare hos qui tam late patent humanos nostros errores, qui etiam conducere praeficas quae lugeant ac plangant consuevimus. Ille vero, quo pacto mortem non alienam, ut illae solent, sed suam deflet? Ipsum audiamus. Cum enim amicos ob eum, qui parabatur ac propinquissimus erat ab eis discessus, tristitia videret affectos, his verbis inter cetera consolatur:

O quantum lucrum est mihi mori, quoniam meum vivere deinceps Christus erit! Ecce terrestris domus huius habitationis dissolvitur, et alia succedet habitatio non manu facta,

his book deploring the misery of the human condition, praises the condition of the dead more than that of the living, and judges that man happiest who was never born.[69] And Job complains that he was brought forth from the womb: 'Would that I had been consumed that no eye might see me.'[70] These things recall Silenus' words to Midas, when, in payment for his freedom, he instructed the king, 'It were best for a man not to be born, and the next best thing to die at once.'[71] True, antiquity always was full of false tales, but for some reason these myths at times please me, and certain of them seem valuable in understanding life. When Cleobis and Biton asked the goddess to reward their piety, they received their death. So too, Trophonius and Agamedes, having built the temple of Apollo at Delphi, after the third day asked for their pay and received death.[72] Doesn't all this seem to teach us by divine testimony that we should prefer death to life? But I think this was more elegantly presented by the Greeks. Let us leave myths aside and listen and look at our own [Christian] authors. For Paul himself, when he was taken up into heaven and saw the mysteries of God, was disgusted with life and longed to loosen the mortal coil and be with Christ.[73]

"It was the same with the saintly Jerome, whom we mentioned 46 a little earlier: with what words, with what zeal did he depart this life? When I read him, I cannot help but condemn the men who broadcast our human fallibility by following the custom of hiring women to mourn and wail. But how did Jerome mourn death — not somebody else's, as women are wont to do, but his own? Let us listen to him. Seeing his friends full of grief as he prepared his imminent departure from them, he consoled them with these words among others:

O how much I gain in dying, for hereafter I will be living with Christ! Behold, the earthly home of my dwelling is dissolved, and another dwelling-place will succeed it, one not

sed aeterna in caelis. Ecce quod mortale est vestimentum exuor, ut aeternum induar. Huc usque peregrinatus sum, iam redeo ad patriam. Ecce bravium capio, pro quo in agone contendi. Ecce portum attingo, quem tanto desiderio deside-ravi. Ecce de tenebris ad lucem, de periculis ad securitatem, de inopia ad divitias, de proelio ad victoriam, de tristitia ad gaudium, de serviente ad dominum, de temporali ad perpe-tuum, de foetore ad odorem suavissimum vehor. Hic caecus sum et illuminor vere, hic vivens et mortuus sum et vere vi-vificor.

Age vero, quanta alloquitur mortem ipsam suavitate orationis! Quis unquam vel sponsam vel amicam suavius?

O mors — inquit — dulcis et iucunda, non certe mors, quae vitam veram largiris, quae fugas, febres et vulnera, famem ex-tinguis et sitim. O mors iustissima, pia bonis et malis aspera, veni, sponsa mea, soror mea, dilecta mea; indica mihi quem diligit, anima mea. Exurge, gloria mea, porrige mihi manum. Ecce tu pulchra es amica mea; noli amplius tardare.

Tandemque se omnibus illam vitae suae diebus quaeritasse confirmat; eamque ‹invenisse› mira quadam laetitia gestire etiam videtur.

47 ʼInnumerae martyrum legiones afferri in medium possunt, qui volentissimis animis ad mortem concurrerunt, ut dubitari iam non possit quantum haec quae appellatur vita non multum diligi, quantum etiam expeti mors, quam vulgus ita horret, debeat. Quae quidem res id efficit in praesentia ut, etsi relictum me esse in vita, minime ex commodo meo factum putem idque doleam. Tamen id me multum consoletur, quod non diutius in vita sum futurus. Id est enim proprium senectutis munus quod plerique contra inter-pretantur obque id accusant et miseram putant senectutem. Mihi

made with hands but one that is eternal in heaven. Now I strip off this mortal dress so that I may put on an eternal one. I have wandered as a stranger thus far, now I return to my country. Behold, I take the prize for which I contended in the games. Behold, I reach the harbor that I have desired with such longing. Behold, I go from darkness to light, danger to safety, poverty to wealth, battle to victory, sadness to joy, servitude to lordship, from the transitory to the eternal, from stench to the sweetest of sweet odors. Here am I blind and there shall I receive the true light, living here I am dead and there shall I be made alive.[74]

Look how he sweetly he eulogizes Death itself! What bride or friend could be more lovingly spoken of?

O Death (he says), sweet and joyful, surely not really death as you offer greater life, as you put an end to exile, to fevers and wounds, to hunger and thirst. O death most just, kind to good and harsh to evil men: come my bride, my sister, my beloved; show me the one my soul loves. Arise, my glory, give me your hand. Behold thou art beautiful, my beloved; delay not any longer.[75]

Thus in the end he confirmed that all the days of his life he had sought death; and he seems to long for it with wondrous joy.

"We could cite countless legions of martyrs who ran toward 47 death with eager hearts, so that no one can doubt how little we should love what is called life, and how much we should desire death, which the vulgar fear so greatly. For these reasons it happens that for the present, though I am left in this life, I do not at all regard that fact as to my advantage and am sorry for it. Nevertheless I am much consoled that I do not have much longer to live. That is the real gift of old age, though many see it the opposite way and blame old age as miserable. To me it seems that, for this

vero ea re sola ceteris omnibus videtur aetatibus senectus ipsa anteferenda esse, quod abitum praeparat nobis ab vivendi laboriosissima vanitate reducitque in caelestem patriam, ubi sine algore, sudore, labore, dolore aevo perfruamur sempiterno.' Haec in me
adspiciens cum dixisset, postea conticuit.

48 Ego vero, 'Optime,' inquam, 'Cosme, nos effecisti miseros, quod
non ad levandum mihi videtur dolorem conferre, quod tibi videri
dixisti, sed id ipsum potius dolendum puto, quod et Carneades
dicebat, quod ita simus misera nati condicione ut id ipsum sit
vel plurimum dolendum. Reprehendere enim Chrysippum solebat
Euripideum illud laudantem carmen:

Mortalis nemo est quem non attingat dolor;

idque penitus dolore dignum asserebat, quod vere id dici ab illo
poeta vel alio quopiam posset. Quid enim magis dolendum esse
dicebat, quam quod ita est naturae constitutum legibus ut non
possit hominum vita multis esse non refertissima doloribus.'

49 Ad haec igitur Cosmus, voce etiam paulo elatiore, 'An tu,' inquit, 'ex his unus es qui naturam et Deum, qui naturae auctor est,
audeas accusare? Quae est enim haec caecitas nostra, quae hae tam
crassae obscuraeque tenebrae ut non possimus quae facta sunt omnia melius non potuisse aut ex nobis ipsis, quod non difficile videtur, si superbi esse nolemus, intelligere aut certe a sapientissimis,
qui scriptis id suis constantissime asseverant, non persuaderi? Ego
vero sic existimo, immo vero certo scio, neque Carneadem ipsum
neque quemquam alium praeter unum ipsum et solum sapientissimum rerum omnium creatorem et patrem Deum melius potuisse
consulere hominibus quam consultum sit. Ut haec ipsa, quam nos
miseriam nec immerito neque praeter Dei vocamus voluntatem,
praecipua putari felicitas debeat, quando quidem non sine magna

reason alone, old age is the best time of life, because it prepares us to depart from the laborious futility of living, and restores us to our heavenly homeland where, free of cold, sweat, labor, and pain, we shall enjoy eternal life." He gazed at me as he said this, then fell silent.

"Dearest Cosimo," I said, "you have done a fine job of making   48 us miserable, and it seems to me that you have not contributed to lightening my sorrow (as you said it seemed to you). Rather, I think, you have made me mourn this very thing, the same thing Carneades used to say, that we are born to such a miserable condition that it is the human condition itself which is most greatly to be mourned. Carneades, indeed, reproached Chrysippus for citing this verse of Euripides:

No man is such that sorrow does not reach him.[76]

And he said that it was worthy of sorrow that this poet or any other could truly say this. But what is even more of a reason for sorrow, he said, is that man is so constituted by the laws of nature that it is impossible for human life not to be replete with sorrows."[77]

In reply, Cosimo spoke, raising his voice a little more. "Are you   49 one of those who dares to accuse nature and God, who is nature's Creator? What is this blindness of ours, what are these dark and dense shadows, that we are unable to see that all things are made for the best? This we could see for ourselves quite easily if we did not choose to be too proud, and surely we could be persuaded of it by the wisest of men, who in their writings steadfastly assure us of this? It is very clear to me, indeed I know it for certain, that neither Carneades himself nor anyone else — except for the one and sole Wisest, the Creator of all things and God the father — could have provided for humankind better than has been provided. For that which we rightly call misery, being in accordance with the will of God, ought rather to be thought our chief blessedness. God es-

quadam ab eo causa ita constitutum est ut scilicet illecebris mundi huius minime allecti, redeundum ad veriores esse delicias non obliviscamur. Mens enim haec nostra et animus ad bonum natura sua, id est Dei iussu, quietemque propensus, si in his quae, ut diximus, nihil in se continent quietis saepenumero decipitur, quid facturum fuisse putandum est, si quid nactus fuisset in quo vel paulum constare se posse animadvertisse? Ita vero fit ut in umbra et fumo nos esse intelligentes, dum secuti animi naturam aliquid stabile conquirimus, illud autem minime in vita hac reperire possumus, oculos ad auctorem ipsum nostrum et necessario quidem dirigamus. Neque aliqua esse vera causa potest cur non tantum non dolere debeamus, quod sine dolore vivere non possumus; sed id ipsum potius inter innumerabilissima Dei in humanum et mortale genus munera praecipuum praestantissimumque existimari debeat, quod tanquam praemonstratorem quemdam dederit et ducem, quem secuti et vanitate reiecta omni aberrare ab caelesti patria, modo velimus, minime queamus.'

50   Quanquam, cum haec dixisset, plura essent praeterea quae ab eo desiderarem, tamen rubore quodam perfusus, cum ille siluisset, non sum amplius percontari ausus. Itaque me tunc quidem continui eo tamen consilio, ut, quandocunque occasio daretur aliqua interrogandi et cum eo colloquendi, non eam praetermitterem. Nullum enim mihi videtur lucrum cum ea utilitate comparandum, nulla voluptas cum illa felicitate conferenda esse.

tablished this for a very good reason, namely, so that being little attracted by the lures of this world, we might not forget that we must return to truer delights. By nature, that is by the command of God, our mind and soul are inclined towards the good and towards peace; and if, as we have said, they are often deceived by things that contain no peace, what must we think they would do if they found something in which they could find rest? Consequently, we understand that we live amid shadow and smoke, and following our spiritual nature, we seek something stable. But we cannot find it in this life, and thus we necessarily raise our eyes to our Creator. Nor can there be any true reason why we ought not to suffer, because we cannot live without suffering. Yet among the countless gifts of God to our mortal humanity, we must consider this the chief and greatest gift of all: that he has given us a guide and leader to follow so that we reject all vanity and, so long as we wish it, we turn not aside from our heavenly country."

After he said these things, there were a number of other things 50 that I wished to ask him; but when he had fallen silent, I blushed and did not dare ask any more questions. And so I restrained myself with the intention that in future I would neglect no occasion that presented itself for asking him questions and speaking with him. No profit seemed to me comparable to this benefit, no pleasure comparable to this felicity.

: 4 :

Praefatio in Collectiones Cosmianas

1   Bartholomeus Scala Laurentio Medici, urbis spei, salutem dicit.

Collegi, Laurenti carissime, scripta compluria et omnia fere in quae manu inciderunt ubi nomen Cosmi avi tui, patris huius urbis, legeretur. Ea redegi in volumen quod mitto nunc ad te. Velim ut tantum otii subtrahas maximis tuis occupationibus, ut mira et legendi et intelligendi divini ingenii tui sollertia omnia percurras; et si tibi videbuntur digna qua‹e› legantur ab hominibus, alicui ex bibliothecis Cosmi ut inserantur curabis. Vale.

2   Dubitare soleo saepenumero iniuriane an iure magis queramur homines de natura nostra, quod qui maxime digni vita sunt, privari vita videamus, tuncque decedere cogantur humanaque relinquere, cum et aetate iam et rerum usu aucta est ad summumque fere perducta sapientia, hominibusque ipsis adeo necessaria ut conspici liceat et civitates et regna saepe cum unius morte hominis vel interiisse funditus vel in damna inextricabilia incidisse. Etsi enim cunctis est mortalibus divinus animus mensque et rerum et causarum omnium acerrima indagatrix, quibus et consultare in rebus dubiis et deligere optima facile possimus, fit tamen cum naturae impedimentis, tum vel multo saepius inertia nostra ut ex infinitis hominum milibus singuli vix reperiantur qui non, ignaviae potius ac turpi otio dediti, ingenii in se lumen penitus extinxerint. Quosdam enim avaritia, multos ambitio, complures voluptas pervertit, adeo ut praeter studia rerum turpissimarum, quibus dies noctesque intentissime invigilant, omnia parvipendentes, quid sit

Preface to the "Cosimo de' Medici Collection"

Bartolomeo Scala greets Lorenzo de' Medici, the hope of our city.[1] 1

I have collected, my dear Lorenzo, numerous writings, including almost all those which have come into my hands, where the name of Cosimo, your grandfather and the father of this city, may be read. These I have edited in the volume which I now send to you.[2] I hope that you may be able to find enough leisure from your important affairs to run through them all with that marvellous cleverness your divine intellect shows in reading and understanding. And if the volume seems to you worthy of being read by mankind, you will see that it is placed in one of Cosimo's libraries. Farewell.

I often wonder whether people are right or wrong when they com- 2
plain bitterly about our nature, that we see people who most deserve to live losing their lives, forced to depart and leave behind their human concerns just when age and experience have brought their wisdom almost to its highest perfection. This often happens when their wisdom has become so necessary to mankind that we may see one man's death plunge cities and kingdoms into ruin or cause them great and insoluble harms. If indeed all mortals possess a divine spirit and mind that delves deeply into the causes of all things, enabling us readily to find prudent counsel in doubtful situations and to choose the best path, still, because of natural encumbrances and more often because of our own inertia, it happens that you will hardly find one of infinite thousands who has not, by devoting himself to indolence and to vile inactivity, wholly extinguished the light of intelligence in himself. For some are corrupted by avarice, many by ambition, and many more by pleasure, so that in their unceasing pursuit of vile things, to which they devote themselves night and day, they care little for all that might contrib-

in vita utile, quid honestum, quid ad bene beateque vivendum maxime conferat, necquicquam norint, nec sit cura aliqua cognoscendi, tantumque abest ut aliis consulere ac prodesse possint ut nunquam quid sibi conducat ipsis, obscuratione rerum obruti, queant dignoscere.

3   Nam quemadmodum in agris fieri videmus, ut feraces etiam natura, nisi agricolarum labor diligentiaque accesserit, inertes primum infecundique iaceant, deinde etiam squalentes atque horridi reddantur, ita ingenia nostra, natura quidem divina, nisi bonarum artium studiis excolantur, non solum nullos ferunt fructus sapientiae, verum etiam ingenita in nobis virtutum semina quasi cum prima herba suffocantur. Quod si aliter eveniret excitarenturque in nobis studiorumque fomentis nostrorum enutrirentur divini muneris igniculi, profecto melius res humanae regerentur, neque tot tantisque erroribus implicaremur, ut saepe quo proram dirigamus ipsi nesciamus.

4   Ex quo fit ut, si quis non vulgarem vitae viam ingressus, avaritiae quidem frugalitatem, ambitioni dignitatem, intemperantiae continentiam, libidini moderationem, turpitudini denique honestatem antetulerit, et quasi perfectionem quandam humanae naturae continuis sudoribus ac vigiliis fuerit consecutus — nam plena rerum est huiusmodi ad virtutem via, ut ait Hesiodus — immortalitate profecto dignissimus esse videatur. Quoque propius ad perfectionem accesserit, quod vitae diuturnitas propter rerum usum affert, eo magis indigna videtur res ut, cum maxime quis potest, aucta iam ac consummata fere humana sapientia, tunc vero sit absque dubitatione aliqua moriendum, tuncque deserendam hominum societatem, cum fuit summa cum utilitate societatis humanae supervivendum.

5   Ut enim cetera omittam, quis, putas, est senilis memoriae fructus, quaeve rerum in vita gestarum recordationis utilitas, quibus cum his quae in dies accidunt collatis, hoc quidem deligendum, illud vero fugiendum esse multo hercle noverunt facilius quam qui

ute to living usefully, honorably, well and happily, nor do they foster such things or care to learn about them. Their unconcern
makes them unable to counsel and benefit others, since they are so
impeded by ignorance that they are unable even to recognize what
would be good for themselves.

For just as we see that fields which are naturally fertile, if left 3
untouched by the farmer's labor and care, lie fallow and unproduc-
tive at first and eventually become dry and rough wasteland, so
our minds, divine by nature, if uncultivated by the study of the
liberal arts, not only fail to yield any fruit of wisdom, but actually
stifle, as though by weeds, the seed of virtue that is innate in us. If,
on the other hand, our divine spark lights a fire to the kindling
found in studies, and if that fire is fed, then, indeed, human affairs
are better governed, and we are not so entangled in errors as not
even to know at times where our prow should be pointed.

Hence if a man avoids the vulgar way of life, prefering frugality 4
to avarice, dignity to ambition, temperance to excess, restraint to
lust, honor to vileness, and achieves almost a kind of perfection of
his human nature through sweat and vigils — for the way to virtue
is, as Hesiod says, packed with obstacles[3] — he will surely become
wholly deserving, it seems, of immortality. And when a man like
this has approached nearer to perfection, which daily life brings
through experience, when he is most able and has expanded human wisdom almost to the full, it seems all the more unfair that it
is just at that point, without any hesitation, that he must die and
so abandon human society right when his survival might have
been supremely useful to society.

To omit the rest, then, what do you think is the fruit of an old 5
man's memory and what the use of his knowledge of all the things
done in his life but to recognize, as he encounters the happenings
of the day, what is to be valued and what is to be avoided — far
better surely than those who arrive at their judgments of things on

rudes adhuc rerum atque inexperti iudicant? Neque enim ita nati sumus ut statim cum luce ipsa sapientiam nanciscamur; sed ea studio ac diligentia nostra nec minus vitae diuturnitate comparatur. Democritum virum egregie sapientem ferunt, cum expletis septem supra centum (tot enim vixit) annis, mori se intelligeret, dolere dixisse quod tunc egrederetur e vita quando sapere incepisset. Et Critias in *Timeo* Platonis refert Atheniensem Solonem aliquando et reprehensum et irrisum ab Aegyptio sacerdote extitisse, quod pueri semper essent Graeci, neque quisquam esset apud illos senex. Novella enim semper esset memoria, neque ulla apud eos unquam cana sapientia. Cur igitur non iure querantur homines naturamque accusent suam, qui tot tantisque utilitatibus vitaeque commodis tunc maxime morte priventur quando his uti commodissime potuerunt et iure debuerunt? Quid enim aliud videtur causae fuisse nisi invidisse naturam generi hominum fortunarumque ipsius iniquissimam se auctorem praebuisse?

6   His, ut puto, rationibus fere moventur plerique, et dum sese inertiamque suam excusare nituntur, naturam ipsam aequissimam sapientissimamque iniquissime accusant. Etsi enim nulla esset quae contra afferri ratio posset, tanta est tamen tamque admirabilis naturae omnibus in rebus sagacissima solertia ut nullus sit, aequus modo naturae velit esse, qui non debeat ex aliis quae manifesto sapientissime facta cernuntur, huius quoque rei facere iudicium, idque potius ignorantiae suae, qui, quo pacto recte id quoque factum sit, nequeat intelligere, quam naturae ipsius sive negligentiae sive invidiae, si fas est dicere, assignare.

7   Quanto vero humanius prudentiusque hi faciunt qui iam tum ab ineunte aetate brevitatem humanae vitae mente ac cogitatione complexi, non quemadmodum ignaviae socordiaeque suae causas excusantes, naturam, quod aevi sit brevis, quod imbecilla aetas, ut

the basis of ignorance and inexperience? For we are not born immediately able to receive wisdom along with the light of day; this is developed by study and diligence and no less by daily experience of life. They say that Democritus, a man of extraordinary wisdom, when at the age of a hundred and seven (for he lived to that age) he realized he was dying, said he was sorry to depart from life just when he was beginning to be wise.[4] And Critias in Plato's *Timaeus* tells how Solon of Athens was once reproached and laughed at by an Egyptian priest, because, the priest said, the Greeks were always children, and none of them was an old man.[5] For their memory was always of the novel and recent nor did any of them have white-haired wisdom. So why are men not right to complain and blame our very nature because they are deprived by death of so many great advantages and useful things exactly at the moment when they could, and by right ought to use them most effectively? What other cause, it seems, could there be but that Nature is jealous of the human race and makes herself responsible, quite unfairly, for its misfortunes?

Many, I think, are moved by such reasonings, and while they 6 try to excuse themselves for their own laziness, they unfairly accuse Nature herself, who is most fair and wise. And if it is indeed impossible to refute their view, yet such is the wonderful cleverness of Nature in all things that no one, provided he wants to be fair to her, can fail to conclude from the other things which are manifestly seen to be done by her with the utmost wisdom, that his accusation against her comes from his own ignorance and inability to understand the reasons behind her actions, and are not to be blamed on Nature's negligence or envy, if one can even say such a thing.

Kinder and more prudent people, who have welcomed in mind 7 and thought from an early age the brevity of human life, do not choose to excuse their laziness and carelessness by blaming nature because life is brief and because age, as Sallust says, is weak;[6] in-

ait Crispus, criminentur, cogitant; verum quo pacto magis brevitatis ipsius damna compensare possint, summo studio, cura et diligentia perscrutantur. Quales et prisca et nostra aetas multos vidit, qui alius alia in laude claruere. Non enim una dumtaxat res est in qua possit animus, aevi brevitatem superans, sese immortalitati commendare. Laudantur enim philosophi, laudantur oratores, laudantur imperatores. Rerum quoque publicarum administratores rectoresque et temperatores populorum summa semper in gloria extiterunt; tantumque abest ut singulis consequendis laudibus humana vita non sufficiat, ut vel in plerisque vel in omnibus simul complures legerimus et audiverimus, et viderimus ipsi nonnullos claruisse. C. quidem Caesar, is cuius arma gentes omnes timuerunt, nonne summus orator fuit scriptorque elegantissimus? M. vero Tullius, cuius de doctrina elegantiaque dici non potest satis, nonne consul ea gessit quae nullus quantumvis egregius imperator vel consultasse gravius vel gessisse gnavius potuisset, quibusque, ut solebat, possit neque immerito gloriari, 'O fortunatam natam me consule Romam'?

8   Quanquam exemplis nobis extraneis non est opus: unus enim Cosmus pro multis quae afferri possent exempla documento certissimo esse debet, quem ego arbitror unum extitisse in quem et ipsa munifica natura suaque ipsa studia et labores tot tantaque contulerint ut maiora nulla aut admirabiliora esse possint. Nam quis unquam aut ingenio acriore aut diviniore memoria fuit aut esse potuit? Quae quidem iam tum ab infantia ipsa excolens, ad eam quam nunc tantopere admirantur omnes fertilitatem bonitatemque perduxit. Quid enim non temptavit, modo aliquid in se haberet laudis; aut quid temptavit quod non sit felicissime consecutus? Legit, audivit, vidit omnia. Nihil unquam excidit quod cognoverit. Nemo disputavit acutius, nemo verum invenit facilius,

stead, they seriously consider how they may be able to make up for the transience of their own lives with devotion, care and diligence. Both antiquity and our own age have seen many such men, who have become variously renowned for different achievements. For there is not just one thing through which the mind, overcoming the brevity of life, can make itself worthy of immortality. Philosophers, orators, and leaders all receive praise. Likewise, those who administer public affairs and guide and moderate the people forever stand in great glory. So untrue is it that human life is just not long enough to win extraordinary praise, that we have read and heard how many men have achieved greatness in many ways, or in all ways at once, and we ourselves have seen some individuals achieve such fame. Did not Gaius Caesar, he whose arms all nations feared, also shine as an elegant orator and writer? And did not Cicero, whose learning and style one cannot praise enough, perform deeds when he was a consul unequalled by any general, however famous, and was he not able in giving counsel and diligent in pursuing matters of state, thanks to which he could deservedly boast, as he was wont to do, "O Rome, fortunate to have me for consul?"[7]

Yet I need not cite examples outside our borders. For in place of 8 many I could name, the case of Cosimo ought to stand as a most convincing example, for he was, I think, preeminently a man in whom both natural gifts and his own studies and labors came together in such a way that no more admirable gifts and achievements could be found. For who ever had a sharper intelligence and so well stocked a memory? Cultivating these qualities from childhood, he brought forth the creativity and goodness which all still greatly admire. What did he not attempt simply to attain some glory; and what did he ever attempt which he did not fully achieve? He read, he listened, he observed everything. Nothing was ever lost on him. No one argued more coherently, no one found the truth more easily, and no one expressed more aptly what

nemo quod invenit expressit commodius. Mirari licet conflu-
entibus ad eum multis quocunque in genere excellentibus viris
(erat enim domus eius tanquam bonarum artium quoddam gymnasium), mirari, inquam, licet neminem unquam ab eo exivisse,
quacunque tandem facultate excelluerit, quin fateatur doctiorem se
a Cosmo recessisse quam accesserit. Sive enim de naturae obscuritate tractaretur, ita omnes summo ingenio suo difficultates callebat
ut habuisse semper putares in manibus Thalem, Pythagoram, Platonem, Aristotelem, Zenonem, Democritum ceterosque omnes,
quibuscunque tandem in scolis paulo praestantiores fuerint. Sive
de religione rebusque divinis, deus bone, quam est inusitata, quam
nova, quam inaudita sapientia? In mores vero, si quando incidit
quam legem non novit, quod eum institutum praeteriit? Quem,
sive ex Graecis, sive ex nostris et philosophis et scriptoribus, non
accuratissime pellegit, quamquam in moribus quidem multo vehe-
mentior illi cura fuit agendi quam cognoscendi aut disserendi studium?

9   Vellem hoc quidem in loco historiam scribere, non prologum.
Dicerem enim quae fuerint in teneriore aetate studia, qui mores,
quae continentia, quae modestia, quamque omnibus in actionibus
senilis prudentia. Dicerem quae accessu aetatis virtutum quoque
facta sit accessio, ut singuli quique anni magnum ad laudes cumu-
lum attulisse videantur, donec ad eam est perductus sublimitatem
quam nedum aequare quisquam verbis, sed ne mente quidem ac
cogitatione complecti totam potest. Ut enim omittam liberalita-
tem, mansuetudinem, eximiamque erga omnes humanitatem, quae
fuerunt in eo profecto divinissimae, magnificentiam ipsam ac ma-
gnanimitatem simul cum eo natas animique ipsius proprias fuisse
iudicares.

10   Testimonio sunt tot templa vel instaurata ab eo vel maximis et
tanto dignis nomine sumptibus extructa, tot aedes, tot palatia et in
sua civitate et in externis summa cum omnium admiratione erecta,

he had found to be true. One may marvel at the numerous men, excelling in every genus of knowledge, who resorted to him (his home was like a school of the humanities) and one may marvel, I say, that no one, in whatever field of study he excelled, ever departed from him without confessing himself more learned when he left Cosimo than when he had entered into his presence. If the subject being treated was the hidden ways of nature, such was the high intelligence and expertise he showed in every difficulty that one would think he had ever in his hands the works of Thales, Pythagoras, Plato, Aristotle, Zeno, Democritus and the rest of the authors who obtained some distinction in any of the schools. If the subject was religion and divine things, good Lord! wasn't his wisdom amazing, novel and unprecedented? As for morality, if something happened that the law did not cover, what relevant knowledge escaped his learning? What author or philosopher did he not read with the greatest care, whether Greek or Latin, though at the same time he was much more concerned with action than with erudition and the discussion of learned matters?

Here I wish I were writing a history rather than a prologue. I would tell what were his studies during his tender years, what was his conduct, what his restraint, his modesty, how wise in all actions he had been as an old man. I would tell how his virtue grew with the passage of time, so that every year still greater praise seemed to accumulate, until it reached such a height that no one could equal it in words, nor could mind or thought encompass it all. To say nothing of his liberality, his kindness, and his extraordinary humanity towards all, qualities which in him were truly divine, you might reckon that his magnificence and magnanimity were born at the same time as he and were the peculiar properties of his own soul. 9

The proofs of this are the many churches, either restored by him or built with a richness worthy of his name; the many buildings and palaces erected to universal admiration both in his city 10

bibliotheca vero tum Marciana, tum Faesulana, quas tanto studio curaque instituit, tot vel ab inferis ipsis revocatis auctoribus atque ex omnibus gentibus ubicunque latitarent luci redditis in eamque collatis voluminibus, neque Latinae modo aut Graecae linguae, sed Hebraicae, Arabicae, Chaldaeae, Indicae, ‹ut› nullis quidem ex antiquis debent videri inferiores. Neque enim Hesdras apud Hebraeos, qui Legum Prophetarumque libros a Chaldeis incensos corruptosque correxit, totque quot sunt apud illos litterae esse voluit; neque apud Graecos Pisistratus Atheniensium tyrannus, qui collegisse in Graecia libros primus dicitur; neque Perses, qui postea Athenis incensis, quae Pisistratus volumina collegerat, devexit in Persiam; neque Seleucus,[1] qui longo post tempore rettulit in Graeciam; neque Alexander, is cui Magno cognomen ab rebus gestis fuit, qui eidem rei non mediocrem operam dedit; neque Ptolemaeus Philadelphus, qui multa librorum milia Alexandriae cumulavit; neque apud Romanos Sulla dictator, qui post firmatam cum Mithridate pacem ad Piraeum cum venisset, Appelliconis Theii bibliothecam exemit, in qua omnia ferme Aristotelis et Theophrasti volumina fuerant, quae adhuc quasi ignota erant, et Romam detulit, quae a Tyrannione postea grammatico in numerum sunt digesta; neque Aemilius, qui, Perseo Macedonum rege devicto, magnum librorum numerum advexit in urbem; neque Lucullus, neque Caesar, neque Pollio, neque paulo ante aetate nostra admirandus vir Nicolaus, summus Christianorum pontifex; neque aliquis tandem qui comparandorum voluminum studiosus fuerit, maiorem videtur laudem assecutus aut librorum numero aut ornatu.

11   Sed et haec ipsa parva sunt prae his quae divinissimo consilio, incredibili animi magnitudine et quasi numine quodam suo pro salute gessit et gloria civitatis suae. Eiusmodi enim sunt quae domi forisque admiranda quadam et plane divina providentia Cosmus

and in other places; the libraries, both at San Marco and in Fiesole, which he founded with such zeal and care,[8] wherein so many authors were called back as if from the the lower regions and brought back from every nation, wherever they might be hidden, and collected into volumes, not only works in Latin and Greek, but in Hebrew, Arabic, Chaldaean, and Hindu, so that these libraries should not seem inferior to any collections of ancient times. No one has ever earned more praise for the number and beauty of his books: not even Ezra among the Jews, who corrected the books of the Law and the Prophets that had been burned and corrupted by the Chaldaeans and who wanted to collect all the books they had; nor, among the Greeks, Pisistratus, the tyrant of Athens, who is said to have been the first among the Greeks to collect books; nor the Persians, who after burning Athens, took the volumes assembled by Pisistratus to Persia; nor Seleucus, who much later brought them back to Greece; nor Alexander, known as the Great for his deeds, who made no small effort to the same purpose; nor Ptolemy Philadelphus, who collected many thousands of books in Alexandria; nor, among the Romans, the dictator Sulla, who after signing a peace with Mithridates came to the Piraeus and bought the library of Apellicon of Teos, which contained almost all the works of Aristotle and Theophrastus, which had hitherto been unknown, and brought it back to Rome, there to be arranged by Tyrannio the grammarian;[9] nor Aemilius Paulus who, having defeated King Perseus of Macedon, brought a great number of books back to Rome; neither Lucullus, nor Caesar, nor Pollius,[10] nor, shortly before our own time, the admirable Nicholas, the highest priest of the Christians,[11] nor anyone else who showed zeal to collect books.

But even these things are trivial compared to the things he did for the welfare and glory of the city by his divine wisdom in counsel, the incredible greatness of his soul and a kind of spiritual presence. Such are the deeds Cosimo performed for us at home and

effecit nobis ut iam neque victoriosissimi reges, quibus et obstiti-
mus fortiter atque adeo laudabiliter superavimus, neque bellacis-
simi aliqui duces, quos iam ex inimicissimis et Florentino imperio
longo iam tempore inhiantibus et amicissimos nobis et coniunctis-
simo foedere astrictos reddidimus, neque potentissimae respublicae, quibus formidini iam et terrori esse coepimus, extimes-
cendae sint.

12   Verum haec quidem historiam, ut supra dixi, non prologum de-
siderant. Itaque comprimam orationem meam haecque ipsa, quae
nunc quoque me magnopere ad scribendum inflammant, ad aliud
opportunius fortasse tempus reservabo. Nam et haec paucula,
quae ex infinitissima suarum laudum copia delibavi, illuc tetende-
runt ut ostenderem exemplis nostris, non iure quidem conqueri
nonnullos de vitae brevitate, cum videamus aliquos eadem brevitate tot tantaque consecutos ut maiora desiderari a modesto homine vix debeant. Quos tamen fateor optandum fuisse immorta-
les, quando quidem ita inertes, ita negligentes nostra certe culpa,
non naturae sumus, ut eorum qui non frustra vixerint quorumque
vita non sibi solum ipsis, sed et ceteris quoque mortalibus utilitati
et ornamento foret, tam parvus sit numerus. Quod etsi desiderari
licet ea quam diximus ratione, minime tamen accusare naturam licet. Illud certo licet potius iureque quodam humano, si grati, si
boni viri esse volumus; ‹immo› nos compellit ut qui tales fuerunt,
quoniam vindicari a morte aliter non potuerunt, quod reliquum
est, litterarum monimentis, quoad fieri per nos potest, immortalitati commendentur.

13   Quae me ratio in praesentia admonuit ut undecunque exquire-
rem quae aliquam in se Cosmi Medicis nostri, qui unicum ‹est›
decus et ornamentum praeclarissimum nostrae civitatis, laudem
continerent. Itaque collegi quaecunque venerunt in manus, et di-

abroad by a wonderful and plainly divine providence. As a result, we must no longer fear the victorious kings whom we had bravely resisted and gloriously defeated,[12] nor other warlike leaders, who have been turned from hostile forces long thirsting for our Florentine empire into good friends and close allies,[13] nor those powerful republics which we had previously begun to fear and regard with great trepidation.[14]

But such things call for a history, as I said above, not a mere 12 prologue. Thus I am condensing my present remarks — much as these matters make me eager to write of them — and shall reserve them as subject for another more suitable occasion. Indeed, even these few words, which I have distilled from the great store of things for which he is to be praised, have become so lengthy only in order to let me show by example that those who complain of life's brevity are not right to do so, since we see that some achieve in that same brief span so many things that more can hardly be expected from a mere man. Further, I confess that one should wish such men immortal, for while we who are so inert and so negligent are not so because of nature but by our own clear fault, there are only a few who have not lived in vain and whose life was not devoted to themselves alone but were of use to other mortals and an ornament to them. Although one may desire this for the reason I've stated, we are still not entitled to blame nature. Rather we are definitely entitled to this by a kind of human right, if we want to be good and grateful men; indeed we are compelled, since such remarkable men as these cannot be rescued from death in any other way, to do what remains, that they may be commended to immortality in literary monuments.

This is the reason that has prompted me to seek everywhere 13 for writings that contain any commendations of our Cosimo de Medici, that unique source of honor and the most famous ornament of our city. To this end have I collected whatever came into my hands, various epigrams of poets and whatever works of ora-

versorum epigrammata poetarum et oratorum ceterorumque scriptorum quicquid ad hanc est rem visum aliquid conferre. Sic enim putavi fore ut et quae passim dispersa essent et facile peritura in unum redacta volumen facilius servarentur, et ipse aliqua saltem ex parte officio meo, quoniam omnes certe multum, ego vero omnia huic viro debeo, satisfacerem. Quanquam non dubito non defuturos qui parci me laboris laudisque opus assumpsisse dicant, qui non eorum quae ipse scripserim, sed quae alii composuerint, non auctor ipse, sed plane librarius volumen confecerim; qui etsi non multum laborasse, certo non omnino indiligentem me fuisse iudicabunt. Quos ego et hortor et oro ut qui maiora possunt atque digniora, iam aggrediantur. Satis enim a me erit factum si tenuis hic labor meus eos qui laboriosa magis magisque laude digna audebunt ac poterunt, ad scribendum concitaverit.

tors and other writers that it seemed would serve this purpose. I thought that in this way works that were scattered around hither and yon and works which might easily perish could be arranged in a single volume, the more easily to be preserved, and I thought that I myself could satisfy, at least in part, my sense of obligation, for while all men certainly owe this man much, I owe him everything. No doubt there will not be lacking persons to say that I have taken on a work that is sparing of effort and sparing of merit; that I have confected a volume, not of my own writings, but those of others, acting frankly like a book-dealer rather than an author; and there will be those who reckon that, though I didn't work very hard, I have certainly been not altogether lacking in diligence. I would encourage those among my critics who can do greater and better things to start doing them now. If my slender effort stimulates those to write who can and dare to do more laborious and praiseworthy works, I shall have done enough.

De legibus et iudiciis dialogus

1 Bartholomeus Scala Laurentio Medici salutem.

Non solum quia permagna est, Laurenti Medices, et quidem magno merito tuo, auctoritas tua in nostra republica, verum etiam quoniam magnitudine ingenii gravitateque atque sapientia facile praestas ceteris, fecerim ipse haud sapienter neque pro modestia civili amicitiaeque nostrae officio rei consuluerim meae, inconsulto te, quem consulit universa iam civitas cuiusque externi etiam populi et principes admirantur exquiruntque prudentiam, si in rebus etiam privatis meis, nedum quae ad rempublicam, ad omne prope humanum pertinent genus, ut ea sunt quae litteris ad iuvandam vitam nostram traduntur, quicquam transegerim. Itaque cum his diebus paucis, quibus Cremonae concilio de administrando bello interfuisti noster legatus, plusculum credo ex abscessu tuo essem nactus otii a meo publico scribendi munere ac disputatiunculam quae mihi cum Bernardo Machiavello de legibus fuit et iudiciis, quemadmodum quidem potui, mandassem litteris, non fuit consilium ut in publicum prodiret nisi te prius, iudicem atque auctorem rerum omnium mearum, salutatum venisset exquisissemque ex te tandem quod esset super his gravissimum iudicium tuum. Quae si non improbaveris et te haec nostra (ut affirmare quandoque soles) delectabunt, curabo equidem quam diligentissime ut in eis quoque operam et studium meum non desideres; modo tantum quietis a publico munere meo sit datum, retenta dignitate, quae quidem mentis tranquillitatem, quae est scribentibus pernecessaria, pulcherrime solet praestare, quantum et ipse, qui et comptius carmen et expolitius orationem condere es solitus, convenire melius multo quam qui laboris et studii huius inexperti, aut nihil omnino legisse

Dialogue on Laws and Legal Judgments

Bartolomeo Scala to Lorenzo de' Medici: 1

In view of your immense and deserved authority in our republic, Lorenzo de' Medici, and of your clearly superior intellect,
gravity and wisdom, I would be imprudent and untrue to myself
as a citizen and as your friend, if I failed to consult you—whom
our entire city consults and whose prudent counsel even foreign
peoples and princes admire and seek—before undertaking any
private project, much less an instructive moral treatise of the sort
that concerns the republic and practically the entire human race.
During the few days that you were in Cremona as our envoy to
the war council, your absence gave me some extra time off from
my duties as public secretary.[1] So I wrote down, as faithfully I
could, a brief discussion concerning laws and judgments which I
had with Bernardo Machiavelli.[2] But I resolved not to publish it
without first sending it with greetings to you, who are the judge
and advisor of all my affairs, so that I might have your valuable
opinion on this subject. If you approve of my studies and find
them pleasing (as you often say you do), I shall strive to demonstrate in them my diligence and zeal as an author, provided I am
given some respite from my public duties, while retaining my position, which affords that peace of mind so necessary to writers. You
yourself often compose both elegant lyrics and polished speeches
and thus know how much leisure I require. Indeed, your own experience has taught you to appreciate such matters more clearly
and more truly than those who, being unfamiliar with our busi-

aut aliena tantum cognovisse contenti sunt, veriusque didicisti. Vale.

2 Cum pedum me dolores detinerent domi, veni in Pinthium Bernardus Machiavellus, amicus et familiaris meus, ut me viseret. Ingressus in cubiculum, cum salutasset, consedit ad focum. Bruma enim erat et per eos dies Boreas cum perflasset impetuosius, oppleverat montes circum vicinos nivibus ut omnia tunc magis rigerent gelu et frigora multo graviora et molestiora viderentur. Rogavit deinde de podagra me ut habuisset, atque ad curandam omni industria valitudinem amice admodum vehementer est cohortatus. Cum autem respondissem aliquot me dies laborasse ex pedibus et egissem gratiam et quod ad me visendum accessisset et quod adeo prudenter curae admonuisset valitudinis, silentii aliquid subsecutum est.

3 Paulo deinde post 'Carnisprivia sunt,' inquit, 'et tu iuventutis huius nostrae percalles mores. Lapidibus omnes urbis infestant vias; sicubi otium est a lapidibus, obstruunt aditus viarum et tigillos opponunt gradientibus quasi repugnacula, nec transire ulterius sine stipe licet. Qua persoluta semel bene (quod aiunt evenire cum Charon‹t›e ad Stygem) agaretur nobiscum si deinde ceteri quoque transitus fierent immunes. Incidis quocumque te vertis in capses novos et nova pretia extorquentur. Quod etsi admodum incivile est, tamen antiqua consuetudine atque indulgentia libere ridetur. Sed ea potissimum causa fuit cur tardius multo quam voluissem ad te venirem. Ardebam enim desiderio videndi tui atque alloquendi, ex quo te in morbum incidisse noveram.'

4 'Tum ipse lepide,' inquam, 'narras. Sed ea mihi carnispriviorum licentia saepe videri nimia solet, et detestari etiam et perniciosam putare Cosmus Medices, pater patriae nostrae, sapientissimus civis, consuevit. Qui quantum etiam non probabat quod usurpasse crebro aiunt Nicolaum Uzanum, male habituram civitatem nostram, cum ea tempora advenerint, quibus iuvenilibus sit his caren-

ness of writing, content themselves with reading nothing at all or with merely browsing the works of others. Farewell.

While I was confined at home by an attack of gout, my good friend Bernardo Machiavelli came to see me at my house in Borgo Pinti.[3] On entering the room, he greeted me and took a seat by the fire. It was the dead of winter, and the strong gusts of the north wind had lately covered the nearby mountains with snow, freezing everything solid and adding to the severity and discomfort of the cold. Bernardo asked how I was faring with the gout, and as my friend he urged me strongly to do all I could to recover my health. I replied that my feet had given me trouble for several days, and I thanked him for coming to see me and for advising me so sensibly to care for my health. We then fell silent a while.

A few moments elapsed before he spoke. "It is carnival season," he said.[4] "You are well versed in the behavior of our youths. They beleaguer every street in town by throwing rocks, and when they take a break from rock-throwing, they block off the roads and set planks as barricades in the way of pedestrians, so that no one can pass without paying their toll. It wouldn't be so bad if we could buy safe-conduct by paying one toll, the way they say Charon charged a fee on the river *Styx*. But wherever you turn, you meet with new traps, and new sums are extorted. Even though it's highly uncivilized, our ancient habit of indulgence lets us laugh at such pranks. In any event, that is the main reason why I arrived later than I wished. Having heard that you were ill, I was eager to come and talk to you."

"You describe the scene quite wittily," I said. "The permissiveness of carnival often strikes me as excessive. Cosimo de' Medici, father of our country and our wisest citizen, used to detest the practice as pernicious.[5] He didn't agree with Niccolò da Uzzano, who, they say, often asserted that our city would be in sad shape if

dum ludis. Instrui, scilicet bonis artibus, et discere prima aetate prudentiam gravitatemque civilem Cosmus malebat, non irritari fervorem aetatis et addi, ut ita dixerim, insanienti, quod magis possit efficere insanum. Et in his quidem quae geruntur ab his, maximum quoddam et ad agendam vitam et ad gerendam rem publicam momenti inest. Sunt enim universarum actionum nostrarum quae principio inhaerescunt nostris animis, ut in aedificiis, quasi firmissima pedamenta, quae si recte ieceris, neque imprudenter, cum ad privata tum ad publica opera viam tibi, qua perhoneste surgant illa quidem atque perficiantur, commodissimam praeparaveris, iterque ad bene beateque vivendum quam apertissimum facillimumque substraveris. Sed de his alias. Sunt enim plura multo iuvenum nostrorum errata quam quae breviter in praesentia corrigi aut comprehendi oratione possint. Alias fortasse dabitur de his accommodatior dicendi locus.

5   'Nunc redeo ad horum dierum intemperantiam, quos quidem arbitror ad Saturnaliorum similitudinem, ut multa praeterea accepimus de antiquis, esse a nostris institutos. Licentia certe eadem, et si nos forte quam antiqui maiores afferimus ad Venerem et ad Bacchum atque ad omnia genera incontinentiarum spiritus, illi (quod et nomen indicat) eius quae erat regnante Saturno libertas (de qua tam multa poetae) quasi quandam imaginem referebant et servi cum dominis liberius versabantur; nos vino et carnibus (si diis placet) non ingurgitari, non prolabi in omnem luxuriem, non obmergi immundis quibusque libidinibus rusticum indecorumque censemus. Et ut illi recte quidem a Saturni expetibili simplici libertate, ita nos multo ut pleraque deterius, quod esu privemur carnium, Christianis constitutis, hos carnisprivia dies appellamus, quasi de summis aliquod malis sit non edisse carnes. Quod tantum apud Pictagoreos non inhumanum modo, sed ferum etiam atque immane est, ut probe nosti.'

our youths had to forego such games.[6] Cosimo wanted them to study the liberal arts and to learn prudence and dignity at an early age, rather than to exacerbate the heat of youth and add fuel, as it were, to a madman's madness. For actions like these shape the conduct of private life and the public state. As in buildings, all our actions rest on firm foundations which are fixed early in our minds. If you lay these soundly and wisely, you prepare a suitable course for the honorable inception and completion of private and public projects, and you pave an open and easy road towards living well and wisely. But that's a topic for another time. The errors of our young men are too numerous to rehearse or redress briefly here. Perhaps we shall find a more suitable opportunity for such a discussion.

"Let me return to the excesses of this holiday. I believe that car- 5 nival was instituted by our ancestors to resemble the Saturnalia, just as we have inherited many other customs from the ancients. There is certainly the same licence, although we seem to show greater enthusiasm than they did in pursuing Venus, Bacchus and every form of dissolution. As the name Saturnalia suggests, the ancients sought to imitate the liberty of Saturn's reign — so often sung by poets — and they allowed slaves to mix freely with their masters. Today, we feel boorish and are ashamed unless we stuff our throats with wine and meat (good heavens!), sink to every kind of debauchery and wallow in all manner of squalid sensual desires. The ancients justly named their holiday after the simple and desirable liberty of Saturn. But as in other things, we are less noble and name these days 'carnival' [*carnisprivium*] because in accordance with Christian custom we forego eating meat [*esu privemur carnium*]. You'd think that not eating meat was one of the worst misfortunes. But, as you well know, the Pythagoreans deemed the eating of meat not only uncivilized but even bestial and monstrous."

6   Tum Machiavellus, 'Novi,' inquit, 'et tangunt mirifice animum quae edisseris. Sed perge, quaeso, siquid praeterea habes quod ad disputationem istam qua de agis pertinere quicquam putes.'

'Habeo equidem,' inquam, 'ac vehementer miror hanc hominum consuetudinem ita omnia detorquendi in vitium resque fere cunctas a bonis initiis ad exitus depravatissimos transferendi, ut etiam ausi sint scribere nonnulli doctissimi homines omnia ferme mala orta fuisse ex principiis bonis. Telesphorus, homo Graecus, anachorita, natus a Simone Petro pontificatu nonus (quantum comprehendi litteris sacris potest) vir bonus fuit, et augendae ornandaeque religionis huius admodum studiosus. Is ergo inter alia quae statuit pontificali auctoritate decreta, ieiunium quoque dierum quadraginta ad ieiunii Christi imitationem atque ad lunae normam primus instituit anno salutis nostrae trigesimo fere nono et centesimo. Qui enim ante hunc rei Christianae praefuerunt, Petrus, Linus, Cletus, Clemens, Anacletus, Evaristus, Alexander, Sixtus, aliis intenti rebus ieiunii nusquam habuerant mentionem. Nam illud quoque quod a quattuor anni temporibus nomen habet ieiunium Calixtus, Demetrii filius, Romanus pontifex, novem et septuaginta ferme annos postea induxit. Et quod ante ad Hebraeorum modum ter quotannis frugum vini et olei gratia faciebant, quarto scilicet et septimo mense et decimo, ad altera aequinoctia alteraque solstitia traduxit. Sed quis tum credat ex indicto ieiunio procuratam ingluviem? Aliquot putarim annos de ieiunando decretum sancte fortasse initio fuisse servatum. Deinde, more humanae naturae ruentibus semper in deteriora rebus, licentia innasci occepit ante principium ieiuniorum ut saturi fierent et implerentur carnibus, a quibus esset toto deinde ieiunio abstinendum. Quae quidem ad eam iam processit magnitudinem ut vitio vertatur si quis omnibus se vitiis atque omni voluptatum genere non coinquinaverit.

7   'Verum, quid id chartae est quod diu versas in manibus? An tu attulisti aliquid de vestris commentaris, quo nobilis illius contro-

"I know," said Bernardo. "What you say strikes a deep chord 6
within me. Please go on, if you have more to say on this topic."

"I do indeed," I said. "I am utterly amazed how humankind habitually perverts all things into vices and corrupts nearly all things
from good conceptions to the most pernicious ends. Some learned
men have even dared to write that nearly all evils arise from good
principles. According to sacred sources, the Greek anchorite
Telesphorus, the son of Simon Peter and our ninth pope, was eager in his goodness to increase and enhance our religion. Among
his other papal decrees, he instituted in AD 139 a forty-day fast in
imitation of Christ, following the lunar cycle.[7] (Busy with other
matters, his papal predecessors Peter, Linus, Cletus, Clement,
Anacletus, Evaristus, Alexander and Sixtus never referred to fasting.) The fast of the four seasons was instituted some seventy-
nine years later by the Roman pontiff Calixtus, son of Demetrius.[8]
Like the Hebrews, the Christians used to abstain from grain, wine
and oil three times a year — in April, July and October. Calixtus
moved the fasts to the two equinoxes and two solstices. Yet who
would have believed then that the practice of fasting would encourage gluttony? I'm inclined to think that initially the decree on
fasting was observed devoutly for several years. But in the customary way of human nature, things always decline and deteriorate.
As the time of fasting approached, the people were overcome by
wantonness and gorged themselves on those meats which they had
to renounce for the entire fast. The practice soon reached such
proportions that it was considered a fault not to defile oneself with
every vice and every sort of pleasure.

"But tell me, what is that paper you are holding? Have you 7
brought me an account of the recent debate between our two cele-

versiae qua duo praeclarissimi inter se iurisconsulti paulo ante contenderunt fiam tuo labore operaque instructior? Quod et rogaram superioribus diebus, et summopere expetebam.'

'Istuc ipsum egi,' inquit Machiavellus, 'tua gratia libenter, tum quia gratum me tibi esse facturum intellexeram, tum ut *Pandectarum*, quae in Palatio inter publica monumenta sancte servantur, auctoritati adderem. Eas autem ego arbitror (etsi assentiri tu non soles) Iustinianum, post emendatam legum priscarum confusionem, ad eum modum ut scriberentur curasse membranis sublucidis tenuissimis, maiusculis litteris antiquis continuatis ne quid abradi aut commutari addive aut demi sine aperta nota posset, ut permaneret id ius, quod se auctore in ordinem erat claritudinemque summa cum gloria redactum imperatoriae maiestatis, intemeratum, incorruptum, perpetuum, et inde ceterorum omnium librorum, petita veritate, emendarentur errores. Arbitror vero factum temporum iniuria (quandoquidem ita variat miscetque fortuna) ut etiam hi libri venirent aliquando in barbarorum victrices manus. Pisanos autem terra marique olim potentes, cum in eos forte incidissent, non magno pretio redemisse, ut puta qui a barbaris rerum ignaris inter res viles haberentur. Pisis demum victis a nobis, nihil antiquius maioribus nostris fuit quam *Digestorum* hos quinquaginta libros huc transferre. Qui positi in Palatio, ut supra dictum est, rerum etiam sacrarum honores assecuntur. Attrectari enim non licet decreto publico nisi funalibus rite accensis, quod tantum in rebus divinis fieri Christianis mos est. Multum vero nomini addidit *Pandectarum*, cum adhuc Pisani possiderent, Baldi Bartolique nobilis controversia. Quam lege iam si placet.'

8   'Placet vero,' inquam, et percurri oculis quicquid ille docte, argute, breviter eleganterque notaverat. Tum ad eum conversus, 'Quin tu potius,' inquam, 'recita memoriter. Malo enim orationem

brated jurists, about which your research will enlighten me? I asked you about this some days ago, hoping to learn more."

"That's precisely what I did," said Bernardo, "and gladly for your sake. I knew I would be doing you a welcome favor and also wished to add to the authority of the *Pandects*, which are religiously kept with other public documents in the Palazzo Vecchio.[9] Now it is my belief (although you generally disagree) that, when Justinian had corrected the confusion of ancient laws, he made sure that the *Pandects* were copied on thin transparent parchment and written in continuous capitals. In this way, any addition or cancellation, even the smallest erasure or change, would leave an obvious mark. This he did so that this code of law, which he had redacted with such order and distinction that it shed great glory on the imperial majesty, would be preserved undefiled, incorrupt and everlasting. And from it the true reading could be sought to correct the errors of all other copies. I think that due to the injustice of history — for fortune alters and confounds all things — these very books eventually fell into the hands of conquering barbarians. But the Pisans, who were formerly a great land and sea power, chanced to find them and bought them back for a small sum, since the barbarians in their ignorance thought them of little value. When we in turn defeated the Pisans, our ancestors' first concern was to transfer the fifty books of the *Pandects* to our city, where they have been placed in the Palazzo Vecchio, as I already indicated, and even receive the honor of religious devotions. For by public decree, it is forbidden to touch these books unless torches have been duly lit, a practice observed by Christians only in sacred ceremonies. While the Pisans still possessed the *Pandects*, the work's fame was increased by the celebrated controversy between Baldus and Bartolus.[10] I urge you to read it now if you like."

"I shall," I said, and glanced through Bernardo's notes, which 8 were learned, insightful, concise and elegant. Then turning to him, I said, "Why don't you recount the case from memory? I would

audire tuam saccaro multo ac melle dulciorem. Nec te non fidere memoriae tuae oportet, quippe qui inter paucissimos civitatis nostrae recordatione rerum praecipue excellas, nec unquam nisi feliciter in ea re feceris periculum.'

9 'Libro igitur,' inquit, 'vigesimo *Pandectarum* ita constat Martianum iurisconsultum respondisse. Quaeritur si pactum sit a creditoribus ne liceat debitori hypotecam vendere vel pignus. Quid iuris sit, et an pactio nulla sit talis quasi contra ius sit posita, ideoque venire possit. Et certum est nullam esse venditionem ut pactioni stetur. Ex re igitur aliquando cum esset orta contentio ex Martiani verbis, duo per id tempus nobilissimi patroni hinc atque hinc stabant. Pro pactione pugnabat Bartolus; venditionem Baldus defendebat; atque uterque verbis Martiani nitebatur; et Baldus quidem pessima industria plerosque regionis eius codices id est quotquot perdiligenter ubique conquisitos potuit nancisci, medicata aqua corruperat et pro venditione conventionem scripserat. Cum iuberet iudex ut inspicerentur libri, et invenirentur conventionem continere non venditionem, petente Bartolo, Pisas missi viri graves, qui ex *Pandectis* tandem quid in ea re veri esset exquirerent. Ita Baldus turpiter cessit causae. Perusinorum decreto corrupti libri ad exemplar *Pandectarum* restituti omnes summa diligentia fuerunt; Baldus prohibitus advocationis honore aliquod ab eo tempus vixit inglorius.'

10 'Perpulchre,' inquam, 'Bernarde. Sed quando legum et iuris a te mentio facta est, atque est otium a carnisprivitis, nisi molestum est, de iure legibusque quid sentias edissere. Sum enim diu dubius commodine an incommodi plus attulerint hominibus hae continuae iuris et legum acerrimae disceptationes, quibus omnia redundant litibus forensibus. Nam mihi quidem tranquillitati vivendi magis esse consentaneum videri solet quod Lacedemonios factitasse quondam comperimus. Scriptam nullam habebant le-

prefer to hear your own words, which are far sweeter to me than sugar or honey. You mustn't distrust your memory. You are one of few men in our city with a prodigious memory, as you have successfully demonstrated many times."

"It is well known," he said, "that in Book 20 of the *Pandects* the   9 jurist Marcianus makes this ruling: "The question is put: if the creditor makes it a term that the debtor may not sell the property subject to *pignus* or *hypotheca*,[11] what is the legal position? Is the agreement void as contrary to law, so that the property can be sold? Such a sale is void, so that the agreement holds good.""[12] Marcianus's ruling gave rise to a dispute between the two greatest lawyers of the day, who took opposite sides in the case. Bartolus fought for the contract, while Baldus defended the sale, both of them relying on Marcianus's words. With wicked zeal, Baldus sedulously located as many codices as he could find and altered them with a special solvent, substituting the word 'agreement' [*conventio*] for 'sale' [*venditio*]. When the judge ordered an examination of the codices, they were found to read 'agreement' rather than 'sale.' At Bartolus's request, a number of prominent citizens were sent to Pisa to ascertain finally the truth of the matter from the *Pandects*. Thus Baldus lost the case in disgrace. By decree of the Perugians, the corrupt codices were carefully restored according to the reading of the *Pandects*. Baldus was discharged from the bar and spent his few remaining years in obscurity."

"Well told, Bernardo," I said. "Since you've brought up the sub-   10 ject of law and justice, and we are enjoying the leisure of carnival, please state your views on justice and laws, unless you object. I have long been in doubt whether humankind derives more good or more harm from the fierce and incessant debates on justice and law which fill our courtroom disputes. It generally strikes me that the tranquillity of society was better served by the former practice of the Spartans. We read that they had no written laws and lived instead according to customs approved by the consensus of the

gem; probatis utentium consensu moribus vivebant. Romani etiam exactis regibus, cum decreta omnia regum rescidissent, viginti annos fuerunt sine legibus.'

11   'Rem tu,' inquit Machiavellus, 'admodum dubiam suapte natura quaeris. Sed in ea quid sentirent gentes, omnium fere consensu hominum declaratur. Quotus enim quisque populus iam est qui aut suo quodam, quod ipse sibi constituerit, aut alieno iure non utatur? Nam quibus suum civile ius non est, aut si qua in parte non omnino plenum atque absolutum est, ius civile Romanorum, quod etiam ex re commune vocant, supplemento est. Neque qui hac tempestate iuri civili ediscendo dant operam, huius aut illius civitatis ius sibi interpretandum sumunt, sed Romanum. Versant continuo *Pandectas* manibus eorumque interpretes. Ita a Romanorum legibus atque institutis interpretandis iuris civilis scientiam consecuti in honore habentur ab hominibus. Nam quattuor *Institutionum* libros, quos suo edi nomine Iustinianus voluit, quibusque admirabili cum gravitate atque sapientia tot tantarum et tam variarum rerum, quot quantasque et quam varias res ius omne civile complectitur dulcissima brevitate atque elegantia omnium elementa continentur, non discunt modo atque interpretantur, sed si qui studiosiores sunt, verba etiam singula, ut scripta sunt, mandant memoriae. Ioannem Bonhieronymum, nostra aetate excellentissimum iurisconsultum, eos tenuisse totos memoria sui temporis homines existimarunt, quod in orandis causis nullo magis quam *Institutionum* iure uteretur. Illud ego de his libris quattuor affirmare ausim: nihil umquam in eis, etsi etiam atque etiam summa cum diligentia lectitarim, desiderare potuisse. Nam saepe accidit ut quae legeris, non his modo nostris legum auctoribus, sed in historia, in philosophia, in oratoria, ceterisque bonis artibus animum non expleant; aliquid continuo occurrat aut verborum aut sententiarum, quod hoc aut illo modo scriptum fuisse velis potius.'

12   'An tu censes, Bernarde,' inquam, 'consensu esse hominum declaratum legibus uti esse commodius?' Cum vero ita respondisset,

wealthy citizens. After the Romans had driven out the kings and rescinded their royal decrees, they too lived for twenty years without laws."

"The question you raise," said Bernardo, "is by its very nature 11 highly doubtful. Yet the consensus of nearly all humankind makes clear how nations have viewed the matter. How few are the communities nowadays who use no legal system, whether developed by themselves or borrowed from others! Those who have no civil law, or an incomplete or imperfect code, supply their need with Roman civil law, which is therefore known as 'common' law. Today's students of civil law examine the problems of interpreting Roman law, rather than that of one city or another, and continually leaf through the *Pandects* and the commentaries on them. Those who master civil law by interpreting Roman laws and precepts are honored in our society. For the most ambitious scholars not only study and interpret but even memorize the very words of the *Institutes*. And these four books, which Justinian had published under his own name, treat an incredible number and variety of authors and subjects with astonishing gravity and wisdom, covering every aspect of civil law with engaging conciseness and elegance. The contemporaries of Giovanni Buongirolami, the greatest jurist of our century, believed that he had memorized the entire work, since he used only the law of the *Institutes* in arguing cases.[13] Having repeatedly consulted these four books with the closest attention, I daresay that they leave nothing to be desired. By contrast, other works in legal studies, history, philosophy, oratory and in the humanities often leave one unsatisfied. One constantly comes across words and ideas which one would wish to change."

"Would you maintain, Bernardo," I asked, "that the consensus 12 of humankind makes clear the preferability of being governed by

'Attamen,' inquam, 'multas esse nationes arbitror quae litteras etiam non norint, atque apud hos quidem vel principis vel viri cuiuspiam melioris arbitrium esse pro legibus. Turcorum certe gentem, quorum tam late in Asia iam atque Europa patet imperium quorumque Italia paulo ante (dum saevit in sese intestinis discordiis) ad Hydruntem arma experta est, consuetudine, non legibus, uti confirmant. Nos vero ita rem haberi intelleximus ex mercatoribus nostris, qui in eorum regnis quaestus gratia plurimi negotiantur. Iudiciis enim praefici *bassias* ab imperatore aiunt. Ita namque appellantur, sive dicundo iuri, sive bello administrando praeficiantur. Verbum (ut opinor) a Graeco nomine, quod regis habet significationem, per corruptionem litterarum ductum, quod illi multis praeterea in nominibus facere consueverunt. Si ius dicendum sit, ascendit *bassias* in tribunal; astant creditor debitorque, sive accusator et reus, aguntque et dicunt causam nudis verbis et veritatem dumtaxat quaestionis significantibus. Sine procuratore, sine patrono simpliciter iudex ab auctoribus controversiarum edocetur. Testes tantummodo adhiberi licet, cunctis praeterea probandi aut diluendi amotis adminiculis, quibus nihil est foris his nostris abundantius. Ea enim adferre ad causam nefas est. In nullum animadvertitur crudelius quam qui dedita opera dolo malo veritatis lucem subtexerit. Iudex autem, sic audita, sic cognita causa, iam nullam iudicando moram facit, verum damnat absolvitque pro arbitrio. Si is a rectitudine iudicii aberraverit idque eum dolo malo fecisse arguatur, morte poenas luit. Mortis genus tale est. Iniuriam qui damnatus [est] perperam defert ad imperatorem statim; si tardior fuerit aut ipse condonaverit culpam, eadem poena plectitur. *Bassias* autem reus factus ex iudice nisi fraudem abfuisse iudicio demonstraverit, adigunt per viscera media praeacutum palum sus-

laws?" When he replied in the affirmative, I said, "Nevertheless, I believe there are many nations which have no written alphabet and for whom the judgment of a prince or a man of high standing substitutes for laws. The empire of the Turk spread far across Asia and Europe, and its military might was recently felt at Otranto in Italy, which was raging with its own internal discords.[14] And some assert that the nation of the Turks relies on custom rather than laws. Yet we have learned the true situation from Italian merchants, many of whom trade profitably in their domains. They say that the emperor places men in charge of legal judgments who are called 'pashas,' a title given to those who sit in judgment or direct the military. The word, I believe, derives from the Greek noun meaning 'king' [*basileus*], with the corruption of some letters, as occurs regularly in other Turkish words.[15] When judgment is to be delivered, the pasha ascends his tribunal; and the creditor and debtor, or the plaintiff and defendant, appear before him to plead their case, expounding the truth of the matter in the simplest terms. The judge is informed solely by the parties to the dispute, with no attorney or advocate present. They may only summon witnesses; all the other instruments of proof and disproof so common in our courtrooms are dispensed with, for these are forbidden as evidence. No one is more cruelly dealt with than a person who intentionally and deceitfully conceals the truth. When the judge has heard and weighed the case, he pronounces sentence without delay, convicting or acquitting as he determines. If the judge pronounces sentence unjustly and is shown to have acted deceitfully, he is condemned to death. The death penalty is administered in the following way. Anyone wrongly convicted at once reports the injustice to the sultan; and if he delays judgment or pardons the offence, the judge must suffer the same penalty. If a pasha, once the judge and now the accused, cannot show that no deceit influenced his judgment, a sharp pole is thrust through his

tolluntque et defigunt humi atque exhibent populo in exemplum horrendumque et miserum spectaculum.

13   'Quot putas praeterea in orbe terrarum nationes esse incultas et rudes atque ab hac civili disciplina quae abhorreant? Cuiusmodi etiam complures Ioannes Lusitaniae rex et novas insulas et antehac incognitas gentes modo pervestigavit, exleges penitus ac naturae ferarum quoque more obtemperantes. Est autem naturae lex ceterarum omnium praecipua, ut mihi quidem videtur, immo vero unicum bene vivendi exemplar documentumque certissimum, unde mores boni, unde iustae leges deducantur. Sine qua neque domos quidem, neque civitates recte gubernari aut constare posse certum est; quae non tempore, non loco, non ulla causa unquam variatur, constantissima, immutabilis, eadem apud omnes, inviolata, sempiterna; quamque qui neglexerit naturamque exuerit humanam volens, huius auctorem legis reformidet, Deum, necesse est. Licet enim ipse maximas poenas, ut ait Lactantius, etiam si supplicia, quae putantur, effugerit, nutasse profecto animum nostrum oportuit, neque quo consisteret loco humanam rationem invenisse, nisi signum natura proposuisset in quod respicientes aberrare a recto atque honesto nequiremus.

14   'Quod in te nolis (inquit natura), in alium ne feceris. Nonne idem et Salvator praecipit? "Diliges," inquit, "Dominum Deum tuum ex toto corde tuo, et tota anima tua; et proximum tuum sicut te ipsum." Quid autem hoc Salvatoris praecepto illi naturae esse similius potest? Nam si ut te ipsum alium itidem hominem dilexeris, quod in te nolis profecto ut in quempiam id fiat non commiseris. Ita diversis verbis et Salvatoris et naturae una eademque de hac lege, id est de hoc fonte, unde omnis recte vivendi ratio emanat, sententia colligitur. Sed quid addit Salvator? "Et in his," inquit, "duobus mandatis tota lex pendet et Prophetae." Tota, inquit, lex in his mandatis pendet, quod apertissime significat ista naturae incommutabili lege omnes omnium gentium et nationum

bowels. He is then lifted up, impaled on the ground and shown to the populace as a terrible example and pitiful spectacle.

"How many other primitive and savage peoples do you think 13 there are in the world who are averse to this civil discipline? King John of Portugal has recently explored many new islands and found previously unknown peoples who live completely without laws, like beasts obeying nature.[16] Yet nature has its own special law which surpasses all others. Indeed, in my view, it is the only certain pattern and example for living well, and from it we derive good morals and just laws. It is clear that without nature's law neither households nor cities could be founded or justly governed. Her law never varies because of time, place or any other reason, but is constant and immutable, the same for all peoples, inviolable and eternal. Should anyone neglect it, choosing to abandon his human nature, he must fear God, the source of this law. Even if one escapes what are considered the greatest punishments and torments, as Lactantius says, our minds would be in doubt and human reason would find no stable point of reference, if nature had not set before us a sign to keep us from swerving from what is right and honorable.[17]

"Do nothing to another person, nature says, that you do not 14 wish done to you. Does not Our Savior teach us the same thing? 'Thou shalt love the Lord thy God with all thy heart and with all thy soul,' he says, 'and thy neighbor as thyself.'[18] What could resemble nature more than this precept of Our Savior? For if you love another person as yourself, you will never do anything to him that you would not wish done to you. Thus, from the different words of Our Savior and of nature we may infer one and the same view of this law, that is, of the source of our entire system for living well. And what does our Savior add? 'On these two commandments,' he says, 'hangeth the whole law, and the prophets.'[19] All the law, he says, hangs on these commandments. This signifies most clearly that the immutable law of nature forms the basis for

contineri leges. Quae multo hercle clarius (mea sententia) comprehenduntur animis bonorum virorum, instituente admonenteque natura, quam cartis his aut quantumvis composita oratione atque industria dicendi, cuius potissimum ars ista fori nostrorum temporum studiosa est, percipiantur.

15 'Neque infitior tamen multa et magna ingenia hac legali in disciplina per omnia tempora extitisse; et Accursios istos vestros, Baldos, Bartolos, Cinos, aliosque innumerabiles minime contemnendos duxerim. Est enim eorum, ut audio, ex vobis in distinguendo, in disceptando atque solvendo industria admirabilis; sed ea iam ad id devenit magnitudinis atque argutiarum ut certo iure nihil possit constare. Neque enim est quicquam adeo apertum aut in promptu, modo adsint clientes, quod non veniat subito in dubitationem et iudiciorum subeat discrimen. Non autem repetamus hoc loco exempla longius; domesticis abundamus et nostris. Nulla enim fere causa est (modo habeat aliquid in se ponderis) in qua hinc atque inde advocati nobiles de victoria non contradicant. Neque autem adducor ut credam tantam in sese vim habere posse lucri aliquam cupiditatem, etsi et ipsum (ut Plato in *Hipparcho* ait) est expetibile, ut bona nostrorum ingenia iurisconsultorum contra veritatem causae cognitam capiant iniusta et nefanda arma.

16 'Semper abundavit nostra civitas his viris qui iurisprudentia multum excellerent. Sed haec nostra aetas (quod sit bona dictum venia aetatum superiorum) ut doctrina certe atque integritate animi nulli cedit, ita profecto adiectu ceterarum quoque disciplinarum, quae merito ornare vitam solent, et dicendi artificio longe iam superior habetur; quorumque non in foro solum causisque forensibus, sed in maximis legationibus, sed in senatu, sed in magistratibus experti sumus experimurque quotidie virtutem, ut nulli omnino non mirum esse debeat si plures huiusmodi inter se patroni eadem in causa sentiant non idem. Quod tamen quoniam fieri omnibus fere in causis videmus, evenire id obscuritate rerum ut concludamus est necesse.

all the laws of all peoples and nations. In my view, such laws are grasped more clearly by the minds of good men when nature teaches and advises them than when they are gleaned from our briefs, our highly polished speeches or that eloquence which our legal profession today most zealously pursues.

"I don't deny that all ages have produced many great geniuses in 15 our legal discipline, and I would scarcely regard with contempt such men as Accursius, Baldus, Bartolus, Cinus and countless others.[20] You lawyers tell me that these men show astounding diligence in distinguishing, arguing and resolving legal questions. But this diligence entails such immense learning and sophistry that nothing can be decided with certain authority. Where clients are involved, no matter is so clear or self-evident that it is not called into question at once, requiring a legal ruling. We needn't look far afield for examples of this, since we have an abundance of local and personal ones. Practically every case of the slightest consequence finds renowned counsellors who vie for victory on opposite sides of the question. Although Plato writes in his *Hipparchus* that profit is desirable,[21] I can scarcely believe that the desire for gain is strong enough to corrupt the good natures of our jurists to take up unjust and abominable arms against an obvious truth.

"Our city has always had an abundance of men who achieved 16 the highest distinction in jurisprudence. But with all due respect for earlier ages, our own is surely second to none in learning and integrity, and is likewise reckoned superior in the art of speaking and in other branches of knowledge which improve our lives. We have witnessed, and continue to witness daily, the excellence of men who speak not only in courts and trials but also in important embassies, in our Senate and highest public offices. No one should be surprised when several advocates of this calibre disagree with each other. Rather, since we see this happen in nearly every case, we must perforce conclude that the obscurity of events is to blame.

17   'Eam autem non a natura esse, quae lumen suum accendit in
nobis et posuit omnem recte vivendi rationem in propatulo, ut est
a me paulo ante supradictum, manifestum est. Sed coacervati libri
rursum, et tot tantaeque eadem saepe de re ac tam diversae disputationes et conatus, quid mirum si animum quid haesitantem in
principiis trahunt in diversa? Nam quod, ducente monstranteque
natura facile quis suopte fuerit ingenio assecutus, congestis ita ar-
gumentationibus modo hanc, modo illam partem confirmantibus
aut infirmantibus, quid veri tandem in re sit nequeunt dinoscere.
Duo librorum milia fuisse quondam legalis disciplinae Romanorum, antequam eam Iustinianus emendaret, memoriae tradiderunt. Quid si plura etiam modo reperiantur? Quid si multo incon-
cinniora et perplexiora? Quis enim est aut fuit paulo doctior
iurisconsultus qui aliquid a se scriptum non reliquerit? Nulla
enim ars est (ni fallor) gignendis libris altercationibusque conse-
rendis civili hac scientia feracior. Ex quo fit, crescente in dies
confusione omnium rerum, ut disceptando atque altercando anni
saepe toti, immo totae aetates, una absolvenda causa conterantur.

18   'Non possum hoc loco praeterire silentio Ulpiani illas quas libro quarto et quadragesimo *Digestorum* exceptiones docte persequi-
tur. Sed ex illis quoque facile monstratur quanta sit inter altercan-
tes producendae litis confundendaeque licentia. Exceptio, inquit,
dicta est quasi quaedam exclusio, quae interponi actioni cuiusque
rei solet ad excludendum id quod in intentionem condemnatio-
nemve deductum est. Et haec quidem ad rerum pertinet. Addit
autem replicationes quae sunt actoris, quibus exceptiones diluun-
tur quibusque reus subinfert triplicationes, rursus et deinceps
multiplicantur nomina, dum aut reus aut actor deiicit. Et ad
centuplicationes dabuntur, puto, vicissitudines contendentibus,
praesertim si ne uno quidem modo tantum excipitur. Sed sunt ex-
ceptionum plura genera, in quibus et illa sunt quae non ad diluci-
dationem causarum, quod ipsum foret tolerabilius, sed ad actio-
nem differendam atque extrahenda iudicia introducta videntur.

178

"It is obvious that nature is not at fault, for (as I said earlier)   17
she has lit a light within us and placed within our view the entire
basis for living well. But when faced with mountains of books and
so many great disputes and struggles on the same questions, is it
surprising if a mind with uncertain standards is torn in several directions? With nature leading and pointing the way, everyone
could arrive at the truth using his own wits; but when arguments
are piled up to prove or refute conflicting claims, no one can distinguish the truth. History records that there were two thousand
books on the discipline of Roman law before Justinian revised it.
Suppose more were found, and suppose they were more incoher-
ent and perplexing—what then? For what jurist of learning, past
or present, has not left some written opinions? Unless I am mistaken, no discipline is more fertile in producing books and fo-
menting discord than this civil science. As the universal confusion
grows daily, entire years and entire lifetimes are often wasted in resolving a single case.

"In this regard, I feel obliged to mention the 'defences' which   18
Ulpian discusses in Book 44 of the *Digest*. They provide a clear in-
dication of the licence which litigators abuse in prolonging and
confusing a case. 'A defence,' he says, 'has been described as some
kind of bar which used to be raised against the action of any party
in order to shut out whatever has been introduced into the accusation [*intentio*] or into the condemnation.'[22] This definition pertains
to the defendant. He then adds 'replications,' which are made by
the prosecution to counter the defences. To these, the defendant in
turn introduces 'triplications,' and thereafter the names are multi-
plied according as either the defendant or plaintiff raises a defence.[23] The litigants may continue the exchanges up to 'centupli-
cations,' I suppose, especially if more than one kind of defence is
allowed. But there are several kinds of defence, including those
which are apparently introduced not to shed light on the case—
which would be more tolerable—but to prolong the suit and to

Adde ad iacturam temporum, quod necesse est ut sumptus fiant
intolerabiles rediganturque ad egestatem longius litigantes. Neque
Cinthia, quam vocant legem, non admodum necessaria fuit, qua
cautum est quondam ne quis ob orandam causam pecuniam acci-
peret aut donum; etsi deinde Claudii Caesaris edicto factum ut
usque ad dena sestertia liceret sine fraude accepisse industriae ac
laboris ergo.

19   'Nunc vero cum multo laboratur magis propter legum scripto-
rumque multitudinem varietatemque paene inextricabilem, si
maiora pretia exposcerint, nihil egisse indigni qui causas modo
multo difficilius tractant fortasse videbuntur. Rei namque, si in eo
vitium est, non artificis culpa est. Suam enim labori cuique pro laboris ipsius condicione constitutam esse mercedem consensu
etiam omnium hominum rationi est quam maxime consentaneum.
Ita contingit ut ad paupertatem facile plerumque devenerint ut de
litigantibus factum sit iam tritum vetustate proverbium: qui in civilibus controversiis fuerunt occupati diutius, qui etiam cum in-
gentia quoque nonnumquam concertando patrimonia consumpse-
runt, tandem suo pretio facti prudentiores, etsi frustra erratum
accusant, qui dum augere ita rem student, omnia per litigia amise-
runt, tamen aliquid fidei esse expertis convenit non usquequaque
morem hunc causarum et iudiciorum comprobandum fuisse.

20   'Maiores nostri ut pleraque prudenter, ita et variarum rerum va-
ria iudicia constituerunt, ut in artibus singulis singularum eruditi
artium iudicarent si quae, ut fit, in sua arte contentiones orirentur.
Sunt igitur in urbe etiam nunc una et viginti artium diversitates,
quarum etiam nomina sunt diversa. Sed communi appellatione vocant capitudines. Conveniunt diversis in locis pro cuiusque com-
moditate habentque singulae suum collegium suosque magistratus, quos appellant consules, quod in rebus suis dubiis (ut opinor)
ceteri sui corporis opifices eorum consilium sequantur. Vetustis-
sima autem lege ab eorum sententiis provocatio non fuit. Quod
ideo factum puto, et quidem sapienter, ne aliquando mutatione iu-

delay sentencing. To the waste of time, you must add the inevitably burdensome expenses, which eventually reduce the litigants to poverty. The so-called *lex Cincia*, which forbade pleaders from accepting money or gifts, was quite necessary, although later an edict of the emperor Claudius made it legal to accept as much as ten sesterces for one's time and effort.[24]

"Today, when we must toil even more because of the perplexing   19 multitude and variety of laws and commentaries, lawyers who take one of the more difficult cases are surely justified in asking higher fees. If there is anything wrong, the fault lies with the practice, not the practitioner. For it is the consensus of all humankind, and clearly in consonance with reason, that compensation for every kind of labor is determined by its nature. Hence it happens that both parties are often reduced to poverty, as our ancient and well-worn proverb has it concerning litigants.[25] By engaging in lengthy civil suits which often consume huge patrimonies, such litigants end by learning a lesson at their own expense. Instead of increasing their wealth as they sought to do, they lose everything in court and regret their mistake too late. Still, when such people say that the present system of cases and judgments is far from perfect, we should believe them as speaking from experience.

"As in many other matters, our ancestors were prudent in   20 assigning different judgments to different circumstances. Thus, when contentions arose in the single guilds, as often happens, master guildsmen would act as judges. Today there are twenty-one guilds in our city, each with its own name, but as a group they are called *capitudini*.[26] Each guild has its own convenient meeting-place with a college of magistrates whom it calls consuls, I suppose because in doubtful matters the other artisans adopt their counsel (*consilium*). An ancient statute prohibits appealing against any of their decisions. I believe that this measure was intended, quite prudently, to prevent decisions from being overturned and cases referred to our system of legal review, whose multiplicity of inter-

diciorum ad hoc interpretandarum legum artificium causa depor-
taretur, fierique ex aperta obscurissima inciperet multiplicitate in-
terpretationum, etsi modo nova lege lata provocant ad sex viros
mercatores (de quibus mox dicemus) tantum in maioribus causis,
et magno quidem provocatoris discrimine, si iniuria provocaverit.

21   'Novi ego paulo ante virum quemdam doctum atque apprime
ingeniosum iurisconsultum, haud nostratem tamen, qui omnes
fere species quae venire frequentius in controversiam solent in
unum ab se scriptum volumen cum redegisset, quid in utramque
partem afferri pro victoria posset diligentissime annotaverat. Ita
omnem sine discrimine causam suscipiebat, neque pro vero, sed
tantum ut vinceret; laborans non mediocres est non longo tempore
adeptus divitias; nomen certe inter iuris doctos quam clarum obtinuit. Tanta vis artis est atque ingenii, ubi tanta scriptorum legumque diversitas omnia confundens, ita obtegere ingenii perversi-
tatem potest. Quem ego ut nominem, si rem teneamus, non opus,
ut a vetere instituto meo non abscedam. Id enim induxi in animum iamdudum, nisi honoris gratia, nominare neminem.'

22   'Satis hic,' inquit Machiavellus, 'intelligo. Et probo istam mo-
destiam tuam, praesertim in his quorum est memoria recentior.
Nam et contigit plerumque ut immeritissimi heredes et propinqui
bene morati et iusti viri aliena affecti nota famae suae et nominis
subeant periculum. Depravata enim consuetudine progenitorum
vitia, praesertim si qua nobiliora fuerint, renasci in iunioribus putamus, et illud probamus satyri poetae quod ait:

Est[1] utile porro
filiolam turpi vetulae producere turpem.

Quod etsi dicitur non indocte, tamen videre licet complures multum parentum moribus dissimiles.

23   'Non autem iverim inficias magnam habere in sese vim ad for-
mandam atque instituendam vitam prima quaeque rudimenta,
quae apud parentes domesticosque imbibuntur. Neque absurdum

pretations would obscure what had previously been clear. Still, a law passed not long ago permits appeals to be made to six men selected from the Merchants' Guild (about which I shall speak later), but only in important cases, and the appellant runs a great risk if he makes a challenge unjustly.[27]

"I recently met a learned and quite ingenious jurist (not a Flor- 21 entine) who has compiled a handbook listing every sort of case that normally comes to trial. For each case, he diligently collected all the arguments on both sides that would contribute to a favorable decision. In this way, he was prepared to undertake all cases indiscriminately. By striving only to win, rather than to find the truth, he made no small fortune in very little time and won a brilliant reputation among jurists. So great is the power of science and intelligence, where the diversity of opinions and laws confuses us, that it can disguise such moral depravity. There's no need for me to name him, as long as my point is clear. I wish to observe my long-standing principle of naming persons only in an honorable context."

"I know the man you mean," said Bernardo, "and I applaud 22 your discretion, especially regarding persons of recent memory. For it often happens that men who are just and principled risk losing their good name and reputation because they are the innocent heirs or relatives of someone in disgrace. We suppose that the habitually corrupt morals of one's forebears, especially the more famous ones, are reborn in their descendants, and we approve the words of the satirist:

It behooves
a wicked woman to raise a wicked daughter.[28]

Yet even if his words are perceptive, we can see many children whose character is unlike that of their parents.

"Of course, I wouldn't deny that the first lessons learned by 23 children from their parents and others in the home exert great in-

est quod aiunt, cuiusmodi sit paterfamilias deprehendi ex familia pulcherrime. Nec liberos modo parentum, sed et servos dominorum mores solere referre, ut in re quoque domestica idem accidere dicamus quod Plato ait evenire in civitatibus. Est enim innata in nobis imitandi quaedam non pusilla vis, quae si ad vitia eorum qui praesint convertatur, incredibile dictu est quam facile coalescat. Virtutis enim, quod ea, ut Aristotili placuit, circa difficiliora versetur, ut est laboriosior imitatio, ita et rarior. Adde etiam quod innascitur nescio quid augeturque consuetudine, quod monere continuo videtur ut ad eorum maxime qui progenuerunt, quibusque convivimus, similitudinem mores et ipsi nostros effingamus. Quod et facit ut soleam stemmatibus istis, quae nonnulli iactant etiam supra modum, et generis nobilitati plus tribuere. Magis certe multo est arduum suo, ut aiunt, Marte sine maiorum adminiculis fieri nobilem. Quod tibi ingenti cum laude tua evenisse pro nostra amicitia vehementer gratulor. Sed perge, quaeso. Etsi enim non probo ex his aliqua quae a te de legibus deque forensi usu disertissime dicuntur, nihilominus tamen nihil est quod aeque cupiam quam audire te de rebus nostris argutissime disputantem.'

24 'Ego vero,' inquam, 'pergam, et tibi geram morem. Tu modo quae aliter sentias aperire deinde non graveris. Non iam usque a principio illuc tetendit oratio mea, ut magistrum me videlicet aut auctorem quemdam non ignarum rerum aliena praesertim in disciplina profiterer, verum ut ex te tandem quae verior sententia esset intelligerem. Quod et tu fortasse facilius cum me audiveris explicabis. Neque ab re, opinor, putabitur si haec ipse haudquaquam doctus homo cum doctissimo, ut in ludis solent et cantibus aliqua praemittere, fuerim prolocutus prius.

25 'Illum igitur nos quanto poteramus modestius reprehendebamus qui non veritati inveniendae studeret, sed victoriae in causa comparandae operam omnem suam conatumque intenderet. Artem scilicet iam vincendi quandam, non dilucidandae atque aperiendae veritatis et iustitiae defendendae studium nonnulli

fluence on the development and direction of their lives. And there is some sense in the saying that you can easily divine the father from his household. Not only do children reflect their parents' nature, but the servants reflect their masters', so that we may say that the same thing happens in the home that Plato describes in the city.[29] We are born with a strong instinct for imitation, and if we are exposed to vices in those who raise us, they take root with incredible ease. Aristotle thought that virtue is concerned with what is difficult and that the attainment of virtue, being more arduous, is also rarer.[30] What's more, we seem to be born with an instinct, reinforced by habit, which constantly urges us to pattern our character after our parents and those we live among. This is the reason I generally give great weight to nobility of birth and family trees, although some exalt them too highly. It is clearly more difficult to become noble through personal efforts and without the aid of one's ancestors. As a close friend, I congratulate you heartily on having achieved this to your great credit.[31] But please continue. Although I don't agree with all your elegant observations about laws and forensic practice, I still feel an overwhelming desire to hear you discuss this subject with your usual shrewdness."

"I shall continue as you wish," I said. "But don't hesitate to tell me if you disagree. From the outset, my remarks have not aimed at proving me a specialist or authority in these matters, which in fact lie beyond my competence, but rather at eliciting your opinion of the truth, which you may find easier to formulate when you have heard my position. I hope no one will think it amiss if I who am the amateur speak first before you who are the expert, in the way that games and songs are preceded by lesser ones.   24

"Now, I have reproached with utmost moderation any lawyer who devotes all his effort and energy to winning his case rather than trying to discover the truth. For there are some who regard our sacred discipline of jurisprudence and law as the art of winning rather than the pursuit of eliciting and illuminating the truth   25

existimant iuris hanc et legum sacrosanctam disciplinam, qua modo fora omnia ita resonant tam dissonis variisque clamoribus perstrepuntque. Opere pretium est ingredi quorundam bibliothecas atque officinas potius causarum et coacervatissimos inspicere librorum cumulos, quos in rota partim libraria, partim ad parietes appensos tabulis tanquam scriniis distenduntur, habentque continuo reclusos praeparatosque legentibus. Ipsi in medio consistentes nunc hos adeunt, nunc illos pro diversitate atque obscuritate causarum. Ita enim putant quod volunt confirmare posse habilius, et clientes multo magis his tot librorum spectaculis eorum esse sapientiam miraturos.

26 'Pandolphum Collenuccium, Pisaurensis principis et Florentinae militiae ducis apud nos oratorem, gravem sane virum atque in omni doctrinae genere excellentem, nosti. Id mihi quod riderem nudius tertius enarravit, cum me forte euntem in curiam quo et ipse proficiscebatur ad archiepiscopales aedes convenisset, atque inter eundum his de rebus, de quibus nunc disputamus, sermo, a me quaesita occasione ut eius super his sententiam pertentarem, incidisset: ventitare scilicet se aliquando solitum in ampullosi cuiusdam atque avari in primis hominis, qui se tamen iureconsultissimum haberi vellet, librariam tabernam, conspicatumque fuisse tres librorum in ea ordines; cum autem quid ea sibi vellet diversitas investigasset diligentius, compertum tamen a se fuisse tot ab illo factos librorum ordines, quot esse possunt advocati partes; atque eos quidem qui pro causa essent, unum eundemque in locum collocatos; in alterum vero eos qui contra causa sentirent; seorsum qui suspensionem causae perplexitatemque inducerent; consuevisse vero adducere, cum litem in se suscepisset atque accepisset de more nummum aureum, a se susceptae litis primum pretium, in bibliothecam ternariam clientem ut, ita conspectis ordinibus, in sua esse manu intelligeret tota iudiciorum fortunam: sive diluere aliena et confirmare tua sive ambiguum facere iudicem atque animi suspensum malis.

and of defending justice, and they fill the courts with a great deal of clamorous and dissonant shouting. You should visit the libraries (or should I say, workshops?) of certain lawyers and see the books they have accumulated, some of them displayed on rotating stands, others in wall-mounted cabinets, all kept ready and open for readers to consult. They stand in the middle, now turning to one set of books, now to another, according to the diversity and obscurity of the cases. They think that such a show both facilitates their preparing a case and impresses their clients with their wisdom.

"You know Pandolfo Collenuccio, a grave and widely learned 26 man who is ambassador here representing the ruler of Pesaro and captain of the Florentine military forces.[32] He told me an amusing tale when we met the other day by the archbishop's residence, both on our way to court. As we walked, we broached the subject we are now discussing, and I took the occasion to learn his thoughts on it. He said that he used to frequent the house of a pompous and greedy fellow who wished to be thought an expert on law. In the man's book nook, he found the volumes divided into three groups. When he examined more closely the meaning of this arrangement, he found that there were as many groups of books as there are roles a lawyer may play. Books for proving a case were gathered in one section; books for refuting it were in a second section; and those for suspending a trial as undecidable were in a separate section. Whenever the fellow took a case and had received a gold florin as the customary initial fee, he would usually invite his client to see his three-part library. The sight of the books thus arranged would show that he completely controlled the outcome of the trial, since he could at will refute the opposition, prove his own case or create doubt and uncertainty in the judge's mind.

27   'Talem fuisse quondam Minoem crediderim aut Aeacum aut Rhadamantum, quod etiam apud inferos Graeci ob iustitiam constitutos esse iudices umbrarum lepide confinxerunt. Atqui, ut ait Homerus, Minos Iovis fuit filius novemque annos quibus Cretae imperavit frequenter cum patre locutus, id est cum ratione et natura. Quid est enim Iuppiter aliud? Regnandi ab eo praecepta edidicit. Unde aureum tenens sceptrum (ut in *Odyssea* idem poeta cecinit) iudex est eorum qui hinc abeuntes sub terram proficisci creduntur ad manes. Qui et solus seorsum sedens (ut ait in *Gorgia* Plato) Aeaci Rhadamantique sententias expendit. Numquid Aristidis, cum Iusto fecerunt cognomentum, aut Catonis, cuius est severitatis et iustitiae apud nos fama insignis, id studium tandem fuit? Persarum pueri, ut est apud Xenophontem in *Cyropaedia,* ad magistros ediscendae iustitiae causa mittuntur, conteruntque diem in agendis atque in dicendis causis. Qui forte est criminis convictus aut falso accusavit, dat poenas. Naturae videlicet semina et rationis, quae sunt in nostris mentibus fundamenta iustitiae, excitare per se volunt, habitusque inducere in animos iuniorum quibus deinde iudicia rectiora fiant quam his tam confusis scriptis, quae poeta in *Satyra* "legum" vocat "aenigmata."

28   'Mercatorium tandem forum civitatis nostrae quid inter naturae pectorisque, ut aiunt, iudicia legumque intersit facile declarat, ubi minus implicatae causae agitari consueverunt et iudicari facilius. Sex viros, non iuris expertos illos quidem, sed natura scitos et bonos deligunt. Hi audiunt controversias quae ex negotiatoribus plurimae oriuntur quodque aequum et bonum sit visum decernunt. Neque ab eorum fas est iudiciis provocare. Huic foro adscriptum supra portam est: "domus aequitatis et veritatis," ut intelligant qui ad id accesserint nihil plus apud loci eius iudices quam veritatis monstrandae studium esse valiturum. Ingens quondam fama fuit apud exteras etiam gentes mercatorii Florentini fori, atque ex uni-

"Of such a calibre, I would think, were Minos, Aeacus and 27
Rhadamanthus, whom the Greeks charmingly fancied to be the
judges of souls brought to trial in the underworld. As Homer says,
Minos was the son of Jupiter, and during the nine years when he
ruled Crete he often spoke with his father, that is, with reason
and nature (which are the same as Jupiter), and learned from him
precepts for governing.[33] Hence, he wields a golden sceptre, as
Homer says in the *Odyssey*, and judges those who are thought to
depart this life to join the shades in the underworld.[34] Seated
apart and alone, as Plato says in his *Gorgias*,[35] Minos reviews the
sentences of Aeacus and Rhadamanthus. Was such zeal for justice
displayed by Aristides, who was nicknamed the Just, or by Cato,
whose severity and justice are still legendary? Xenophon writes in
his *Education of Cyrus* that Persian boys were sent to teachers to
learn justice and spent their days arguing and pleading cases.[36]
Whoever was convicted of a crime, say, or made false accusations
paid a penalty. The Persians wished to foster the seeds of nature
and reason, which are the foundations of justice in our minds, and
to instil in their youths mental habits by which they could make
better judgments than by our confusing legal texts, which the poet
in one of his *Satires* calls the 'enigmas of laws.'[37]

"The Merchants' Court of our city, which usually tries less 28
complicated cases and judges them speedily, readily distinguishes
between judgments of nature and conscience (as they say) and
judgments of law. They appoint six men who are not legal experts
but who are by nature shrewd and good. These men hear the disputes that frequently arise between merchants and decide what
seems just and fair, and their judgments allow no appeal. Above
the door to the court is written 'The House of Equity and Truth,'
so that whoever enters will understand that nothing carries more
weight with the judges who sit there than their zeal to ascertain
the truth. The Merchants' Court at Florence once enjoyed enormous fame among foreign nations. Cases that seemed very com-

verso prope orbe si quae viderentur causae implicatiores, huc afferebantur, quemadmodum Dodonam olim et Delphos et Delon in rebus suis dubiis scitatum oracula veniebant. Quod sex viri statuissent, referebant ad suos et ad oraculi modum venerabantur.

29   'Nos eam iudicandi gloriam amisimus ex eo iam tempore, arbitror, quo litigandi hae civiles formulae huc quoque sensim irrepsere. Illud me commovere multum solet quod non ratione, non causa leges ubi latae sunt semel, non bono, non aequo aliquo, ne syllabam quidem immutaverint. Ex quo lepidiusculus in illas est noster apologus huiusmodi:

> Nobilis spurius in Leges invehebatur acriter quod et locupleti hereditate et honore familiae ac patriae immeritissimum privavissent; inique fecisse profecto et crudeliter, quae adeo insontem indicta etiam causa condemnavissent. Insolescere eas iam nimium et exercere regnum, neque rationi quid aut occasioni aut necessitati, quod modeste facerent, quicquam velle concedere. Severitatem modo prae se ferentes, quid boni aequique sit in rebus, nihil quaerere, surdas, inexorabiles, neque precibus neque lacrimis miserarum unquam fortunarum commoveri didicisse. In auctores etiam suos saepe exercuisse immites poenas et terrifica exempla constituisse posteris. A natura tandem, quae omnia progenuisset, impie descivisse ad tyrannidem, eiusque leges constitutis suis (si diis placet) insolentissime abrogasse. Non tulit Natura diutius lamentari spurium, quem ex abdito recte ita argumentantem exaudierat. Citatas itaque Leges, quibus et ipsa diu succensebat, male defensa causa damnavit vertitque in reti-

plicated were referred to it from nearly the whole world, just as people long ago went to consult the oracles at Dodona, Delphi and Delos when in doubt about their affairs. The rulings of the six men were reported to the enquiring parties and venerated like oracles.

"I think we lost our pre-eminence in judging when the formulas   29 of civil litigation began to creep gradually into this court as well. It often distresses me that not even a syllable of our laws, once passed, can be changed for any reason, case or consideration of justice and fairness. This is the subject of a witty fable I wrote about the laws, which runs as follows:

An illegitimate son of noble parents bitterly attacked the Laws by which the wealthy wrongly deprived him of the rich inheritance of his family and the honor of citizenship in his country. He said that the Laws had acted wrongly and cruelly in condemning an innocent man without a trial, and had become insolent in their power to govern, with no allowances for motive, circumstance or necessity. While they made a grim display of severity, they never enquired about the goodness and justice of a question. Deaf and inexorable, they had never learned to feel compassion at the pleas and tears of those who suffered misfortune. The Laws had even condemned their own authors to the worst penalties and had established terrifying examples for posterity. They had impiously abandoned Nature, who had given birth to all things, and degenerated into tyranny, setting up their own laws and (good heavens!) abolishing those of Nature. Nature had secretly overheard the illegitimate son's just arguments and could no longer bear to let him complain. She summoned the Laws, who had long provoked her wrath, and when they made but a poor defence, she found them guilty and changed

cula aranearum et dixit condicionem ut nisi minutioribus insectis non obsisterent.

30 'Id enim est etiam in his, etsi non est id quidem vitium a legibus. Qui plus possunt, earum vix ferunt ut teneantur imperio, severiores modo esse consueverint, si sint magis abiectae magisque afflictae miseraeque fortunae, severitudinem quoque redarguunt, neque iniuria (ut mea est opinio), quod ea ad crudelitatem quam proxime videatur accedere, et feritatis cuiusdam nonnumquam atque immanitatis naturam imitari. Quis laudarit Brutum vindicem Romanae libertatis de filiis sumentem tam dirum, ferox supplicium? Qui dum animo (ut sibi forsitan videri poterat) magno excelsoque sedet et solvi fasces imperat nudatisque corporibus colligari ad palum infelices liberorum manus, verberarique et percuti securibus, populus tam triste horrendumque spectaculum aspicere oculis vix poterat, miserebatque homines non poenae magis quam sceleris, quo poenam meriti fuissent, ut ait Livius, et turbam certe crediderim, quae spectabat, in consulis filios multo patre quoque ipso indulgentiorem futuram. Quamquam ferociane id innata fecerit, an conventorum inter se in tyrannidem pro libertate tuenda necessitate potius, incertum est. Ego necessitatem malim, etsi et ipsam probare nullo pacto possum.

31 'Multa enim evenire quotidie videmus, tot versantur res humanae casibus, tot sunt quae quotidie emergunt earum diversitates, in quibus merito solutiorem facultatem liberiusque iudicium desideres. Fieri namque vix natura potest ut comprehendere animo nomotheta queat universas rerum species quae unum sub decretum possint venire. Si quid inest in lege vitii, tempus arguit, quod etiam philosophi solent ob eam ipsam causam appellare sapientissimum. Multa enim ipsum detegit datque in lucem, quae tu non arte ulla, nullis studiis, non viribus quibusvis conatibusque per te

them into spider's webs, stipulating that they were to obstruct only the tiniest insects.[38]

"Our courts share this defect, although the laws are not to 30
blame. People with the most power bridle at being subject to the authority of the laws, especially when these tend to be rather severe. People in more abject and miserable circumstances also reprove their severity. In my opinion, they are right, since it seems that severity borders on cruelty and sometimes imitates the spirit of savagery and brutality. Who would praise Brutus, the champion of Roman liberty, for inflicting such a dire and fearful death on his sons? Sitting in judgment with what he may think a great and lofty spirit, he orders the fasces unbound and his wretched sons stripped and tied to the stake by their wrists, and then beaten and battered with the axes. The populace can scarcely bear to witness such a sad and terrifying spectacle, and 'pitied the men not more for their punishment than for the crime for which they deserved it,' as Livy says.[39] I'm inclined to think that the crowd of onlookers would have been much kinder to the consul's sons than their own father. It is unclear whether he acted out of natural brutality or whether he was compelled by his pledge to defend liberty against tyranny. I would like to think he was compelled, even though I can in no wise condone the fact.

"We are witnesses each day to new events unfolding. Human 31
affairs are shaped by so many chance circumstances, and so many diverse situations arise each day that to face them calls for unrestricted powers and freedom of judgment. It is by nature practically impossible for a legislator to foresee every species of event which may fall within the scope of a single decree. If a law has defects, they will be revealed by Time, which philosophers, for this very reason, are accustomed to call most wise. For time lays bare and brings to light many things which you will not discover by any art or study, by any force or striving, unless time assists you. Thus,

sine adiutore tempore consequare. Ita necessarium fit, cum quid
tale evenerit, aut recedere ab legum observantia, quo vos nihil esse
detestabilius putatis, aut certe tale agere aliquid quale non probasse animis populum Romanum in Bruto, auctore libertatis, supra diximus. Nam ut in aedificiis, dictante natura, inconcinna non
probant, sic in iudiciis abhorrent maxime a crudelitate animi nostri, ac quidquid rationi naturaeque, quae regnum obtinere in mentibus nostris debent, non vident convenire, vitium habere in sese
putant et probris consectantur.

32   'Quanto igitur, ne longius faciam, vivi potuit melius ad boni viri
bonique iudicis arbitrium, duce natura (quae libera est semper, nec
aliquibus obnoxia extraneis constitutionibus, ipsa sibi pro tempore, pro rebus, pro causis, pro casibus quid decerni oporteat
abunde subministrat), quam eam sibi imposuisse homines necessitatem, ut velint nolint sit obtemperandum, in his etiam saepe rebus in quibus multo in rem fuit aliter ut decerneretur! Ex quo probare totam illam non soleo sententiam, cuius arbitror fuisse vos
auctores, et dici graviter a quibusdam sapienter putatur: aut non
ferendas esse leges, aut certe latas inviolabiliter sancteque esse ser-
vandas. Illud fortasse sapientius, si ferendae sunt leges, eatenus eis
esse parendum quatenus naturae legibus, qua ipsa in nobis immu-
tabiles sempiternasque constituit, non contraveniant. Ipsa enim
sola est quae recte instituit sine praeceptoribus, quae aperit dubi-
tationes sine altercatione, quae verum cognoscit, neque falli potest,
quae recte diiudicat et nemo coarguit. Ipsa tandem est, a qua si
quis recedere ausit confidentius oblitus ipse sui, immo vero sibi
ipsi ac naturae suae adversatus, inextricabiles incidat perniciosissi-
mosque in errores necesse est.

33   'Ut enim nautae gubernatore amisso huc atque illuc temere cir-
cumaguntur, pereuntque saepe illisi scopulis vel absorti fluctibus,
aut certe acti ventorum flatibus eo deferuntur, unde postea regredi

it becomes necessary, when the unexpected arises, either to depart from a strict observance of the laws (than which nothing is more execrable, according to you lawyers) or else to take actions such as I have described earlier, which the Roman people condemned in Brutus, the author of their liberty. Just as we object to incongruities in buildings, our minds are repelled, with nature's guidance, by cruelty in legal judgments. When we see something inconsonant with reason and nature, which should rule our minds, we decry it as imperfect.

"In short, how much better we could live by following the 32 judgment of a good man and good judge who is guided by nature than we can under the constraint men have imposed on themselves, which they must needs obey willy-nilly, especially in the frequent cases when a different judgment would be more appropriate! For Nature is always free and subject to no outside decrees; of herself Nature supplies abundant reasons for rendering decisions according to the time, the matter, the causes and the chance circumstances of a question. That is why I generally reject the opinion (which I believe you lawyers formulated and which some regard as a wise and grave utterance) that one must either pass no laws or else observe those passed as inviolable and sacrosanct. It would perhaps be wiser to say that, if laws must be passed, they should be obeyed insofar as they do not contravene Nature's laws, which she herself established as immutable and eternal within us. For it is Nature alone who correctly instructs us without tutors, resolves dubious questions without contention, perceives the truth without error and judges rightly without contradiction. In sum, if anyone boldly dares depart from her, he forgets himself, or rather betrays himself and his nature, and must inevitably fall into inextricable and pernicious errors.

"Now, if the helmsman is lost, the sailors are driven helplessly 33 this way and that; often they perish, dashed on the rocks or engulfed by waves, or gusting winds drive them so far away that no

humana aliqua opera non licet; quemadmodum dispergi consueverunt oves, gregis pastorem si percusseris; sicut milites, si quis imperatorem casus subtraxerit, confusione opplentur variaque in pericula et mortes corruunt; ita si rectorem, si custodem, si ducem
rerum omnium actionumque humanarum naturam neglexeris,
contempseris, abieceris, nihil est omnino eorum quae timere et fugere merito homines consueverunt non formidandum, non expec-
tandum, non ferendum.'

34   Cum finem fecissem dicendi, Bernardus aliquantisper obticuit,
expectans, credo, prae modestia, quoniam praeterea dicenda resta-
rent quae quidem quas ego tueri velle partes videri possem confirmarent. Cum autem ex illius silentio id fuissem conspicatus,
'Congessi,' inquam, 'plura etiam fortasse quam necesse fuit. Te
modo habeo audire, ut quid tu tandem censueris, non quod mihi
ita occurrerit, sequendum putem. Meministi enim hac me condicione ad dicendum supra venisse, ut tu demum quae esset tua his
omnibus fere de rebus sententia explicares.'

35   Tum ille, 'Memini,' inquit, 'et quando pro legibus mihi habenda
oratio est, non fecerim modeste si peccare incepero in leges nec
stetero ipse nostris iam conventis. Prius autem quam ad ea veniam
quae a te sunt prudentissime disputata, necessarium videtur ut aliqua de origine iuris ac legum deque eorum generibus appellationi-
busque brevissime percurram. Sic enim fiet, arbitror, quod quaeri-
mus inventu multo facilius. Neque vero unum dumtaxat naturae
ius est, de quo paulo ante tam multa, quod et ipsum non hominis
modo, sed omnium quoque animantium commune est, atque
unde fateor cetera quoque iura tamquam a parente quadam fecun-
dissima producuntur. Verum tamen differt a iure hoc, quod natu-
rale appellant, illud, quod, quia gentes tacito inter se consensu
utuntur, eam subministrante natura convenientiam, dicitur ius
gentium, quod quidem non transit in alienas species, sed homines
modo et quidem ubique terrarum omnes eo iure comprehenduntur. Hinc emptiones sunt, hinc venditiones, hinc constantia dicto-

human power can bring them back. If the shepherd of the flock is slain, the sheep are dispersed. If soldiers lose their commander through some mishap, they are filled with confusion and expose themselves to various dangers and even death. By the same token, if you ignore, despise or reject Nature, who is the guide, guardian and leader of all human affairs and actions, you must dread, must expect and must suffer every ill that humankind has wisely feared and fled."

When I had finished speaking, Bernardo was silent a while, waiting modestly, I think, to hear what further arguments I would make to prove my point. Surmising this from his silence, I said: "Perhaps I have heaped up more arguments than were needed. I am now in a position to hear you, so that I may embrace what you believe rather than what occurred to me to say. You recall that I agreed to speak only if you explained your view of this entire question." 34

"I do," he said, "and since I must speak in defence of laws, it would be improper if I began by breaking them and violated our agreement. Yet before I respond to what you have so wisely said, it seems necessary to review briefly the origin of justice and laws, as well as their types and designations. I think this will greatly simplify our search. Now, the law of Nature, as you have just argued at length, is common to all animals as well as to humankind; and I concede that all laws derive from Nature as from a most fertile mother. But this natural law is not the only kind, for there is a difference between this 'natural law' and what is called 'the law of nations,' which nations use between themselves by a tacit agreement which Nature herself provides.[40] Now, the law of nations does not extend to other species, but applies solely to humankind, embracing all human beings everywhere on earth. It is this law which introduced buying and selling, the observance of verbal 35

rum conventorum, hinc rerum permutationes ad hominum utilitatem commoditatemque vivendi, quae magna ex parte nunc constant pecuniarum usu, sunt introductae. At quoniam diversi admodum sunt mores, diversa item cuiusque fere civitatis constituta. Tertium iuris genus fit, et civile nominatur. Didicisse furari apud Spartanos olim ex Lycurgi legibus in pretio fuit. Duodecim tabulae quadrupli poenam statuerunt furibus; nos vero, si quis furti est convictus, ignominioso mortis genere damnamus, atque e furca suspensum laqueo guttur perstringimus.

36   'Ceterarum quoque rerum apud diversos non diversa modo sentiuntur, sed contraria etiam penitus instituta servantur. Gaetulae mulieres agros colunt et virilia exercent; miscentur quibuslibet praesertim advenis sine rubore. Idem et Bactrianis mos est. Contra apud Arabos adulterae interficiuntur, neque deprehensae modo hanc fortunam subeunt, sed in suspectas quoque saevos sese ostendisse quam decorum est. Babylonii (ut ait Herodotus) lege lata medicos non admittunt, deferunt in forum aegrum, neque viatori transire prius licet quam omnia fuerit diligentissime ex ipso percontatus et siquid sibi acciderit eiusmodi edocuerit. Padaeorum gens quae vocatur, quae incolit ad auroram, vescitur crudis carnibus, affectos morbis interficiunt exeduntque; senio item appropinquantes mactatos devorant. Tamen apud plerosque sancta admodum est ac venerabilis senectus. Sunt et qui coeunt in propatulo, quod tamen et Cynicorum secta philosophorum assentitur. Sed id mihi brutis convenire magis nihil ratione utentibus quam hominis excellentiae videri solet. Natura certe genitalia non in promptu ut oculos, ut frontem, ut aures collocavit, sed apte modesteque occuluit. Unde nos pudere (quod hominis proprium est) didicisse percommode debuimus, quandoquidem hinc quoque pudibunda nomen acceperunt.

37   'Sexcenta huiuscemodi afferri possunt. Sed haec quoque sunt plura fortassis quam necesse fuit. Res enim ipsa per se sine his

agreements and those exchanges of goods, today largely effected through the use of money, which enhance and advance our lives. But since customs differ greatly, practically every city has different statutes. Hence, a third kind of law is called 'civil law.' Under the laws of Lycurgus, the ancient Spartans admired the ability to steal.[41] In Rome, the Twelve Tables imposed fourfold penalty damages on thieves.[42] Today, when someone is convicted of theft, we condemn him to an ignominious death and hang him by the neck from the gallows.

"In other matters, different peoples have customs which are not   36
only different, but even completely opposite. The women of the Getae till the fields, perform men's work and engage without shame in intercourse with anyone, especially strangers — customs which the Bactrians share.[43] By contrast, the Arabs put adulterous women to death, and women caught in the act are not the only ones to meet this fate, for the men think it honorable to deal harshly with any women they even suspect.[44] Herodotus writes that the Babylonians had a law banning doctors; instead, they would carry a sick person into the square, and no traveller was allowed to pass until the patient had questioned him at length and learned whether he had ever witnessed a similar disease.[45] The people known as the Padaei, who lived in the Orient, fed on raw meat, killing and devouring anyone who fell sick or grew feeble with age.[46] Yet some nations regard old age as very holy and venerable. There are others who copulate in public, an act which philosophers of the Cynic school also endorse. But it strikes me that such behavior is more suited to irrational beasts than to the excellence of human beings. Indeed, nature did not place our genitals in the open, like our eyes, brow and ears, but aptly and modestly hid them. This is why we appropriately learn to feel shame, a peculiarly human emotion, which gives us the word *pudenda*.

"One could adduce countless such examples. Perhaps these are   37
more than sufficient, since the issue is clear even without the aid

exemplorum adminiculis in aperto est. Ius igitur civile quod suo quodam more rationeque singulae sibi civitates excogitaverunt tale est. Constant vero civitates publicis et privatis rebus. Unde et publica et privata iura deducuntur. Et publica quidem, quae ad statum pertinent rerum publicarum, bifariam dividuntur. Aut enim ad rem divinam cultumque ordinantur sacrorum et ad religionem religiosaque vocantur, aut curant magistratus illa quidem profanaque dicuntur.

38   'Hactenus (nisi fallor) nulla mihi tecum controversia est. Privatum vero ius, in quo tota omnino discrepantia futura est, id autem duas distribuitur in partes. Aut enim scriptum aut non scriptum est, quod tu probasse magis videris. Et scripti quidem iuris Romani sex species constituerunt; ut hi fuerunt qui apud eos condendarum et scribendarum legum facultatem sunt nacti. Quae tamen et aliis quoque civitatibus possunt accidere plura, item et pauciora, pro numero et varietate eorum quibus constituendi potestas est a populo attributa. Quae constitutiones communi nomine appellantur leges, dictae ut arbitror a legendo, ut a regendo reges, neces a necando, et greges ab antiquo verbo gregare, quod in nostrum usum non venit, sed ab eo congregare atque aggregare verba sunt ducta; ut et defaecare ab eo unde eodem itidem modo dictae sunt faeces.

39   'Verumtamen apud Romanos proprium genus lex obtinuit. Nam quod populus, senatorio interrogante magistratu quasi consule, constituebat, id dicebant legem, ut plebiscita, quae plebs magistratu interrogante plebeio, veluti tribuno. Nam senatusconsultum id est quod iuberet senatus, cui statuendi pro populo auctoritas fuit, cum is auctior factus difficilius conveniret. Lege etiam regia lata, omnis populi potestas in principem translata est. Quae illi placuerant, legis vim habebant; et principum placita huiusmodi constitutiones appellantur. Licuit et praetoribus atque aedilibus curulibus iura condere, quae dicuntur magistratuum edicta. A nonnullis vero, quod ea ab his qui honores, id est magistratus ge-

of examples. Now, civil law is what individual cities have devised according to their own usage and reason. But cities consist of public and private elements, whence we derive public and private laws. Public laws pertain to the status of public institutions and are divided into two kinds. When they govern religious rites, holy worship and religion, they are called religious. When they concern public offices, they are called profane.

"Unless I am mistaken, you will agree with me thus far. It is 38 the private law which will cause us to disagree. Private law is also divided in two parts, either written or unwritten; and you seem to approve this view. Concerning the written law, the Romans established six species, and some men of Rome were assigned the task of framing and recording laws.[47] But for regulating events, both many and few, that could occur in other cities as well, the people of Rome appointed officials according to their number and variety. In common parlance, their regulations are called 'laws' [*leges*], a word derived from 'choosing' [*legendo*], just as 'kings' [*reges*] comes from 'ruling' [*regendo*], 'slaughter' [*neces*] from 'killing' [*necando*] and 'flocks' [*greges*] from the ancient verb 'to gather' [*gregare*], a word no longer current, but which gives us 'congregate' and 'aggregate.' Likewise, 'defecation' and 'feces' have the same root.

"Now, among the Romans, each law had its own separate sta- 39 tus.[48] For when a senatorial official, such as a consul, raised a question, the decree of the people was called a law. A plebiscite was the decree of the plebs when a plebeian official, such as a tribune, raised a question. And a decree of the Senate was whatever was ordained by the Senate, which had assumed the authority for decisions on behalf of the people when the latter grew so large that it could scarcely be convened. Later, by a royal law, all the people's power was transferred to a sole ruler. His decisions had the power of law, and the ruler's decisions were called constitutions. Praetors and curule aediles were allowed to make laws,

rerent, componerentur, honoraria sunt nominata. Demum quae prudentes respondebant, observabant vocabantque, ea responsa prudentum, opiniones scilicet eorum qui iuris habere maiorem notitiam putabantur, quibusque Augustus Caesar, quid illis videretur, in dubiis rebus declarandi fecerat potestatem. Apud nos praeter populum leges fert nemo, nisi ex causa cuipiam ad tempus ipse auctoritatem delegaverit. Quae tamen suum aliud quoddam nomen non sortiuntur, sed nostro vocabulo, tum provisiones, tum reformationes appellantur, sive sciverit eas populus, sive populi vicem gesserit populi iussu magistratus alius. Verum haec quoque atque illa communi nomine appellantur leges.

40   'Est autem lex, ut iurisconsulti diffiniunt, sanctio sancta iubens honesta et prohibens contraria. Quid autem dici aut excogitari potuit ad recte vivendi rationem ista definitione accommodatius? Quid hac voce melius? Quid sanctius? Quid divinius? Utrum huiusmodi aliquid a ratione naturaque esse alienum potest? An est in vita quicquam his sanctionibus ad bene beateque vivendum magis necessarium? Duobus stare pedibus civitates Bias, ille Prienaeus sapientiae fama insignis, dicere erat solitus: altero quidem quo bonos, quo malos; altero sua condigna factis pretia manerent. Quid aliud tandem leges curant? Quid sibi volunt leges? Quid expectamus a legibus? Quid pollicentur? Quid praestant? Nonne accendunt ad decora egregia animos honore praemiisque propositis?

41   'De fortitudine, de continentia, de iustitia ne philosophi quidem vel disputant prudentius vel accuratius dant praecepta. Quo te geras pacto edocent leges, neque tantum modo instruunt ut vivendum sit tibi, sed etiam quid cum alteris contrahas sine iniuria constituunt. Illae quae ad familiam, quae ad civitatem, quae ad omne prope humanum genus pertinent exactissime persecuntur. Etenim quod recte domum instituis, quod cum uxore, cum liberis, cum servis, cum colonis tuis sine invidia versaris, quod te amant, quod reverentur tui, quod formidant imperium, quod te virum parentem dominum observant, quod ferunt, quod tibi obsequuntur

which were called magistrates' edicts. Laws made by others were called *honoraria*, because they were framed by those who held honors such as public office. Finally, the responses of jurists were observed as binding and were called *responsa prudentum*, in other words, the opinions of those regarded as most learned in law to whom Augustus Caesar granted the power of decision in ambiguous cases. In our day, only the people make laws, unless they temporarily delegate their authority to someone else. While such measures do not have a special name, we sometimes call them 'provisions' and sometimes 'reformations,' whether they are adopted by the people or by a magistracy appointed to represent the people. Both kinds are called by the common name of 'laws.'

"According to the definition given by jurists, a law is a sacrosanct ordinance prescribing what is right and prohibiting what is not.[49] Could anyone devise or formulate a definition more conducive to living wisely? Could any utterance be more noble, more holy or more divine? Is it conceivable that such a notion could contradict nature and reason? Is anything in life more essential to our living well and wisely than this ordinance? Bias of Priene, a man celebrated for his wisdom, was accustomed to say that cities stand on two feet: from one good citizens, and from the other evil ones, received their just rewards.[50] Isn't this in fact the sole concern of laws? What is the purpose of laws, and what do we expect of them? What do they promise, and what do they deliver? Don't they incite our souls to noble deeds by placing before us honor and rewards?

"Concerning courage, moderation and justice, not even philosophers reason more wisely or offer more valuable precepts. Laws teach you how to act. They not only teach you how to live with yourself but also prescribe how you must deal fairly with others. Laws examine in the greatest detail everything that pertains to one's family, one's city and nearly the entire human race. Do you govern your household justly and deal generously with your wife,

et parent, fit pulcherrime legum beneficiis. Quae bonum deceant civem et bonum virum, unde haurias quam a legibus facilius? Nam si cum peregrinis res est, inde officium quid sit tuum cognoscendum est. Tuentur hospitalia iura leges, conciliant amicitias, quibus nihil est in vita melius, et vicinitatis bonae atque affinitatis ut sunt illae quidem praeclarae auctores, ita earum quoque munere atque opera commodissime conservantur.

42   'Illae militiae victorias, illae domi triumphos parant, et in pericula, in mortes pro salute et magnificentia civitatis ceterarum oblitos rerum solent impellere, si quibus animi adsunt periculis maiores et virtus ea viget in pectore, quae possit cum supremo etiam terrore humanarum rerum secura cum gloria decernere. Arcem iustitiae leges appellare Cosmus consuevit, quo, cum oppugnaretur, ut tuta esset a vi illata atque iniuria refugeret (quod tamen tu noveris oportet melius, qui cum eo vixisti familiarius), sed illam, cum omnes prope gentes quondam inferrent bellum, desertis terris (ut Graeci aiunt), ascendisse in caelum, nec prius verentem vim reverti ad nos voluisse quam leges, quibus uteretur ad salutem, conderentur. Quod quidem dici mihi non prudenter modo et graviter videri solet, sed summo etiam cum lepore ac venustate, ut referre sic facile Cosmum dixerim excultam illam quae in Socrate fuit olim ornatamque Platonis mellita deinde elocutione sapientiam.

43   'Quis verum primum tulerit leges, ut multarum quoque praeterea rerum inventores, in ambiguo est. Cereri quidem tribuunt eam gloriam, et legiferam ea gratia dictam putant. Nonnulli Phoroneum Inachi filium ex Niobe, qui Argis imperitavit rex secundus. Nos Moysem quem, cum Deo fertur locutus, ut amicus ad amicum solet, tabulas dictante Domino quas scripsisset postquam cum eo quadraginta dies totidemque fuisset noctes, quibus quidem nec panem gustavisset aut aquam, tradidisse hominibus primum leges pie credimus; etsi Minoem alii, nonnulli Rhadamantum primos in Creta posuisse leges tradunt, et Minoem fama est

children, servants and tenants? Do they in turn love and revere you, fear your command and respect you as husband, father and master? Do they heed and obey you? If so, it is thanks to laws. If you wish to know what befits a good citizen and husband, what better source is there than laws? If you have dealings with foreigners, you must learn your duty from laws. For laws protect the rights of hospitality and win us friendships, which are our most precious possession in life. With neighbors and relatives, they nobly create goodwill and offer us aid in preserving it.

"Laws furnish the victories of our troops and the triumphs at 42 home. They often cause men to forget all else in defence of their city's safety and splendor, so that men's spirits overcome all perils and their hearts swell with courage that serenely routs all human fears. As his close friend, you remember how Cosimo de' Medici used to call our laws the 'Citadel of Justice' to which, when attacked, Justice would flee to escape force and violence. The Greeks say that, after nearly every nation had declared war on her, Justice left the earth and ascended into heaven, resolved in her fear of violence never to return, unless laws had been framed to protect her.[51] I am often struck that Cosimo spoke not only with wisdom and gravity, but with the greatest grace and elegance. Indeed, I would readily call his wisdom as refined as that of Socrates, embellished by Plato's mellifluous style.

"As with many other inventions, it is unclear who first created 43 laws. Some ascribe the honor to Ceres and think that she is called the lawgiver for that reason. Others think it was Phoroneus, Inachus's son by Niobe, who was the second king to rule the Argives.[52] As people of faith, we devoutly believe that Moses spoke directly with God, as a friend speaks to a friend, and having spent forty days and forty nights without tasting bread or water, passed on to humankind the tablets which the Lord had dictated as the first laws.[53] Others say it was Minos, and some Rhadamanthus, who first framed laws in Crete. According to leg-

cum Iove patre locutum, ab eo quod deinde referret in leges accepisse, ut tu quoque paulo ante dicebas. Bonum quidem illum virum iustumque regem, etsi poetae quidam Athenienses, credo ut
oppugnatae patriae iniurias ulciscerentur, immitem et durum ceci-
nerint in tragoediis; Rhadamantum vero ipsum non condidisse leges, neque regnandi scientiam didicisse, sed eo usum Minoem mi-
nistro atque interprete in urbe Gnoso in qua regnavit eorum quae
a se Iove monstrante patre decernerentur, quemadmodum Talo, ut
eas ad alios quoque deferret populos quibus imperabat aeneis inci-
sas tabulis publicaretque leges, utebatur.

44   'Hoc certe constat Cretensium leges omnibus totius Graeciae
legibus fuisse antiquiores et ad longissima etiam tempora perdu-
rasse, ut puta quae Iove, deorum omnium maximo, conderentur
auctore. Quem si quis errare existimat potuisse [et] secretiores an-
tiquae theologiae mysticos sensus ignorasse, merito a doctioribus
reprehenderetur. Quae enim putas causa est cur nos quotidie
(quod et aliis quoque vereor evenire itidem civitatibus) condimus
leges novas, abrogamus conditas, nisi quia praedominantur affectus et sine Deo pleraeque res mortalium inveterata peccandi
consuetudine aguntur? Nam si, ut Socrates disputat in *Minoe* Platonis, lex quoque inventio est veritatis, nec cuncta quae principes
civitatum statuunt recte dicuntur leges, sed tantummodo quae
iusta atque honesta sunt decreta, quis non videt iam quae sic erunt
constituta esse immutabilia? Fieri enim non potest ut quae vera
sunt comperta semel, falsa tamen quandoque quavis etiam causa
efficiantur. Est enim veritas incommutabilis quaedam et divina vis,
rebus immixta mortalibus, ipsa nihilominus immortalis et sempiterna est.

45   'Quae si vera sunt, ratio quoque cur non eadem de re eadem,
quae videri possit, apud diversos constituuntur, haud obscura est.
Aut enim diversa sunt opinati, et aliquorum non fuerunt verae
opiniones (nam non semper est facile veritatem adinvenire in rebus) aut certe diversitas rationis, quam attendere potissimum le-

end, Minos spoke with his father Jupiter and learned from him what to make into law, as you were saying just now. Minos was a good man and a just king, even though some Athenian poets (presumably avenging the siege of their country) portrayed him as harsh and cruel in their tragedies. But Rhadamanthus did not himself frame the laws, nor learn the art of ruling. Instead, he acted as Minos's agent and ambassador in ruling the city of Cnossus and in promulgating the laws which Minos had framed with the advice of his father Jupiter. In the same way, Talus used bronze tablets in order to publish his laws and bring them to the peoples under his rule.[54]

"In any event, it is certain that the laws of Crete were older 44 than any others in the rest of Greece and lasted a very long time, since they were framed at the instance of Jupiter, greatest of all the gods. Anyone who thinks that Jupiter erred will rightly be reproved by the learned as ignorant of the more arcane mystical senses of ancient theology. How can you explain the fact that each day we frame new laws and rescind old ones — as I fear happens in other cities as well — unless our emotions dominate us, and most human affairs are conducted without God's help and with an inveterate tendency to err? If law is an invention of truth — as Socrates argues in Plato's *Minos*[55] — and if only the just and honorable decisions of legislators may correctly be called laws, can anyone fail to see that laws so established are immutable? For once something has been found to be true, no cause whatsoever can later render it false. Truth is an inalterable and divine force which, even while involved in mortal affairs, remains immortal and eternal.

"If these things are true, it is also not difficult to explain why 45 different people do not make the same decision about what seems the same issue. For such people either hold different views of the issue, and some of them hold false ones (the truth being often difficult to ascertain); or else different principles, which lawmakers must above all respect, rightly create a difference in the law. There

gum latores debent, merito legis quoque diversitatem facit. Sunt
etiam quae ad tempus feruntur leges; quae quoniam cum tempore
ipso etiam moriuntur, non absurde quidam mortales leges vocant.
Quamvis et has si paulo acutius inspexeris, immortalitatem et ipsas aliquo modo retinere invenias. Nam nisi legislator ab ratione
aberraverit, certum est, si redierint eadem tempora, idem quoque
de re eadem decernendum fuisse. Legem Oppiam in medio ardore
Punici belli M.Oppius, tribunus plebis, tulit cum Hannibal victor
in Italia insultaret, iam iamque Romam obsessurus videretur; qua
muliebri mundo convenientem tempori modum Romani posuerunt. Eam post viginti annos, mutata fortuna civitatis, abrogavere
pristinaque feminis ornamenta restituerunt. Quis vero dubitet non
Romanos modo, sed omnes prope gentes, si urgeat res eadem et
ratio decernendi non sit diversa, semper eandem de ornamentis
fuisse feminarum decreturos legem atque abrogaturos, nisi quid
habes ad haec?'

46   'Ego vero,' inquam, 'nihil. Nam vere mihi duas legis species fecisse videris. Ut altera mortalis sit, quae tempori inservit; oritur
vero cum eo deperitque, ut de Hamadryadibus tradunt poetae,
quae nascuntur cum sua arbore, cum qua et moriuntur. Altera
immortalis, de his rebus quae mutationem, varietatem diversita-
temque aliquam non recipiunt; quae, quoniam rationem non mu-
tant, immutari legem nihil convenit. Itaque manet cum sua ratione, quae immutabilis, quae aeterna est, immutabilis quoque
atque aeterna lex.

47   'Nam dicere de his, quae non recte homines opinantur, legem
esse absurdum est. Sed illud velim explices, existimesne extempo-
rales quoque illas, quas tu appellavisti mortales, in Iovem esse refe-
rendas? An in Saturnum potius, quem vocant Graeci Κρόνον et
praeesse tempori magis putaverunt, unde et ab annorum saturitate
Cicero dictum autumat, quandoquidem divisae sunt rerum potes-
tates et singulis iam suum est numen ab antiquitate attributum?
Haud docte nos fecerimus, ut mihi quidem videtur, si quae illi

are also laws passed temporarily; since they 'expire' with time, some reasonably call them "mortal" laws. Yet if you examine them more closely, you will find that even these laws contain an element of immortality. For unless the lawmaker deviated from reason, the recurrence of the same conditions would require an identical ruling in the matter. The tribune of the people Gaius Oppius moved the Oppian Law in the heat of the Punic War, when the victorious Hannibal was triumphant in Italy and seemed about to lay siege to Rome. Under this law, the Romans set limits to feminine fineries that were suited to the moment, but they abrogated the law twenty years later, when the city's fortune had changed for the better, and reinstated the previous luxuries of women.[56] But can anyone doubt that practically every nation, not merely the Romans, would enact and abrogate the same law about women's luxuries, if it were pressed by the same emergency and had similar legislative principles? Did you have something to add?"

"Nothing," I said. "You seem to me to have defined correctly   46
two kinds of law. The mortal kind serves the moment, arising and passing away with it, as the poets describe the Hamadryads, each born together with a tree and dying with it. The immortal kind concerns those things which admit of no change, variation or alteration; and since its principles do not change, this type of law cannot be changed. A law founded on immutable and eternal principles remains immutable and eternal.

"It is senseless to speak of what people mistakenly consider to   47
be laws, but I would like you to clarify a point. Would you ascribe to Jupiter those temporary laws which you have called mortal? Or to Saturn, whom the Greeks call Chronos, believing him to be in charge of time? Cicero maintains that Saturn takes his name from the fullness [*saturitas*] of years, following the ancients' division of all things into powers and assigning each to a specific divinity.[57] In my view, we would act ignorantly if, in pursuing the truth by every means, we were to confuse things which the ancients so carefully

sunt singulatim tanta prosecuti diligentia, ipsi confuderimus, antiqua tractantes praesertim, dum rei qua de agimus omni modo inquirimus veritatem.'

48   'Recte tu quidem,' inquit, 'addubitasse mihi videris. Sed rem admodum implicatam, multisque ambiguam involucris et quasi praestigiis quibusdam inanibus atque inextricabilibus, ut soleo dicere, in disputationem adducis; nec quae huic tempori, huic sermoni conveniat. Satis enim modo videtur, sive id ab Iove, sive ab alio quovis deorum id sit, legum primordia a divinitate esse profecta ostendere. Quod et earum auctores vario modo apud diversos comprobaverunt, nonmodo quia sic putaverunt posse populos reddere praeceptis suis obsequentiores auctoritate interposita deorum, verum etiam ut id quod nos supra diximus de vera legum origine his accommodatissime confictis fabulis significarent.

49   'Et Zoroastres quidem, qui Bactrianis leges tradidit et Persis, Oromasium (id est enim apud illos grande numen) eorum quae tradidisset commonstratorem affirmavit; Charondas, qui Carthaginiensibus, Saturnum. Trismegisti quoque est apud Aegyptios in veneratione ingenti alibi numen, sive ipse Mercurius fuit, sive Mercurii scriba, ut quidam memoriae prodidere. Eas certe, quas illis dedit leges, dictasse Mercurium populis persuasit; quemadmodum Lycurgus Lacedaemoniis Apollinem; Dracon et Solon Atheniensibus Minervam. Pompilius, rex Romanus, cum Egeria Nympha secreta consilia inibat; Zalmoxis, Scytharum legumlator, cum Vesta. Maumettus tandem sub imperio Arabes Gabrielis contubernio, quod iactabat et cum quo esset ei frequens consuetudo, continebat; et angeli, id est divinae nuntiationis, auctoritate obnoxiam sibi et praeceptis obtemperantem suis barbaram multitudinem effingebat, atque adeo quidem ut et ad nostram iam aetatem Maumetti improba secta pervenerit audeatque etiam cum nostris multis variisque per superiores annos elata victoriis de veritate religionis deque armorum gloria contendere.

distinguished, especially since the topic of our discussion is an ancient one."

"Your perplexity strikes me as well-founded," he said. "The   48
question you raise is very complicated, obscured by many layers of
ambiguity and fraught (as I often remark) with illusory and impenetrable mystifications. Since it is hardly suited to our present
discussion, I think it will suffice to show that laws had their origin
in divinity, whether Jupiter or another god, as in fact the authors
of laws have variously demonstrated in different nations. For they
not only sought to make the masses more obedient by invoking
the authority of the gods but also wished to portray the true origin of laws, which we discussed earlier, by means of fables invented for this purpose.[58]

"Zoroaster, for example, the lawgiver of the Bactrians and Per-   49
sians, asserted that their great deity Oromasius aided him in
framing his laws; and Charondas, lawgiver of the Carthaginians,
credited Saturn. The Egyptians, in turn, held in highest awe
Trismegistus, who was either Mercury himself or Mercury's
scribe, as some have recorded. In any event, he persuaded the
people that the laws he gave them had been dictated by Mercury.
In this way, Lycurgus named Apollo to the Spartans; and Draco
and Solon named Minerva to the Athenians. The Roman king
Numa Pompilius took secret counsel with the nymph Egeria; and
Zalmoxis, lawgiver of the Scythians, did so with Vesta. Mohammed kept the Arabs under his rule by vaunting his familiarity with
Gabriel, whom he said he saw frequently. Thus, through the authority of the angel, that is, of divine communications, he made
the barbarous masses submissive to him and obedient to his precepts. He was so successful that the wicked sect of Mohammed
has survived to our day and, elated by many victories in recent
years, even dares contend with us for the truth of religion and the
glory of arms.

50   'Quae quidem omnia illuc tendunt profecto, ut supra dixi, ut legum primordia in divinitatem referantur. Quod ego convenire cum
tua illa sententia opinor, qua in cognoscendis causis atque iudican-
dis naturam esse audiendam proposueras. Nam ita versatos esse
legumlatores omnium prope nationum cum diis familiarius quid
aliud interpretemur quam citasse eos naturam, quae pro diversitate
religionum diversa nomina accipiat et quae ratio recta, quae simulacrum est divinitatis in nobis, dictaverit, decrevisse, quod et tu
paulo ante de Minoe in Iovis alloquiis sensisse visus es?

51   'Platonis ego, summi viri et ingenii plane divini philosophi, novi
te saepe solere admirari sapientiam, et laetari plurimum quod
illius scripta, Cosmi, praecipue patris patriae nostrae, opera qui illius libros summa diligentia paulo ante conquisitos civibus suis le-
gendos atque admirandos tradidit, magis venire in hominum notitiam occeperint.

52   'Iuvat vero hic referre quae ille philosophus et qui eum secuti,
qui se appellari Platonicos voluerunt, senserint de legibus, quo
modo diffiniant, quae genera faciant, unde unumquodque earum
genus accipiat exordium. Lex igitur est, inquiunt, vera gubernandi
ratio, quae ad finem optimum per commoda media quae guber-
nantur dirigit; saeva illa quidem contumacibus, benigna parentibus. Atque hanc illi legem constituunt aeternam. Nam si quae recipiunt mutationes, haud veras esse eas leges arbitrantur. Quattuor
autem species ex *Timeo Phaedro*que et *Gorgia* colligunt: divinam,
caelestem, moventem, humanam. Et divinam quidem in dei collocant mente, quam Plato ipse appellat providentiam, quae dicitur et
Saturni lex. Nam caelestis altera, quam vocant fatum, dicitur Iovis, eamque in superiori animae mundi parte positam putant. Moventem dicunt eandem et naturam, et versari eam in inferiori illius
potentia, et primae Veneri attribuunt, quemadmodum secundae

"As I said before, all these examples surely suggest that laws 50
have their origin in divinity. I think this view tallies with your
proposal that we must obey nature in hearing and deciding cases.
For if the lawgivers of nearly every nation have been intimate asso-
ciates of the gods, we can only interpret this to mean one thing:
they called upon nature, which assumes different names in
different religions, and decreed what was dictated by right reason,
which is the likeness of divinity within us. That is what you apparently meant just now in describing Minos's conversations with
Jupiter.

"I know that you often express amazement at the wisdom of 51
Plato, a noble man and a philosopher of nearly divine genius. And
I know what pleasure you take in seeing his writings win increasing popularity. This has happened especially through the efforts of
Cosimo de' Medici, father of our country, who recently showed the
greatest diligence in collecting Plato's works and in making them
available to his fellow citizens to read and admire.[59]

"In this context, it is worthwhile to record the views regarding 52
the law held by this philosopher and his followers, who chose to
call themselves Platonists: how they define laws, what categories
they set and what are the sources of each category. They say that
law is the true basis of governing, which directs the governed towards their highest end through appropriate means. Law is harsh
to those who resist her and benign to those who obey. They define
law as eternal, for they do not regard those which suffer change as
true laws. From the *Timaeus*, the *Phaedrus* and the *Gorgias*, they
derive four types of laws: divine, celestial, 'moving' and human.
They locate divine law in the mind of God, which Plato calls
providence and which is also called the law of Saturn. They say
that celestial law, also called fate, is the law of Jupiter and is located in the upper regions of the world soul. They identify 'moving' law with nature and place it in the lower potency of the world
soul. They assign this law to the first Venus and assign to the sec-

quoque Veneri humanam, quae est in mente hominis et prudentia appellatur. Rursum a summo bono deflectunt omnia legum genera referuntque in deum, utpote in principium non legum modo, sed rerum quoque omnium ceterarum, et incommutabilem causam atque permanentem.

53 'Viden ut cuncta illuc tendant ut sint legum origines a diis immortalibus, quandoquidem non earum tantum latores, sed philosophi quoque graves atque eruditi illarum principia referant in deos? Non igitur recte faciunt mea sententia qui non colunt, qui non venerantur sacrosanctas has legum sanctiones quique ad illarum sacratissimam normam ac plane divinam non vivendum sibi, aut res omnes humanas regendas atque administrandas putant. Quae profecto nisi moderentur affectibus, nisi avaritiae, ambitioni, libidini obstiterint animorum, misceantur omnia et confundantur funditus est necesse; atque haud scio sine his ferarumne vita et brutorum sit expetibilior. Aguntur enim minoribus multo perturbationibus pastum modo et latibula quaeritantes; nisi quandoque Veneris actae stimulis raro tamen inter se belligerant aut naturae statutis, quibus moventur solis, non obtemperant. Genus autem humanum saepe ratio, deorum summo beneficio inserta mentibus, quae continere in officio nos debuit, emancipata libidini transversum agit, unde bella et contentiones, quibus assiduo inter se miserrimae dissentiunt prope gentes, oriuntur.

54 'Contra vero capiunt arma leges, et praecipue natura et ratione duce faciunt in perturbatores impetum et, dispersis pro viribus pacis otiique vitae nostrae violatoribus, ipsae pulcherrime regnum tenent; si tamen qui apud homines rerum potiuntur illarum non adversentur conatibus iustitiamque, cuius gloriae volentes inserviunt leges, non excluserint; quod tamen, quia praevalente cupiditate, fieri ab his frequentissime videmus qui praesunt hominibus et habent rerum gubernacula in manibus. Ita fluctuant, ita vexantur res

ond Venus human law, which is found in the human mind and is called prudence. They derive all the types of law from the highest good and refer them to God, who is the first principle not only of laws, but of all other things, and their immutable and permanent cause.[60]

"You see, then, how everything points to the origin of laws in 53 the immortal gods, for their first principles are ascribed to the gods not only by the lawgivers, but by grave and learned philosophers as well. This is why I regard as mistaken those people who do not worship and venerate the inviolable decrees of the laws, or who do not think that their conduct and all human affairs should be governed and administered according to the holy and divine standard of laws. Indeed, if laws did not moderate our emotions and hold in check avarice, ambition and desire, human affairs would inevitably be confused and utterly chaotic. Without laws, I am inclined to think that the life of beasts and brutes would be preferable to ours, for they are driven by far weaker impulses than ours and seek only food and shelter. Except for the times when they are goaded by Venus, they seldom fight each other or disobey the decrees of nature, which alone inspire them. But when desire overcomes our reason, which the gods generously planted within us to remind us of the bonds of our obligations, the human race is soon thrown off course. This is the source of those wars and conflicts which cause the continual strife and misery of nearly all peoples.

"But laws take up arms against these ills and, with nature and 54 reason to guide them, assail the forces of unrest. By their might, laws rout those who violate the peace and tranquillity of human life and hold fairest sway over it. If those who control our affairs did not interfere with the operations of our laws, they would not obstruct justice, whose glory laws willingly protect. But all too often we see how immoderate desires dominate those who rule and hold the reins of power. This is why human affairs are so tempes-

hominum, dum inter se, neglectis legibus, id est unica recte vivendi ratione, de imperiis, de honore, de divitiis digladiantur ab natura atque a vero longissime aberrantes. Ex quo inter maiorum recte instituta illud quoque vehementer probare sum solitus atque admirari, quod bimestribus singulis in senatu praetoribus magistratibusque atque aliis dicundo iuri praepositis assidentibus de iustitia accuratissima habetur oratio; quodque illi qui summum gerunt magistratum ab ea virtute, qua sola civitates conservantur, nomen indiderunt addideruntque eiusdem vexillum appellationis; quod quidem ceteri in iudicando atque administranda publica intuerentur, imitarentur, sequerentur, formarent.

55   'Non fugit scilicet maiores nostros quanta esset in animis peccandi facultas quantumque fuit, ut ipsa tenere posset imperium, adversus appetitiones rationi opitulandum. Quae si non deiceretur ex arce ac suam ipsam dignitatem perpetuo, ut par fuit, retineret, fateor nihil fuisse opus ut bene beateque secundum naturam viveremus legum adminiculis. Verum quando ita sumus ad peccandum proclives, ita ab via facile aberratur, non committendum profecto fuit, etsi aliter paulo ante dicebas, ut libera sic humanis animis rerum iudicia relinquerentur, quibus potestatem nacti iudices plerique ad suum potius commodum quam ad eorum qui cuique forent commissi fidei, utilitatem fuerint relaturi. Omnes enim placemus ipsi nobis, vixque invenias qui in se amando honesti limites non transgrediatur. Ex quo fit ut, paulatim gliscente cupiditate, iudiciorum potestas evadat in tyrannidem, ut apud Athenienses legitur de triginta tyrannis. Et Appius Claudius, decemvir apud Romanos, dum dat vindicias libertatis prae amore in servitutem, decoris omnis honestique obliviscitur. Lacedaemoni tandem Lycurgi susceperunt, hisque usi sunt Romani. Sive post viginti (ut legitur *Pandectis*) annos sive, ut Livio placere magis videtur, octo et triginta a pulsis Urbe Tarquiniis, leges quibus uteretur populus constituerunt. Tribus enim in Graeciam missis legatis, ut inclitas

tuous and tormented, for in disregarding the laws (which are our sole guide for living justly) they abandon nature and truth, and battle for political power, prestige and wealth. As a result, I often strongly approve and admire one of our forebears' wise institutions. Every two months, they convoke the senators, praetors, magistrates and all others charged with legal judgments, to hear a detailed speech about justice. I also laud them for naming their highest officers after that virtue which alone preserves cities, to which is joined the title of standard-bearer.[61] Truly this is a precedent which others who judge and govern should contemplate, imitate, follow and adapt.

"Clearly our forebears were aware what great capacity for misdeeds we harbor in our minds, and what great assistance our reason needs in order to control our appetites. For if reason were not toppled from its citadel but could forever preserve its dignity, as is right, I admit that we would have no need of laws to help us live well and wisely according to nature. But since we are so inclined to misdeeds and we stray so readily from the right path, the judging of our affairs could not be freely left to human minds, despite your arguments to the contrary. Many judges would use their power for their own advantage rather than for the good of those who were entrusted to their care; for we all think well of ourselves, and it is hard to find anyone who would not be led by self-love to overstep the boundaries of propriety. Hence, as ambition gradually intensifies, the power of judging can change to tyranny, as we read in the case of the Thirty Tyrants in Athens. So too, the Roman decemvir Appius Claudius, while avenging the cause of liberty, in his love for it transformed it into servitude and forgot all decorum and honor.[62] The Spartans adopted the laws of Lycurgus, and the Romans used them too, whether (as we read in the *Pandects*) twenty years after expelling the Tarquins or (as Livy seems to prefer) thirty-eight years later, when the Romans established the laws the people should use.[63] Three envoys were sent to Greece in order

55

Solonis leges describerent aliarumque civitatum iura moresque cognoscerent, decem tabulas primum Romanarum legum composue-
runt, quibus deinde duas cum adiecissent, omne ius Romanum,
quod duodecim tabularum appellaverunt, aeneis incisum tabulis
absolutum est.

56   'Nam quod multas existimas incultas et rudes nationes etiam
litteris carere, nedum legibus, quae scripto constant, primum vix
ita rem habere persuadeor. Videmus enim animantes quoque quae
rationis atque orationis usu carent, quasdam tamen sibi notas
quasi litteras constituisse, ad quas conveniant vel ad escam vel
opem ferendam, vel ad cantus edendos et laetitiam animorum
exercendam. Operae est pretium ululatus nonnumquam luporum
attendere atque eorum varietatem, ut lingua quadam sua colloqui
eos inter se possis putare. Id certe accidit, ut tota silva, quantum
exaudiri ululatus potest, citissime quicquid est in ea luporum con-
gregetur. Turdum aucupes in cavea conclusum collocant inter
fruteta, qui modulis suam gentem variis ad praeparatum viscum
pertrahit. Turtures quoque capiunt industria haud dissimili. Sci-
pionem tres longum cubitos ubi devolare consueverint altera parte
affigunt humi, apte tamen ut moveri et levari altera commode
queat, in qua intexunt iunceam plagellam turturemque ligatum pedibus imponunt; deinde sustollunt cum plagella turturem funi-
culo, quo mox laxato volatuque, dum ad terram plagella redit, exci-
tato, convolant turtures, ut vocatos fuisse alarum ligatae planctibus
facile dixeris. Ciconiae cum advolare aut revolare quoque volunt
(nam quo de loco ad nos veniant incompertum est), Asiae patenti-
bus in campis congregatae inter se commurmurant. Quae novis-
sima advenit discerpunt, atque ita abeunt. Plura sunt praeterea
quae afferri possunt de his animantium inter se significationibus
quam quae dicere in praesentia conveniat.

57   'Verum qui haec animadverterit, et muta ac ratione carentia ea
tamen notasse inter se quibus sensa sua demonstrarent cogitaverit,
non arbitror facile adducetur ut alicubi terrarum inveniri gens pos-

to transcribe the famous laws of Solon and to learn about the laws and customs of other cities. At first, they composed ten tables of Roman laws. Later, they added two others, and with the name of the Twelve Tables, they had the completed code engraved on bronze tablets.[64]

"Now, as for your opinion that uncivilized and primitive na- 56 tions have no written alphabet, not to mention written laws, I am not convinced that this is the case. For we see animals that are incapable of reason and speech, and yet have agreed on signs as a sort of alphabet, which they use to offer each other food or help, or to produce songs or cries expressing their inner joy. It is worthwhile sometimes to listen to the howls of wolves, for their variety suggests that they can speak to each other in this language. At least, it happens that, as far as their howling can be heard, all the wolves in an entire forest will gather together very quickly. Fowlers shut a thrush in a cage and place it in the shrubbery, so that its melodic singing lures its fellows to the bird-lime set for them. They catch turtle-doves in a similar manner. Finding a gathering-place of these birds, they fix one end of a six-foot pole in the ground, leaving the other end free to move. To this end they fasten a net woven of rushes, in which they place a dove with its feet bound. Next, they lift the net holding the dove by a rope; then slackening it, they let the bird fly while the net falls to earth. Other doves flock there, so that you can see that they were summoned by the beating of the bound dove's wings. When storks begin to migrate here or return to their home (a place as yet undiscovered), they gather in the open fields of Asia and murmur to each other. The last stork to arrive is torn apart, and then the others fly off. Further instances of animal communications could be adduced, but they are too numerous to recount here.

"If one bears these examples in mind and reflects that even ani- 57 mals lacking speech and reason can make signs to each other to indicate their intentions, I think it will prove difficult to believe that

sit tam rudi, tam hebeti, tam plumbeo ferreoque ingenio quae suas et ipsae sibi notas, quibus valeat inter se animorum exprimere affectus, quas litteras vocamus, non excogitaverit. Sed sint sane illitterati atque exleges quidam. Numquid ab his propterea qui sine industria, sine litteris, et ad naturam vivunt, ut dicitur, sine laude, sine nomine, an ab eis potius qui ceteris nationibus et belli et pacis gloria praestiterunt, bene vivendi exempla sumenda sunt, iusque hoc, quo certe genus humanum protegitur, coalescit, alitur, ad barbarorum negligendum modum, non ad eorum qui sapientiae laudibus excellunt, complectendum atque excolendum est?

58   'Quo profecto ut re quoque nihil habent homines divinius, ita etiam praeclarum nomen est sortitum ut id quoque admonere dignitatis atque utilitatis facile possit. Sive enim a iuvando ius sit dictum, sive a Iove, qui iuris, ut supra dixi, auctor putatur a quibusdam, afferet nominis eius deductio auctoritatem. Quid enim est praeclarius quam iuvando bene mereri de humano genere, ut de Hercule, de heroibus adhuc etiam Graecia gloriatur? Et Iovem, quod astrologi illius sidus salutare terris putant et iuvare eum res humanas, ita appellaverunt. Qui si iuris auctor est, atque ab eo nomen accepit, nihil est omnino Iovis numine in terris, aut esse potest, salutarius, et astrologis, a quorum ego opinionibus saepe soleo discrepare, praesertim cum rerum futurarum tenere se scientiam profitentur, hac in re fides haud abnuenda est. Iustitia certe, sive dederit ipsa, sive acceperit ab eo nomen, iuris in sese habet significationem. Quae sola potest in societate continere homines et diuturniores reddere civitates et regna (quae quid tandem sunt sine iustitia, nisi latrocinia?). Quod et crediturum te sine iuramento mihi arbitror (quae tua prudentia est). Quod et ipsum tamen a iure appellationem sumpsit, ut non sit iurare aliud (ut opinor) quam iura testari atque eorum auctores, deos.

people anywhere on earth can be found whose wits are so unrefined, dull and leaden that they have not devised those signs for expressing their thoughts which we call letters. Still, suppose there are some people lacking letters and laws. Should we derive our models for living from them because they live according to nature, as they say, without industry, letters, praise or renown? Shouldn't we rather derive our models from those who have surpassed other nations in the glorious achievements of war and peace? Should we, like barbarians, neglect justice when it truly protects, unites and nourishes the human race? Or should we embrace and cultivate it, like those whose wisdom is extolled above others?

"Just as humankind possesses nothing more divine than law, so law has obtained a name, *jus*, which readily reminds us of its distinction and usefulness. Whether the root of *jus* comes from *juvare* [to aid] or from Jupiter, whom some consider the creator of law, as I said earlier, the very derivation of the word lends it authority.[65] What is more glorious than to aid the human race and earn its thanks, as even today Greece boasts of Hercules and other heroes? The planet Jupiter is so named because astronomers think that it is salutary to the earth and aids [*juvare*] the human race. If Jupiter is indeed the creator of law [*jus*] and took his name from it, there can be nothing more salutary on earth, in practice or in theory, than Jupiter's divinity. And although I often disagree with the views of astrologers, especially when they profess to possess a knowledge of future events, I think we must lend them some credence in this matter. The term "justice" [*justitia*] contains the meaning of law [*jus*], no matter which noun is derived from the other. Justice alone binds people together in society and renders permanent our cities and kingdoms which, without her, would be nothing but bands of robbers.[66] As an intelligent man, I am sure you'll believe me without my adjurations — another word derived from *jus*, since swearing an oath is, I think, merely calling the laws to witness, and the gods who created them.

58

59   'Quae tandem si obscuriora nonnumquam redduntur, vel multitudine et diversitate earum rerum quae veniunt in usus nostros, vel
eorum qui ea enucleandi partes sibi arrogaverunt vitio, indigne
proculdubio nos fecerimus si eam in iura et leges culpam, non in
conditionem rerum perversitatemque eorum qui perperam interpretantur, rettulerimus. Est enim admodum absurdum si quae
sunt artificis errata, arti vortas vitio, ut in medicina. Si ab sanitate
medicus aberraverit quam aut reddere aut conservare propositum
est, utrum medicinae scientia, an minister est potius medicus vitu-
perandus? Idem nonne recte dicimus si in philosophia quid tale
aut in oratoria ceterisque liberalibus disciplinis acciderit? Servant
enim perpetuo omnia haec quae laudem sua natura in sese habent
propriam dignitatem, nec possunt cuiusquam fieri fraudibus aut
adventiciis quibusquam confictis mendaciis ignobiliora.

60   'Multis ego quoque modis hos fori rabulas minutioresque, cau-
sidicos quos vocant, soleo insectari qui non leges iam ad defenden-
dam causam, sed legum quoddam versutum callidumque artificium efferunt ad tribunalia. Neque hanc scriptorum tam amplam
tamque argutam et confidentem multitudinem non improbandam
duxi, ut puta quae dubitandi etiam in rebus apertissimis ingentem
materiam praebere videantur, et quasi praecidere ansas quibus
multo fuit facilius iudiciorum munus obeundum. Estque iam iam
et nobis Iustinianus aliquis ab inferis excitandus qui rursum inter
tot librorum milia quam severissime diiudicet ponatque scriptoribus et ipsis iam modum ne tanti tamque necessarii labores emen-
dati clarificatique Romani iuris iterum ac tertium recidant in irri-
tum procacitate ac petulantia eorum qui, cum tenere iuris se
prudentiam putent idque pro certo sibi persuaserint, vana turgidi
ambitione doctissimorum sibi hominum scribendi provincias de-
sumunt. Qui, si quod subeunt onus intelligerent, etsi audax est illud genus et confidens, tamen fieri posse quin exterreantur rei magnitudine non existimaverim.

"If the principles of law are sometimes obscured by the multi-   59
plicity and diversity of their applications or through the fault of
their interpreters, we would clearly be wrong to blame the laws
and their principles, rather than the peculiar conditions of their
interpretation or the perversity of their misguided interpreters. It
is quite absurd to fault the discipline for the practitioner's mis-
takes. In medicine, if a doctor loses sight of health, which it is his
aim to restore or preserve, is it the science of medicine we should
censure, or isn't it rather its practitioner, the doctor? When the
same thing happens in philosophy, oratory or the other liberal
arts, won't our answer be the same? All the disciplines which are
by their very nature laudable can never lose their intrinsic worth,
nor can they be debased by the chance circumstances of a practitioner's fraud or lies.

"I am accustomed to denounce in many ways the proliferation   60
of these ranters and pettifoggers, as they are called, who in defending a case in court exalt not the laws but cunning and crafty legal
stratagems.[67] I would likewise censure the astute and arrogant
multitudes of juridical authors, who in even the most clear-cut
cases seem to produce mountains of material for doubt, while
hacking away anything which offers a handle by which to judge.
Soon we shall have to raise from the dead a second Justinian who
can adjudicate most rigorously between so many thousands of
books and finally set limits to the writers on law. Otherwise, the
immense and invaluable toils which once emended and clarified
Roman law will be rendered useless a second and third time by the
effrontery and impudence of these writers. For they are convinced
they have mastered jurisprudence, and swollen with vain ambition,
they claim for themselves the literary province belonging to the
greatest scholars. I daresay that, if they understood the onerous
task they are taking on, even such audacious and arrogant men
would all be deterred by its magnitude.

61   'Nihil est enim tam arduum mea sententia tamque laboriosum
et difficile quam se auctorem et scriptorem rerum profiteri. Primum namque opus est multa et magna cognitione omnium rerum,
aut earum saltem de quibus futura oratio est; in quibus si vel tan-
tillum quid fuerit aberratum, illa etiam quae recte scripseris errati
fortuna secum trahit in eandem ignominiae calamitatem ignorata-
rum rerum. Deinde quae cognoveris, nisi docte, nisi breviter, nisi
diserte ornateque litteris mandaveris, vix qui tua velit legere reperias. Ita quod vigilaveris, quod sudaveris, quod alseris frustra est.
Saepe ante auctorem suum incondita poetae carmina et oratoris
ineptae atque inconcinnae orationes perierunt. Sed ipsi sese ra-
bulae complectuntur, se observant atque admirantur; scriptis ipsi
suis nituntur in causis, Romanum ius ne legunt quidem, nec quid
aut quomodo Ulpianus, Sulpitius, Paulus, Marcellus, Scaevola,
Africanus aliique prudentissimi legum auctores Romanorum
atque eloquentissimi scripserint cura est. Ineptiarum modo atque
argutiolarum harum, quibus ipsi dies totos noctesque conterendo
involvuntur, peritiam nacti confundunt fora obtunduntque clamoribus, quasi nebulam quandam obscuritatemque iudiciis prae-
texentes. Ita mihi haudquaquam digni videntur qui veniant in collegium iurisconsultorum: grave sane genus, venerabile ac sanctum,
quorum nos opera non in privatis modo rebus, sed in publicis, sed
in divinis cum legum dignitate et maiestate utimur. Neque enim
quam ab his melius sacrorum ritus caerimoniasque percipiemus
profanaque a religiosis segregabimus.

62   'Quod nos de industria ad hoc loci servavimus ut cum rebus divinis orationem et ipsi nostram clauderemus. Partem enim publici
esse iuris religionem constituimus ut hinc, quid ad sacrorum ordinem, quid ad templorum curam, quid ad sacerdotum officia pertineat, petendum sit. Nam quod profanum dicitur publici et ipsum
pars iuris, curam potius gerit magistratuum, atque adeo ab religione differt ut interesse non initiatos quibusdam sacris fas quon-

"For nothing is so arduous or difficult as the profession of au- 61
thor and writer. To begin with, one must have a vast and profound
knowledge of all subjects or at least of the subject at hand. For if
you make the slightest error, bad luck will taint all your good
points with ruinous charges of ignominy and ignorance. And unless you write what you know with learning, brevity, elegance and
eloquence, scarcely anyone will want to read it. If you spent sleep-
less nights and suffered heat and cold, it was all in vain.[68] Often
unpolished poems perish before their poet, and inept and inele-
gant orations before their orator. But these ranters embrace each
other, courting and admiring themselves. During a case, they rely
on their own writings, and don't even read Roman law, indifferent
to the substance and style of Ulpian, Sulpicius, Paulus, Marcellus,
Scaevola, Africanus and the other learned and eloquent authors of
Roman laws. Having mastered the art of those frivolities and
sophistries which occupy them day and night, they confound the
courts and deafen everyone with their shouting, as if obscuring
men's judgments in a dark fog. They strike me as unworthy of entering the guild of jurists. For jurists are a venerable and sacred
race who aid us in applying the dignity and majesty of laws not
only to our private affairs, but to public and divine ones as well. It
is they who best teach us to understand the rites and ceremonies
of religion and to separate what is profane from what is sacred.

"I have intentionally saved this subject until now, so that we 62
may conclude our remarks with divine topics. We define religion
as part of public law, from which we must derive whatever pertains
to the order of rites, the care of temples and the duties of priests.
For the part of public law which is called secular is administered
by magistrates, and it differs from religion in that the uninitiated
are occasionally not admitted to certain rites. Thus Virgil de-

dam non fuerit. Unde apud Vergilium Sibylla, cum esset facturus manibus Aeneas,

> procul hinc, procul este, profani,
> conclamat vates, totoque absistite luco.

Religionis autem unde sit factum nomen non una sententia est. Cicero in libro *De natura deorum* a relegendo dictam putat quod ea quae ad culturam pertinent deorum retractet; et quasi relegant qui religiosi appellantur, Lactantius ea homines condicione natos putat ut auctori vitae, Deo, iusta ac debita pietatis obsequia reddamus, Deum noverimus, Deum sequamur, Deo nos natura obstrictos et quasi religatos arbitremur; unde et religionem sumpsisse suum nomen existimat. Quod et Lucretius sensisse videtur cum ait,

> et artis
> religionum animos nodis exolvere pergo.

Servio autem Sulpicio apud Macrobium ideo dictam religionem placet quod rerum excellentia divinarum remotior esse a nobis videatur a relinquendo ut a carendo caerimoniae. Quod et Maro summus poeta testari est visus cum inquit:

> est lucus ingens prope Caeritis amnem,
> religione patrum late sacer; undique colles
> inclusere cavi et nigra nemus abiete cingit.[2]

63   'Sed utut verum habeat illud est attendendum potius ut quid ipsa sit et quae vera sit religio cognoscamus. Quod Iacobus apostolus decem tribubus quae in dispersione sunt divine scripsit. 'Si quis autem,' inquit, 'religiosum esse se putat non refrenans linguam suam, sed seducens cor suum, huius vana est religio. Religio autem munda et immaculata apud Deum patremque haec est: visi-

scribes the Sibyl when Aeneas is about to sacrifice to the spirits of the dead:

> Far off, stand far off, you uninitiated
> the seer cries, leave all this grove behind.[69]

There is no one view on the origin of the word 'religion.' In his work *On the Nature of the Gods*, Cicero thinks it comes from *relego* [to go over again], since it examines what is appropriate to the worship of the gods, and is 'gone over again' by men of religion [*religiosi*].[70] Lactantius thinks that we human beings are born in such a condition that we should show devotion and deference to God as the creator of life. Since we know God, we obey God and we deem ourselves naturally obliged and bound [*religatos*] to God, he believes that 'religion' takes its name from this fact.[71] This seems to be the view of Lucretius when he says:

> Now I proceed
> to release souls from the tight bonds of religions.[72]

In Macrobius, Servius Sulpicius is inclined to believe that, because the excellence of divine things seems far removed from us, 'religion' is derived from *relinquo* [to leave behind], as 'ceremony' is from *careo* [to lack].[73] Virgil, our greatest poet, seems to subscribe to this view when he writes:

> There is a grove near the river of Caere,
> all hallowed by our fathers' religion; on all sides valleyed hills
> enclose it, surrounding the wood with dark fir-trees.[74]

"Whatever is true, we must rather address the problem of rec- 63 ognizing what religion itself is, and what is true religion. The apostle James wrote divinely to the dispersed tribes: 'If any man thinketh himself to be religious while he bridleth not his tongue but deceiveth his heart, this man's religion is vain. Pure religion and undefiled before our God and Father is this, to visit the

tare pupillos et viduas in tribulatione eorum, et immaculatum se custodire ab hoc saeculo.' Colendi vero deos et sacrificandi ritus admodum varius apud primae aetatis homines fuit usque ad Nini tempora, cum primum idola colere institutum. Quod et nostra tempestate pro varietatibus gentium proque opinionum, quae de diis habentur, diversitatibus accidere videmus. Nobis, in hereditatem caelestis patrimonii electis, Iesus Christus, Dei filius, salvator noster, veram et sacrificandi et colendi sui viam ipse aperuit. Quos etiam nominis proprii dignitate condecoravit. Iam aberrare a casta, ab immaculata sanctaque eius religione non licet quam ipse nos edocuit, quam vita comprobavit et stabilivit morte aeternamque constituit.

64   'Legibus tamen pontificiis praesertim et nostris nihil est quod ad Dei nostri optimi maximi culturam religionemque et sacra pertineat praetermissum. Signati dies sunt festi nefastique, ac quae cuique sacrorum genera conveniant declaratum est. Ordines distincti eorum qui sacris administrandis praesunt modusque quidam positus in sacrificando, quo non antistites dumtaxat sacrorum et sacerdotes quid se operari sit pium clarissime intelligunt, sed populo quoque quo habitu mentis, quo corporis et membrorum gestu adesse sacris oporteat in promptu est positum. Diversa sunt nomina ministrorum, diversa item officia, ne quid possit per oblivionem, per negligentiam praetermitti, quod ad religionem ritumque sacrorum pertinere quoque posse modo videatur. Hocque agunt videlicet ostiarii, exorcistae, accoliti, cantores, lectores; hoc agunt subdiaconi et diaconi, presbyterique atque episcopi; hoc tandem archidiaconi, hoc archipresbyteri, hoc primicerii thesauriique curant quam diligentissime. Nam de summis quoque pontificibus, quos iam communiore nomine vocant papas, quibus non sacrorum modo et religionis praecipua cura est, sed et qui ligandi quoque atque solvendi potestatem habent, quid mirum si pauca dixerim in praesentia?

fatherless and widows in their affliction and to keep himself un-
spotted from the world.'[75] Now the rites for worshipping and
sacrificing to the gods varied until the age of Ninus, when the
worship of idols was first established. In our day, we see the same
happen according to the variety of peoples and the diversity of
their beliefs concerning the gods. To us who were chosen to in-
herit the heavenly patrimony, Jesus Christ, the son of God and
our Savior, has shown the true way to offer him sacrifice and worship, and he has embellished it with his lofty name. We may no
longer stray from the chaste, immaculate and holy religion which
he himself taught us, which he confirmed by his life and which he
established as eternal by his death.

"Everything concerning the worship and religion of God the   64
Highest and Best is covered by our laws and in particular by
pontifical laws. All sacred and profane days have been marked, and
the observances appropriate to each feast have been set forth. Various orders have been distinguished for those who administer the
rites, and certain rules have been set for the mass, so that not only
the celebrant and other priests understand fully how to act with
piety, but even the people have clear models for their behavior
during the mass. The priests have different titles and different
functions, so that nothing can be omitted, through forgetfulness
or negligence, which seems essential to religion and sacred rites.
Ostiaries, exorcists, acolytes, cantors, lectors, subdeacons, deacons,
elders and bishops all play their parts. And archdeacons,
archelders, precentors, superintendents and treasurers perform
their functions diligently. Is it surprising if I say little here about
the supreme pontiffs, more commonly known as popes, who not
only oversee rites and religion but also have the power to bind and
to loose?

65   'Et reformidabit horrebitque vicarium Christi humilis ista nostra pusillaque oratio, praesertim vero si neque ut nunc plura dicantur est necesse. Non enim propositum est modo nostrum quae ad sacra caerimoniasque pertinent deorum prosequi omnia accuratius, verum enimvero id tantum ostendere, non humanarum modo rerum curam, sed etiam divinarum et sacrorum leges suscepisse, ut non una solum et simplex illis habenda gratia sit, sed quod ad normam virtutis formamus nostros mores, quod familiam domumque recte instituimus, quod uxor nobis natique et servi obsecuntur et imperio nostro parent, quod reipublicae, quod amicis, quod nostris, quod peregrinis non sumus iniurii, non molesti, non inutiles, quod ipsis tandem diis non ingrati famulamur pietatemque excolimus ac vitam tandem homine ipso dignam, quem Deus ad imaginem et similitudinem suam creavisset, ducimus, ingentissima referenda.'

66   Haec habui quae de legibus in praesentia dicerem et iudiciis, hortante maxime ac cogente te. Non equidem quo contra sententiam tuam disputarem, sed ne legum et iudiciorum causa nuda sic atque indefensa derelinqueretur. Fieri vero ita posse putavi ut qui haec quoque cognoverit, quae nos brevissime modo et quasi per rerum capita percurrimus, veluti qui celerius iter habent nihil usquam morae faciunt in diversoriis praeter necessitatem, poterit quid veri tandem in re sit haudquaquam iudicare difficilius.

"Our humble and weak discourse will fear and tremble before   65
the vicar of Christ, especially when, as now, there is no need to say
more. It is not our aim to discuss in detail every aspect of divine
rites and ceremonies. Rather, we have tried to show that laws su-
pervise not only human affairs but divine matters and holy rites as
well. We cannot offer our laws a single and simple expression of
gratitude. For if we shape our character to the standard of virtue;
if we govern our families and homes correctly; if we organize our
family and household properly, so that our wives, children and
servants obey us and accept our authority; if we are not harmful
or troublesome to our government, our friends, our family and
foreigners; if we are agreeable servants to the gods and cultivate
their worship; and if we lead a life worthy of man, whom God created in his own image and likeness[76] — for all these things we must
render enormous thanks to our laws.

"This is what, at your urging, I had to say concerning laws   66
and legal judgments. I spoke not to contradict your view, but in
order to protect and defend their cause. Although we have moved
quickly through each aspect of the question, stopping only when
necessary, like travellers at a way-station, I believe that anyone who
reflects on these matters will now find them less difficult to judge."

Apologia contra vituperatores civitatis Florentiae

1 Petrus Crinitus salutem bonis.

   Saepenumero mecum dequestus sum, cum Rempublicam Florentinam viderem turpiter lacerari, tam ab imprudentibus quam
ab his etiam qui se velint haberi prudentiores, accusantes passim
ipsius administrationem, perinde ac puerilia et levicula tractentur
in civitate, quodque minus tolerabile, flagitiosa quoque et deridi-
cula. Sed evenit praeter spem ut istis omnibus offam quasi quandam sim obiecturus, quam[1] obrodentes necesse sit obmutescant
nec virulentis, ut antea, sibilis in quemque desaeviant. Siquidem
Bartholomaeus Scala, nostri utique studiosus, apologiam nuper
contra viros istiusmodi, si viri sunt, felicissimis noctibus elucubra-
vit, quae me mihi reddidit, refecit, exhilaravit ingenio, prorsus ut
statim cogitaverim, invito etiam auctore ac renuente, opifici exhi-
bere, qui hanc ipsam, ut fit, formis excudat.

2   Adeste igitur cuicui cana veritas cordi, quae latere aliquandiu
potest, perire nunquam. Unde nec ineleganter aut de nihilo theo-
logi quoque veteres Saturni, hoc est temporis, filiam dixerunt.
Sed ne sim impendio longior, ad ipsam Scalae defensionem te
invito. Laetaberis scio et mihi gratias egeris, qui tam assiduis
precibus atque adeo conviciis a Scala nostro apologiam efflagitavi,
ut id muneris tandem aliquando impetrarim, quod et tibi usui sit
legisse et voluptati meminisse. Vale feliciter. iii Non. Octobris
MCCCCLXXXXVI. Florentiae.

*   *   *

Defense against the Detractors of Florence

Pietro Crinito sends greetings to good men.[1]   1

It has often given me cause for inward complaint when I see the Florentine Republic being shamefully taken to task by those who lack wisdom, as well as by those who wish to seem wise. Everywhere they accuse its government of conducting its affairs in a childish and inconsiderate fashion, or even, less tolerably, in ways that are disgraceful and laughably absurd. But beyond all hope it happens that I am going to throw them a morsel which will shut them up while they chew on it and stop them from savaging anyone with their venomous hissing, as they have hitherto been doing. Seeing how Bartolomeo Scala, a man zealous on our behalf, has burned the night oil (and fortunate nights they were too) to write an apologia against these men—if men they are—and how this apologia has put me right again, refreshed and cheered me, it immediately came into my mind to show the work, despite the author's opposition, to an artisan who might print it, as is widely done.

So come then, all you to whom white-haired truth is dear,   2
truth which can sometimes be hidden but never perishes. Hence it was that the old theologians, neither inelegantly nor without purpose, said that Truth was the daughter of Saturn, that is, of Time.[2] But so as not to expend more of your time, I invite you to read Scala's defense. I know you will enjoy it and thank me for having induced our friend Scala, through my prayers and even my reproaches, to write it. I would ask only this reward, that you find it a useful thing to have read and pleasurable to remember. Farewell and be happy. Florence, 5 October 1496.

*   *   *

3   Petrus Crinitus Bartholomaeo Scalae Salutem.

    Heri forte oblata mihi a Trebatio nostro apologia tua, quam in Florentinae urbis gratiam contra ipsius calumpniatores nuper scripseris. Legi eam, ut cetera fere soleo, avidissime. In qua re, Scala, vir optime (admittatur Veritas), aperte probas qualem te virum pro amicis, qualem pro patria geras, qui tam strenue, tam viriliter in maledicos istos et perinde cerebrosos homines feceris impressionem ut nullibi cedas, nullibi tumultueris. Et Hercle tu unus Florentiae cuius eruditioni non auctoritas, non eruditio desit.

4   Ceterum quoniam eo semper fueris ingenio prorsus ut nullis unquam rationibus adduci potueris ex tuis quicquam scriptis in lucem proferri, donabis hoc tandem pro re ipsa amori saltem nostro, hoc Crinito tuo, quamvis nec mihi tantum, sed tempori, sed amicis omnibus, sed patriae, ut patiaris te deflecti quasique de gradu isto deici. Effice, obsecro te Scala suavissime, effice, inquam. Id quoquo modo exoremus, quod et Trebatio quoque nostro mirum quam placeat, quam cordi sit, ut qui Reipublicae nostrae non dico studiosus, sed plane sit zelotipus, persuasum, exploratum, apud multos me pridem inter tuos receptum, quibus tu quidem nunquam voluisti quicquam denegatum, propterea, credo, ne de iure amoris violato in ius te vocarent litemque apud iudicem contestarentur. Et nos igitur nostram quoque operam libere ad hoc muneris promittimus, curaturi mox in amicorum et patriae gratiam apologiam hanc tuam calcographis exhibendam, qui eam formis exprimant tam exacte, tam diligenter ut nihil omnino videatur ab archetypo dissentire. Bene vale. Pridie nonas Octobris MCCCCLXXXXVI. Florentiae.

5   Rem fecisti tu quidem, mi Trebati, dignam te et tua nobilissima familia, qui restitisti fortiter accusatoribus nostris non fortunam

Pietro Crinito sends greetings to Bartolomeo Scala. 3

Yesterday our friend Trebatius[3] chanced to bring me the apologia you recently wrote in favor of the city of Florence against her detractors. I read it with my usual voracity. Best of men (and Truth will allow you that title), you clearly prove in this regard the sort of man you are on behalf of your friends and your country — a manly fellow who pushes back against these detractors and *enragés*, giving no ground and no quarter. By Hercules, you're the one man in Florence who lacks neither the authority nor erudition to do so.

But since you've never been of a mind that any arguments could 4 induce you to have any of your works published, you will, please, grant this to our love, to your Crinito — although not to me only, but to the circumstances, all our friends, and our country — and suffer yourself to be swayed and, as it were, wrong-footed in this matter. Please allow this, sweetest Scala, please, I beg you. Let us somehow prevail upon you in this — a thing that our friend Trebatius too approves of wondrously and holds dear, being a man who is not so much zealous as a zealot on behalf of our Republic. It is a thing that I have canvassed and persuaded many of your friends to accept, and you would never deny them anything, since, I believe, you wouldn't want them to bring a suit against you for violating the laws of love and to contest their case before a judge. As for myself, I freely promise my help too in performing this duty; I will see to it that the apologia you have written in favor of your friends and country is turned over to the kind of typographers who will print it with such care and precision that they will reproduce the archetype exactly. Be well. Florence, 6 October 1496.

Defense against the Detractors of Florence

You, my Trebatius, have acted in a way worthy of yourself and 5 your noble family in standing firm against the detractors who con-

modo nostram, quae minus in se habet vituperationis, sed prudentiam Reipublicae administrandae criminantibus. Qua quidem in re
ut pro tua modestia visum esse tibi scribis, quippe cui minus Reipublicae causa nota fuerit, magno afficeris dolore, quod ne tibi
quidem potueris satisfacere, nedum nonnullis quibuscum tibi res
fuit, qui arroganter adeo magis quam vere in dignitatem nostrae
civitatis per ambitionem et fastum, ut utar tuis verbis, inveheban-
tur. Petisque a me ut gravis videlicet cliens te edoceam quid in
causa sit apertius ne te inveniant adversarii, si sit rursus congre-
diendum ut modo, rudem indoctumque defensorem. Geram vero
tibi morem magis adeo, ut neque in hoc, quantum in me est, de-
sim patriae, quam te instruendi satis confidentia quamvis ea causa
est nostra, in qua etiam non mediocriter eruditi eloquentiae sibi
laudem in tanta iustitia consecutos facile videri possunt. De qua
quidem iam dicere incipiam, si de Fortuna prius, quae (ut aiunt)
versat suo arbitratu res mortalium hisque gaudet, breviter pauca
percurrero.

6   Sunt igitur qui existiment regi a Fortuna omnia quae etiam
produxerit, utputa qui principia quoque creatarum rerum fortuitae
cuidam concursioni indivisibilium minutorum tradiderint. In qua
quidem sententia multi profecto philosophi, non Graeci modo, sed
et Latini extiterunt. Et Lucretius poeta admirandus, cuius etiam
carmina rex ipse, ut ita dicam, Latinorum Virgilius suo inserere
operi integra non erubuit, hanc naturae partem versibus est elegantissimis prosecutus. Quod etsi diserte dicatur, et patroni eius
sententiae non contemnendae sint auctoritatis, tamen haudquaquam id mihi omnino persuadent. Vero autem illi similiora dicere
aliquo modo videntur qui fortunam penitus tollunt de rebus humanis, traduntque rerum omnium nostrarum prudentiae palmam.
Opitulari vero huic putant opinioni, quod neque apud Homerum
τυχῆς appellatio usquam inveniatur; utputa qui ne nomen quidem ad id usque temporis recepissent. Ita enim id nonnulli interpretantur acutius. Quemadmodum de podagrae quoque morbo re-

demn, not only our misfortune — for it is hard to blame us for that — but also the wisdom by which our Republic is governed. On this subject you write, in your modest way, that you feel you hardly know the state of our Republic and are sorely grieved that you can meet neither your own expectations nor those of certain men you deal with when, with more arrogance than concern for truth, they rail against our great city, driven (in your words) by pride and ambition. So you ask me, as your respected client, to clarify what should be said for our cause, so that, if you meet them again, your opponents will not find in you an inarticulate and ignorant spokesman. I shall do what you ask, more to serve our country as best I can than to presume to teach you adequately, although our purpose is such that even not particularly learned men can win praise for eloquence, speaking on behalf of so great and just a cause. Let me introduce the subject by first taking up briefly the question of Fortune, who (as they say) enjoys overturning human affairs according to her whim.

Now, some think that Fortune rules and even produces all 6 things — those, for instance, who have attributed the very origin of created things to a fortuitous conjunction of tiny atoms.[4] Many philosophers, both Greek and Roman, have held this view. Lucretius, a wonderful poet whose lyrics even the king of Latin writers (if I may so describe Virgil) did not blush to incorporate into his own work, expounded this idea of nature in elegant verses.[5] Though this doctrine is eloquently presented and the authority of its patron[6] is not to be despised, still I am not at all convinced. More plausible views, somehow, seem to be expressed by those who completely deny the power of Fortune in human life, and give the palm in all our affairs to prudence. They find support for their view in the fact that the word *tuche* is not to be found in Homer, suggesting that not even the name was current in his day.[7] Such is some people's clever interpretation. By the same token,

fert Plinius, quod quia Romani nomen non habuerunt, morbo quoque ipso eos caruisse autumat. Quod etsi dicitur speciosius, tamen desideratur saepenumero prudentia, nec potest aliqua hominis industria in rebus quae veniunt in nostram deliberationem quid optimum factu sit dignoscere, ubi rem committere fortune necesse est, id est, eventum expectare earum causarum quas ignoraveris et duci non arbitrio tuo et ratione, sed naturae necessitate.

7   Quae quidem ab omni profecto incertitudine longissime est, neque ipsa causas rerum quarum auctor est, ignorat aut fortunam habet. Sed nos, ignoratis causis quas sequi eventa sua pernecessarium est, sorte cecidisse asserimus quae videmus tantum evenisse. Non etiam cur ita evenerint perspeximus. Nam Fortunae quidem nomen nobis ipsi confingimus, quae per se procul dubio nulla est. Sed 'nos deam facimus caeloque locamus', ut Satyrus ait. Quid igitur dicemus? Quam sequemur sententiam? Natura certe fortunam non habet, apud quam nihil fit nisi a causa notissima naturae, quae et Deus est, qui in verbo veritatis suae omnia constituit, non temeritatis aut sortis. Ergo in rebus quae pertinent ad hominem fortuna non est? Non asseruerim id quidem, cum multa saepe accidant incommoda hominibus, quae volunt evitare omnes, quibus etsi cunctis ingenii viribus occurreris, eveniunt tamen atque afflictant animum resque faciunt vivendi deteriores. Non igitur fortassis absurditer dicetur quod, quanvis ipsa sine fortuna est, naturae tamen factum sit condicionibus ut pluribus in negotiis imploremus Fortunam et fortunata ea appellemus, quae illius, ut videtur, beneficio nulla nostra opera, ex animi tamen nostri sententia contigerunt. Quod in his modo rebus accidit quas explicare satis animus per se non potest, itaque sorti mandat quod eventurum est, atque hinc fortunae nomen est, id est, ab his rebus quae forte sua contingunt, non hominum labore studioque pariuntur. In quo satis fuerit, ut arbitror, praestitisse in agendis rebus diligentiam ne quid, quod vitari cura rationeque potuerit, perpetiendum sit. Nam quod

Pliny tells us that since the Romans had no name for gout, the disease itself , he alleges, was absent from their world.[8] Though all this is plausibly argued, yet often prudence is wanting, and no human efforts figure out what to do when situations come before us in our deliberations where one must entrust the matter to Fortune — when, that is, we cannot rely on will or reason but must await the course of nature and the outcome of unknown causes.

Nature indeed is far from indeterminate, and the causes of those things of which she herself is the author are well known to her and are not truly a matter of fortune. But we, not knowing the causes that make certain outcomes inevitable, assert that a great deal of what we see happen occurs by chance. For we do not understand why things happen. So we have ourselves given the name of Fortune to something that doubtless in itself is nothing. As the Satirist says, "we create a goddess and place her in heaven."[9] So what shall we say? What conclusion can we come to? Fortune is no part of nature, since in nature nothing happens without a cause known to herself, who is also God, who governs everything according to His word of truth, not by accident or chance. Does it follow that in human affairs there is no such thing as fortune? Let me not say that, since many misfortunes do occur which everyone wishes to avoid, and which, though you counter them with all your mental powers, still happen and afflict the spirit and make life very hard. And though chance has nothing to do with it and it is nature that shapes events, it should not be considered absurd that in many of our doings we ask for Fortune's help and call those things fortunate which seem to happen by her beneficence rather than through any effort of our own, exceeding our own expectations. In these cases things happen that the mind cannot fully explain to itself, so it ascribes them to what we call fortune, that is, to the source of events which seem to happen, not through any human effort and zeal, but by chance. In my opinion, it is enough to practice diligence in our affairs so that we need not suffer any-

omnino immunes malorum in vita simus, in potestate procul dubio nostra non est, sed Fortunae, si ea his tantummodo rebus praeest quarum ab hominibus nesciuntur causae, quod nos ei numen nomenque indidimus. Neque vero iverim inficias plus minusve posse Fortunam in rebus nostris pro prudentum hominum differentia, sed nullam tamen adeo esse exactam natura‹e› disciplinam, nisi Deus aliter indulserit, ut videre supra hominem quisquam possit atque omnes declinare Fortunae impetus, si ipsa suo more quandoque desaeviat, ut nobis modo contigisse manifestum est, ut iamiam redeat unde digressa est oratio.

8   Paulo ante etiam fortunati putabamur, cum Politianum, nobile oppidum, quod et a civitate nomen habet Graecum, in Senensium finibus, cum Pisae et ager prope omnis Lunensis nobis pareret, cum multis magnisque polleret Respublica amicitiis et floreret opibus. Quae nunc nulla nostra culpa, sed Fortunae conversa praebere videntur quibusdam contra nos occasionem ut obloquantur liberius. Sed certe quod in nobis iure accusent nihil habent, nisi me amor rerum nostrarum patriaeque caritas a vero longe pertrahit. Quam enim nos causam praebuimus Politianensibus posthabendae fidei et tot tantorumque in se nostrorum beneficiorum obliviscendi? Quibus, praeterquam quod intra haec moenia nati non forent, nihil deerat ut meliore etiam viderentur conditione quam si hinc orti extitissent. Nos tuebamur. Nos armis nostris eorum iniurias propulsabamus, propter quos, ut omnis novit Italia, maxima quandoque bella gessimus et variorum plenissima periculorum. Quis vero putaverit his artibus, nisi in fortunam referas, datam esse Politianensibus deficiendi a nobis bellumque inferendi aliquam causam, qui etiam invitos prope olim ut sese in fidem reciperemus sociorum compulerunt?

thing that reason and prudence could have avoided. For to live lives entirely free from suffering is surely not in our power, but depends on Fortune, if that word refers to those many things of which men do not know the causes, for which we have given her the role and name of a divinity. I shall not deny that Fortune's power in our affairs varies as men vary in their ability to be wise, but there is no science of nature that suffices to ward off all the blows of Fortune, unless God shows His favor, so that one may see beyond mortal vision and avoid Fortune's assaults, even when at times she rages, as clearly happened to us recently. Let me now return to the point whence I digressed.

Not long ago we were actually considered fortunate, when   8 Montepulciano—a noble town on the Sienese border, whose name [*Politianum*] comes from the Greek word for city [*polis*]— and Pisa, with all the territory of the Lunigiana, were subject to us, and when many great alliances strengthened our wealthy and flourishing Republic. The present reversal of these circumstances, because of Fortune rather than through any fault of our own, seems to have offered an opening for some boldly to revile us.[10] Yet surely, unless my love of our customs and country leads me far astray, there is no justice in their criticisms. For what reason have we given the people of Montepulciano to abandon loyalty and quickly forget all that we did for them? Indeed, although they were not born within these walls, they enjoyed in every way even better conditions of life than if they had been. We protected them. We mobilized our army against those who threatened them and, as all Italy knows, for their sake fought a great war and exposed ourselves to many and varied dangers. Who would think, unless you give all credit to fortune, that by these good deeds we gave Montepulciano cause to defect and declare war against us, when they had only recently pleaded, despite our misgivings, to be joined to us as allies?

9   Pisae vero captae quondam iustissimo bello, quod innumerabili-
bus paene provocati iniuriis suscepimus. Nemo vi fuisse captas
dixerit; colonia potius quaedam nostra iudicari poterat. Nihil est
usquam in cives, in aedificia, in agros desaevitum, nisi quantum re-
tinendae civitatis coegit necessitas, nihil omnino factum, quod illi
iure expostulent, sed habitare nobiscum commodisque uti omnibus in perdita patria permisimus, qui olim, ut haec nostra deperi-
ret, tantopere curaverant. In eo enim hostium concilio, in quo ad
Emporium oppidum de Florentia consultatum est, ut cetera modo
praetermittam, Pisani oratores, qui et ipsi eo convenerant ad deliberandum de rebus communibus, primi omnium evertendam esse
a stirpe hanc urbem censuerunt. Quam crudelissimam sententiam
cum multi praeterea secuti fuissent, Farinata ille Ubertus, magnus
vir, ne quid tale fieret, prohibuit. Sed minime per Pisanos stetit
quin perirent Florentini funditus, qui paulo ante, cum in Baleares
expeditionem paravissent atque a Lucensibus per eam armorum
absentiam impeterentur antiquis hostibus, ne ipsi perirent effece-
rant.

10   Sed antiquiora omittamus, siquidem plus habere virium recen-
tiora solent. Superioribus enim annis, quid praetermissum est a
nobis ut Pisani sublevarentur? Quid excogitare animis potuere aut
petere a nobis quod non sit datum quam liberalissime? Remissa
vectigalia. Concessum ut honoribus atque magistratibus, tanquam
Pisae liberae forent, fungerentur. Locus ad conveniendum datus.
Permissum tandem ut curiam, ut priores senatumque haberent.
Quae tamen indulgentia nostra, ut res ipsa demum declaravit, ad
eorum in nos superbiam addidit atque ingratitudinem, nec quicquam (quod evenisse fuit convenientius) ad fidem erga nos suam
obsequiumque retinenda profuit. Desciscunt ergo a nobis Pisani,
atque eo quidem tempore quo nobis eorum constantia et virtute
magis opus fuit. Occasione enim praerepta, quod in constituenda
libertate res videretur nostra publica perturbatior, quos iuvare
dubiis quoquo modo in rebus debuere, impetiverunt armis bel-

Pisa, by contrast, we had at one time defeated in war, a most   9
just war after we had suffered innumerable unprovoked offenses.
Yet no one would have thought that they had been captured by
force; one would rather think that they were our colony. We
never vented our rage against the town, its buildings, or its territory beyond what was required to retain the city. Nothing at all
was done that they might with justice challenge, and those men
who had once done all they could to destroy our city we let live
side by side with us, enjoying every benefit in their defeated city.
Yet in that conference of enemies in which the fate of Florence was
debated at Empoli, to say nothing of other instances, the Pisan
ambassadors, who were there to discuss matters of common interest with others, were the first to recommend that our city be razed
to the ground.[11] When many favored this cruel measure as the
best, Farinata degli Uberti, a great man, blocked it.[12] But the
Pisans did not care at all whether the Florentines would perish,
even though a short time before, when the Pisans mounted an ex-
pedition to the Balearic islands and were attacked while unarmed
by their old enemies, the Luccans, the Florentines kept them from
being destroyed.

But let us omit such old stories, since more recent events usu-   10
ally have more impact. In recent years, then, what did we not do
to assist Pisa? What could they think of or demand that was not
generously given? Taxes were rescinded. Posts of honor and magistrates were allowed to continue in place as if Pisa were free. They
were given a place to assemble. They were allowed to keep their
court, as well as their priors and senators. As events have at length
shown, our indulgence only added to their pride and ingratitude,
and it was of no profit to us (as would have been the more appropriate outcome) in retaining their loyalty and deference to us. The
Pisans revolted, and just at a moment when we most needed their
constancy and courage. They seized the chance when our republic
was struggling to maintain its liberty, and when they owed us help

lumque intulere, et Lucensium quosdam male fidos populos ac regulos ad easdem artes pertraxere, sollicitatis etiam contra nos finitimis amicis et foederatis Senensibus et Lucensibus. In quibus quidem ad hanc diem maior gravitas fuit quam quae Pisanorum talibus studiis permoveri quiverit. Sunt vero nonnulli iam quos incepti paenitere sui perfidiaeque necesse est, quibus multo aliter res cecidere quam a principio ipsi existamaverint. Saepe enim accidit ut fluctuet melior causa, sed ut faciat penitus naufragium accidere non potest, gubernatore atque administratore rerum humanarum Deo. Neque nos de reliquis dubitamus, quin, recognito tandem errore, redituri sint in viam veteremque nostrae Reipublicae clementiam imploraturi.

11   Sed interea respondeant nobis, mi Trebati, qui nos vituperant, quid hac in parte non probent. An nos plura indulsisse quam oportuerit reprehendent et facilitatem et benignitatem publicam, quae peculiaris est nostrae civitatis, condemnabunt? Quae enim ex omnibus Italiae urbibus — nam de extraneis modo dicere nihil attinet — quae, inquam, urbs, qui populi unquam extiterunt, qui didicerint nobis aut imperare mansuetius aut culpas condonare facilius? Aut plura et praestantiora indulgere his qui quoquo modo reguntur a nobis? Unde saepe accidisse vidimus ut non minore prope obstinatione animorum sese quidam nostris opposuerint hostibus restiterintque ad extremum sanguinem quam si ipsi Florentini essent cives atque ad eos primum belli cura pertineret. Testis est in agro Casentinate paulo ante Nicolaum oppidum, in Clante Castellina, in valle quae ab Elsa flumine ducit nomen Collensis obsidio, non multos ante annos toto urbe nobilitata, quanquam hic quidem locus multo est manifestior quam qui multa asseveratione testibusque indigeat.

12   Ex quo etiam multo videtur magis esse detestanda eorum improbitas qui hoc tempore ab nostrorum more recedentes ipsi sibi

in a crisis, they chose instead to take up arms and start a war, dragging certain disloyal peoples and leaders of the region of Lucca to do the same, even soliciting support against us from our neighboring friends and allies, Siena and Lucca. Indeed to this day these latter cities have shown more dignity than the Pisans could overcome by their partisanship. There are some who now have cause to regret their traitorous acts, for things turned out very differently for them than they at first intended. Often, indeed, the better cause is tossed and buffeted but cannot be brought to suffer shipwreck, thanks to God who governs and regulates human affairs. Nor do we doubt that the other cities, perceiving their mistake, will return to their old path and ask our Republic for clemency.

Meanwhile, my Trebatius, ask those who rail against us what parts of this story they find untrue. Do they reprove us for being more indulgent than we should have been and condemn our policies, characteristic of this city, as too easy-going and benign? Which of the cities of Italy — for there is no point in talking of those outside Italy — what city, I say, what people ever existed who learned to rule in a gentler and more forgiving manner than we have? And what peoples have ever been treated with greater and more marked indulgence than those whom, after a fashion, we rule? Hence we see how it has often happened that certain [of our subject] peoples have opposed our enemies and resisted them to the last drop of their blood with no less obstinacy than if they themselves were Florentine citizens and the conduct of the war was primarily their business. Witness the recent case of Castel San Niccolò in the territory of the Casentino, of Castellina in Chianti, or of the siege of Colle Val d'Elsa, renowned throughout the world a few years back and too well-known to require demonstration or witnesses.[13]

All the greater then is the despicable wickedness of those who have abandoned our way of life and perpetrated novel and utterly

novum prope atque inusitatum penitus facinus desumpsere. Nec mihi quisquam Volterranam direptionem obiciat, qui cum sine causa et ipsi rebellassent atque obstinatius in suscepto facinore perdurarent, occasionem praebuerunt militibus nostris, qui urbem obsidebant, agendi cum illis durius. Ipse vero testis sum quantum senatus populusque Florentinus, quantum viginti viri, qui eius belli curam gererent, ne quid tale accideret restiterint, quantum etiam ob eam ipsam causam victoriam magnis et sumptibus et periculis protraxerint. Verumenimvero fatum quoddam ex ignoratis, ut supra diximus, causis proveniens et illam tunc et hanc modo necessitatem attulit rerum ita mutandarum. Nisi forte ex honestissimis causis, idest, pietate, clementia, benignitate ista sequi eventa putant, quod absurdissimum est.

13   Sed leviora quidem haec fortunae vulnera sunt. Illud vero gravius quod in mores, in prudentiam, in religionem tandem hominum nostrorum invehuntur acerbius. Sed de moribus quidem pauciora dicenda sunt, ne et nos morosiores contra morum disputantes petulantiam videri cuipiam merito possimus. Sese expendant qui nos reprehendunt. Et de oculi trabe sui (ut aiunt) quam de alieni festuca solliciti magis esse velint. Quanquam tota haec pars de moribus melius arguitur quam colitur. Sumus enim natura omnes ad peccandum proni. Et qui deterior est, idem est ad maledicendum prontior. Meliores esse in vita cuncti possumus. Sed ne ille quidem, qui Dei manibus in paradiso creatus ex luto est, ex quo et nomen habet apud Hebraeos Adam, ‹absque peccato fuit. Nam› mandatum transgressus formatoris sui Dei, peccavit in mores, et septies in die iustus peccat. Ut de Lucifero eiusque sequacibus angelis taceamus, cuius maior culpa fuit quam quae condonari potuerit, aut de qua hoc in loco fieri sermo oporteat, nostra condonabiliora errata sunt; quippe qui ex humo (unde et apud nos homini nomen est ad Hebraeorum nominis similitudinem) ducamus stirpem et facile dilabamur. Sed magnitudines scelerum potius aspiciendae sunt atque detestandae: rapinae, prodi-

unprecedented crimes. And let no one cite our sacking of Volterra as a counter-example, for since they rebelled for no reason and persisted in their crime, they gave our soldiers, who were besieging them, reason to act harshly.[14] I myself can bear witness how the senate and people of Florence, as well as the Twenty in charge of war, tried to prevent this and so postponed victory at great cost in money and lives. Thus fate, coming from unknown causes, as I have said, created the necessity then, and likewise now, of changing our ways. Or do they think perhaps that our honorable customs — that is, our piety, clemency and benevolence — themselves brought on what happened, which is completely absurd?

But these wounds inflicted on us by fortune are relatively light. 13 It is worse that people harshly criticize the morality of our people, their wisdom, and their religion. Yet let us say little about morality, lest we appear to anyone, and deservedly so, overly punctilious about their scurrilous attacks on our morals. Let them consider their own faults before reproving us. Let them consider the beam in their own eye (as they say) rather than the mote in another's.[15] It is easier to argue about morality than to improve our lives. We are all inclined by nature to sin; and the worse one's sins the more inclined one is to slander others. We can all improve the way we live. But even he who was created from clay in Paradise by God's own hands (whence his Hebrew name is Adam) was without sin. For he disobeyed the command of God his Maker, and though a just man, sinned in his actions, and the just man sins seven times a day. I say nothing of Lucifer and the angels who followed him, for his great fault went beyond what could be forgiven, and also beyond what is appropriate to speak of here. Our own errors are more forgivable, for we are rooted in earth, humus (from which in Latin, as in Hebrew, man, *homo*, takes his name), and we fall easily into decay. Yet we must scrutinize and condemn great crimes: rapine, treachery, sacrilege, impiety and other things of this kind, to which the human race is rightly hostile and which even the laws

tiones, sacrilegia, impietates, et alia praeterea generis eiusdem, quibus merito infestum est genus humanum, quaeque arma etiam et leges barbarorum facile persequuntur. Nam quae communiora sunt atque leviora naturae infirmitati et consuetudini ita aberrandi facile ignoscimus et alter alteri condonamus. Unde et illud aureum divinumque praeceptum est, ut debita dimittamus quia eadem mensura qua metiemur aliis mensurabitur et nobis. Quid igitur ais, maledice? Quos reprehendis mores? Fortasse qui perferunt atque in quos peccatur persequeris, atque eos, ut vulgus et facinorosi homines quandoque solent, qui astutius intulerunt calumniam extollendos putas. Qui decipi ob bonitatem et morum simplicitatem potuerunt, condemnandos censes, ut de Lycurgi legibus aliquibus in erratis fertur: in eos qui damno afficiebantur, ob cavendi negligentiam animadvertebat. Sed malim de moribus alii scribant nostris, ne quis me de patriis dicente rebus referat in affectum, quod veritati potius concedendum fuit. Verum percommode quidem accidit ut bene aut perperam facta ubique locorum per se loquantur de se deque auctoribus suis satis, atque erunt omnia quaecumque homines vel in occulto gesserunt hac (quam cernis) solis luce clariora. Nam corda etiam et secretiora eius aperire et ponere in propatulo tempus solet. Prudentiam tueri difficilius est. Quae virtus nisi praesit omnibus in actionibus, subeant erroris ac vitii taxationem necesse est.

14   Plura sunt autem quae in hac prudentiae parte vituperant. Sed inprimis rem nostram publicam male administrari dicunt ac paene pueriliter: quod non sit iam in ea ullus personarum delectus, sed confluant in populi contionem, ubi de summa rerum deliberatur, tanquam in sentinam, omnes etiam illi, quorum ob imperandi desuetudinem atque imperitiam nullae fuisse partes debuissent. Illi item qui propter tenuitatem census multo intersi‹n›t magis rei consuluisse propriae quam publicis. Addunt quod quemadmodum doctorum atque imperitorum discrimen nullum in consulendo et

and arms of the barbarians are quick to punish. As for more common and lighter lapses of our natural character and customs, we readily forgive and pardon them in each other. Hence the golden and divine rule that we should forgive debts since the measure by which we assess others shall be applied to us.[16] So what do you say to this, slanderer? What customs are you condemning? Perhaps you would punish the victim, and, as the mob and the wicked often do, think those who cleverly devise false accusations should be praised to the skies. Do you think those whose very goodness and simplicity makes them easy to deceive should be condemned? That is what is reported of the laws of Lycurgus in the case of certain lapses: he punished those who had suffered some loss for their negligence in taking precautions.[17] But I prefer that others write about our way of life lest, when I say what must be granted as true about my country, someone think that I am rather speaking out of partiality. It is highly convenient that actions well or badly done should everywhere be enough to speak for themselves and for those responsible, so that whatever things men have done, even in secret, shall be clearer than sunlight. For time usually reveals the heart and its secrets and brings them into the open. It is more difficult to preserve prudent conduct. And when this virtue is not present to all our actions, a measure of error and vice will inevitably be found to have crept in.

They vilify us for many things that relate to this matter of prudence. First of all, they say that our public life is badly and almost childishly governed: that there is no longer any selectivity of persons, but rather that the people's council, where the most important matters are considered, is like a sewer, full of people who ought not to be there owing to their lack of experience and knowledge of government. Having little property, moreover, they are much better employed taking care of their own affairs than public ones. They also say that since there is an indiscriminate mingling of learned and unlearned persons in consulting and deliberating, 14

deliberando sit, ita bonique et mali indifferenter conveniant, quae quidem in bona republica recteque constituta repudianda sint. Quibus quidem si sit absque levitate vanitateque respondendum, erit forsitan non inutile ut aliquid, antequam ad has descendamus proprias accusationis partes, aliqua de rerum publicarum natura et conditione breviter disseramus. Sic puto et adversarii quid accusent, et nos quid diluamus, facilius explicatiusque cognoscent.

15 Est autem respublica, ut in mentem modo venit, in unum aggregata multitudo commodorum gratia propriorum, ex pluribus melius quasi adiutoribus quam ex solitudine provenientium. Arbitror enim non aliena causa sed sua in coetum convenisse quandoque homines et communi utilitati inservisse ut ex publica tandem facilius consequerentur suam. Falluntur vero quidam, qui ex hoc principio privata putant anteferenda publicis. Verum si in publico bono melius fit privatum atque facilius, quis dubitaverit illud anteponere propter quod alterum sit melius? Neque nunc est mihi de finium nobilitate disserendum. In quibus quidem, si quod animus mihi ratioque suadet explicaverim, invidiosum erit propter eos qui de his scripserunt, a quorum forte necesse foret opinione aliquando dissentire.

16 Sed ista omittantur. Redeamus ad rempublicam. Ea vero primum duplex est, humana et civilis. Et humanam quidem eam appello quae natura solum, non etiam hominum opinionibus continetur. Quam si sequeremur ducem, omnes eisdem uteremur institutis et legibus, nec essent cur aut hi imperare aut illi liberi esse contenderent. Et beati viveremus, nudi et sine rubore tuentes singuli eum locum, in quo creavit nos Deus ac de ligno boni et mali ne comederemus praecepit. Sed nos transgressi divinum mandatum, id est, naturae limites desciscentes, a patria exulamus ac tot tantisque implicati malis, incommodorum sectantes diffugia,

the good and bad gather without distinction, which is unacceptable in a well-constituted republic. To answer such charges without levity or vanity, it may perhaps be useful, before we descend to particulars, to say a few things about the nature and condition of republics. In this way, I think, all will have a readier and more detailed understanding both of our adversaries' accusations and our rebuttals.

A republic, in conception at least, is a gathering of many into 15 one body for their own advantage, which they are better able to attain with the help of many others than all alone. I think that, whenever men have united, they did so not for some else's sake but for their own, and when they serve the common interest, they do so to derive their personal advantage from the public one. It is wrong, however, to infer from this that private advantage is to be put before public good. For truly, if private good is better and more easily to be found when the public good is served, who can doubt that the latter must be preferred even for the sake of the former? But this is no time to discuss the nobility of ends. Indeed, if I were to explain what my mind and reasoning ability lead me to believe on this subject, my remarks might arouse hatred because they would perhaps contradict at times the views of writers on these matters.

But let us set these things aside. Let us go back to the republic. 16 First of all, it is twofold, human and civil. I call that one human which is held together by Nature alone, and not by human beliefs. If we were to follow her as our leader, we would all practice the same customs and laws, and there would be no contention as to who should command and who is free. And we would live happily, naked and without shame, maintaining each one of us the place where God created us and taught us not to eat of the tree of knowledge of good and evil. But having disobeyed the divine commandment, that is, having broken out of the limits of nature, we

commutandis locis moribusque veterno huic vitae adeo immedica-
bili remedia inde petimus, unde incrementa saepe malorum super-
veniunt. Atque hinc quidem, ut videri mihi solet, orsum habet illa
respublica quam civilem appellavimus quamque supra diffinivimus,
et de qua nobis nunc habenda oratio est. Nam illam alteram ius-
tiorem multo sanctioremque rempublicam in praesentia describere
alienum est. Civilis autem tot prope sunt species quot gentes;
ex diversitate namque regionum diversitas fit vivendi. Unde fiunt
leges consuetudinesque non diversae modo, sed plerunque contrariae inter se. Ex quibus diversitates quoque et contrariae posi-
tiones oriuntur rerum publicarum. Inter quas difficilius forsitan
fuerit quaenam eligenda sit potius dignoscere quibusque sua et
quos imbiberint a primis annis mores praeponentibus. Nos autem
non quae ad mediocritatem respiciat magis, ut quidam putaverunt,
sed quae accesserit ad naturae rationem propinquius, reliquis
praestare dicimus, quae illo quasi relicto vertice, immo vero sole
nostrae peregrinationis, multis saepe aguntur erroribus ad interi-
tumque maturant[2] gressum.

17   Tamen quae minus improbantur tres sunt regendarum formae
civitatum. Aut enim unus recte gubernat, et dicitur regnum. Aut
omnes qui civitatis ius habent, et nominatur respublica. Aut de-
lecti quidam moribus praestantiores, quod genus Graeci aristocra-
tiam vocant, ut nos quoque a melioribus imposuimus vocabulum
imitati Graecos, optimatium hanc rempublicam appellantes. Civitas nostra regnum semper abhorruit, utputa quod possit soleatque
facile verti in tyrannidem, quod genus est omnium deterrimum.
Nam ad suam haec, utilitate neglecta civitatis, cuncta administrat.
Et cum sibi licere omnia putat, qui ita rerum est potitus, sacraque
et profana omnia confundit, nec diis tandem aut hominibus quicquam parcit. Cui non multum dissimilis illa quae optimatium videri vult, quia apud pauciores est imperandi potestas, verum tamen ad tyrannidem declinat magis quam ad regnum. Unde et

are exiled from our homeland. Entangled in many evils, seeking to flee our troubles, changing our place and way of life, we seek cures for this incurable lethargy of life that often produce an increase of our woes. And this, as I see it, is how the civil republic originated, such as we have defined it above, and such as we must now consider—for to discuss that other much more just and more holy republic is not to the present purpose. There are, however, as many kinds of civil republics as there are peoples, for regional diversity leads to diversity of ways of life. Hence come, not merely different but entirely contrary laws and customs, from which arise diverse and contradictory arrangements of republics. It will perhaps be difficult to choose the best among them for people who prefer their own constitution and the customs they imbibed from their earliest years. For myself, I do not consider best, as some have believed, the constitution that more closely approximates a middle position, but rather the one that comes closest to natural reason.[18] If we leave behind this peak or rather sun of our pilgrimage, the remaining constitutions are often driven into error and hasten towards their death.

Three types of constitution are the least subject to criticism. In the first, which is called kingship, a sole ruler governs rightly. In the second, which is called a republic, all who enjoy the rights of citizenship govern. In the third, those whose conduct is best are chosen to rule. This kind of government the Greeks call *aristocracy*, and we imitate them by using our word for "best," and call it a republic of *optimates*. Our city has always hated kingship, thinking that it easily can and often does turn into tyranny, which is the worst of all constitutions. For the tyrant governs entirely for his own advantage and neglects that of the city. And as he thinks he is free to do anything he wants, and is all-powerful, he confuses sacred and secular matters, and spares neither gods nor men. The constitution which would like to appear to be that of the optimates is not much different from this, since all power belongs

aliud est sortita nomen: oligarchiam vocant, nos recte paucorum principatum dicimus. Atque hanc quoque speciem—tantus est tyranni metus—abiecimus populumque Florentinum asseruimus in libertatem.

18   Num tu id accusas, maledice? Neque tibi libertas placet quae tot viris quandoque nostris atque externis adeo cara fuit, ut vitam quoque ipsam pro ea servanda ponere non dubitaverint? Exemplis omnis apud quosque historia refertissima est. Et nonnulli paulo ante apud nos praeclarum periculum fecere, quorum et nunc est in admiratione nomen, adeo ut referant id quidam in Deum potius et facinoris eum auctorem putent, quia supra humanam virtutem rem gessisse adeo magnam vixque credendam posteris videantur. Certo scio, mi Trebati, ne hiscere quidem audebit contra libertatem adversarius. Quotus enim quisque est qui divini huius praeclarissimi muneris expers esse in vita velit ac non potius omni id sibi ope vendicet paretque paratumque tueatur? Nihil est enim libertate melius, ea praesertim quam non ambitio aut vanitas ingesserit, quae appellari potius licentia consuevit, sed naturae nostrae praerogativa, ut ita dixerim, decorque suaserit.

19   Sed non est satis, inquies, liberum esse se velle, quod plerique omnes volumus, verum didicisse liberum fieri atque uti libertate, id vero magnificum atque ingenuo dignum est ingenio. Nos certe ex tribus illis administrandae civitatis generibus, quae modo diximus, popularem desumpsimus nobis, quam proprius rempublicam appellant, cuique praeter ceteras cura sit tuendae atque excolendae libertatis, ut non veriti sint quidam finem reipublicae constituere libertatem, ut paucorum divitias, optimatium virtutem esse propositum censuerunt. Nam regis et reipublicae, etsi diversum nomen est, finis tamen idem est, nisi aberret uterque a recto, et hic ad tyrannidem, illa ad plebis status inconditaeque multitudinis plebis-

to a very few, yet it is more likely to turn into a tyranny than to become a kingdom. Hence it has been alloted another name: [the
Greeks] call it *oligarchy*, and we correctly call it "the primacy of the
few." And this kind of constitution too we Florentines reject —
such is our fear of tyranny — and assert our claim to liberty.

Is this what you are attacking, slanderer? Do you disapprove of 18
liberty, which has been to our people as well as to others so precious that to preserve it they did not hesitate to risk their very
lives? All of history is crammed with examples of this. And even
in the recent past some among us have put this famously to the
test, whose names are still spoken in wonder, so much so that
their deed, as an act surpassing human ability, is attributed to God
and seems hardly believable to posterity. I know, Trebatius, that
my opponent will not dare utter a word directly opposed to liberty. Indeed, there are few who would want to be bereft of this divine and most excellent gift, who would not rather lay claim to it
with every resource, who would not obtain it and preserve it when
obtained. Nothing is better than liberty, especially that liberty
which is not guided by ambition or vanity — a better name for
which is license — but is urged by the prerogative, as it were, and
dignity of our nature.

But it is not enough, you will say, to want to be free, as most of 19
us do; but to have learned how to become free and to make use of
freedom: that is what is truly splendid and worthy of a noble
mind. Of the three kinds of constitution just mentioned, we have
certainly chosen popular government, which is properly called a
republic, and this, more than the others, demands the defense and
cultivation of liberty. Hence some do not hesitate to maintain that
the purpose of a republic is to establish liberty, as the purpose of
an oligarchy is wealth, and of an aristocracy, virtue. For a kingship
and a republic, as different as they are in name, have the same ultimate purpose, unless they diverge from what is right, and the former lapses into tyranny, or the latter into the rule of the plebs and

cita dilabatur. Quid enim sibi rex vult in populis civitatibusque gubernandis nisi eorum omnium ipsorum qui ab se reguntur otium securitatemque vivendi rerumque propriarum pro arbitrio proque privati cuiusque usus commodo agendarum facultatem? Nonne eadem et reipublicae intentio est? Sed illic imperio, hic legibus, illic edicto, hic suffragiis geritur res atque obtemperatur. Dictum est autem cur unius nobis nomen odiosum sit. Nunc vero reipublicae partes, quam complexi sumus, defendendae sunt. Quae, quanvis et ipsa perpetuum servare tenorem non potest semperque esse eadem, tamen corrumpitur tardius; et minus affectum sapiunt, qui in deliberando agere saepenumero animum in transversum solent rerum publicarum decreta quam principum, aut ubi contingit civitatem gubernari a paucioribus. Et causa quidem in promptu est, ut mihi videtur. Minus enim mutationibus dant operam ad quos minus ex rebus novis sit utilitatis commodique perventurum. At qui sperant cupiditatibus sic consulere suis melius, saepe his quae adsunt rebus contenti non sunt. Nam qui nihil inde plus habituri videantur, cur mutari velint atque in periculum adduci suam libertatem?

20   Nunc ex quibus constet respublica videamus, ut quid nostri vituperatores insectentur magis in apertum veniat. Praetermittentes autem modo quid alii senserint, nobis ita occurrit ut sint in republica inprimis sacerdotes et profani. Quanquam de sacerdotibus mox, cum de religione disputabimus, suo magis loco dicendum erit, nunc profanos explicemus, quos percommode quidem duo in membra dispertiemur: aut enim senatus erit aut populus. Nam magistratus in populo comprehendimus, ex quo et deliguntur aut sorte fiunt. Senatum segregamus et virtute constare magis atque aetate, unde et nomen habet, existimamus. Neque rempublicam appellare convenit, ubi senatus auctoritas non sit, id est, ubi publicum consilium desideretur — id enim senatus est — aut desit populus, qui civilibus muneribus possit sufficere.

the vote of the disordered masses. For what does the king seek in governing peoples and cities if not peace and security for those who are governed by him, and the ability of each to pursue his own affairs according to his personal will and his ability to manage things suitably? And isn't this same thing the aim of the republic? Government is conducted and submitted to in the former by command, in the latter by laws; in the former by edict, in the latter by votes. Now we have said why the name of one-man rule is hateful to us. Now I must defend our partisanship of the republic we have embraced. Although the republic cannot keep on course and be consistent, it is slower to become corrupted; and those whose minds are often driven in opposite directions while deliberating about the decisions of a republic show better sense and less passion than do the decisions of princes, or the decisions of states ruled by a few. And the reason for this is, I think, obvious. People are less likely to promote instability when they are going to get less advantage and profit from revolution. Those who hope to satisfy their own desires are often discontented with things as they are. Indeed, if people do not expect to gain from it, why would they make changes and endanger their own freedom?

Now let us see what parts constitute a republic, to make quite 20 clear what our detractors are attacking. Leaving aside the opinions of others, to us it seems that a republic contains, first of all, the priesthood and secular authorities. As we will soon discuss religion and speak at some length of the religious authorities, let us now talk about the secular, which we may conveniently divide into two branches: the senate and the people. For the magistrates, in our view, fall under the people, from whom they are either elected or chosen by lot. We set the senate apart and reckon it greater both in virtue and in age, whence the name.[19] Nor should the word republic be used where there is no senatorial authority, that is, where a public council—a senate, in other words—is lacking, or where there is no people capable of filling the civil positions.

21   Et populi quidem plures sunt differentiae. Nam alii bellicis idonei negotiis propulsant iniurias, et appellantur milites. Eorum vero conventus dicuntur exercitus. In quo etiam sui sunt magistratus: imperatores, praetores, legati, quaestores, praefecti, centuriones, et minorum dignitatum nomina, qui fiunt ex populo omnes, et dicuntur belli propulsatores a nonnullis, a quibus quidem defenditur respublica pulcherrime. Nam si externo repugnandum bellatoreque et duce fuerit, ut nobis quoque aliquando ingruit necessitas, multo est fortunatius si res populo prospere ceciderint. Alterum genus est eorum qui terrae exercendae ad victus abunde subministrandos praesunt, quos vocant de re agricolas, optimum hominum genus, neque ulli publico muneri inutile, nisi nos ambitiosiores simus. Sed optimae olim respublicae huiusmodi homines non fastidierunt neque pastores qui sunt reipublicae negotiis quibusdam pernecessarii. Unde enim coriaria erit, unde armorum quadam genera equosque et iumenta comparabimus? Quibus certe respublica indigent, nisi pastores admiserimus. Nam adventitia ea esse et peregrina non decet si sufficere sibi et perfectam esse volumus rempublicam. Restant opifices, inter magis necessaria membra civitatis, non modo ad arma ad defendendum fabricanda navesque et proeliares machinas, sed ad populares quoque usus calceorum supellectilis vestimentorum. Nam de mercatoribus, de poetis, de oratoribus, de philosophis, quorum minus videtur indigere respublica, ut in praesentia multa dicamus haud est necesse. Ad opes tamen et ad dignitatem populi multum conferre quis dubitaverit? Neque audiendi mihi videntur, qui mercaturam damnant — non dico omnem, sed quae exportandis atque importandis mercibus commoditatibus rerum publicarum favet, ut in nostra republica saepe evenit, quae multas magnasque belli et pacis temporibus inde reportavit opportunitates. Sed haec alias. Neque enim nunc de republica scribimus ut philosophi solent, sed obiecta in nos diluimus.

Among the people one can distinguish a number of kinds. 21
Some are suited to the business of war and ward off injuries; these
are called soldiers. Collectively they are called the army, within
which we find their own magistrates: generals, praetors, legates,
quaestors, prefects, centurions and the lesser ranks, all drawn from
the people. Some call them guardsmen, and they defend the republic in the most seemly way. For if we have to fight off a foreign
warrior and leader, as sometimes we must, the outcome is much
more favorable if the task falls to the people.[20] A second kind of
people consists of those who work the soil and are in charge of
providing abundant food. Such men are called farmers, an excellent class of men, by no means useless in public office, if we are
not overly ambitious. Indeed, the best republics in the past did not
disdain this kind of men, nor herdsmen, who are essential to meet
certain practical needs of any republic. For whence will come
leather, whence certain sorts of arms, and horses and beasts of
burden? The republic will surely lack these if we do not include
herdsmen. For if we want the republic to be self-sufficient and
perfect, it is not advisable to import such goods from abroad.
Then there are the craftsmen, among the most necessary members
of a city, not only for the manufacture of arms for our defense,
ships, and war machinery, but also for everyday items like shoes,
furniture, and clothes. As for merchants, poets, orators, philosophers, they seem less necessary to a republic, so that we hardly
need to say much about them here. Yet can one doubt that they
contribute a great deal to the wealth and dignity of the people?
Nor do I think we should listen to those who condemn com-
merce — certainly not all forms of it, since the export and import
of goods helps the republic, as often happens in our city, and has
brought many and great advantages in times of war and of peace.
But of this elsewhere. For we are not writing about the republic as
philosophers do, but are refuting accusations.

22   Quid vero est in his quae modo de populari diximus administratione quod tantopere vituperandum putent? Contionem fortesse hanc populi, quam nos Magnum Consilium vocamus, quidam propter magnitudinem non probant, verentes, credo — quod de Mylesiorum templo ferunt, quod propter amplitudinem sine tecto remansit — ne ullum hos quoque, qui sunt cogendi, tectum accepturum sit. In quo quidem non solum tarditatem conveniendi difficultatemque arguere videntur, et negligentius peragi publica negocia, verum etiam quia indigni ad consultandum deliberandumque conveniant. Ante ergo de perferendi difficultate, demum de dignitate atque indignitate disputabimus.

23   Primum igitur quis non videt id esse praecipuum libertatis argumentum, si fiant rerum decreta cum pluribus, etsi plus id habeat difficultatis et laboris? Nihil enim magis ad peccandum videtur impellere quam apertae ad nequitiam fores, ut vetus est tritumque de penu servando proverbium. Adde quod nihil videtur ad recte deliberandum veritatemque in rebus perspiciendam tempore accommodatius, quod multas solvere plicas, si paulo incesseris gravius, consuevit. Animi certe perturbationes in multitudine minus habent virium quam si pauciores deliberent, praesertim si sit inde ad eos aliquid accessurum earum rerum quarum desiderio saepe anguntur. Populus magis communia commoda respicit, in quibus recognoscit sua. Nam ut quicquam ad se usque speret seorsum perveniat utilitatis ex his quae per affectus decernuntur, ita longe abest ut illis etiam qui omne id tale praeriperent potentia vehementer invideat, defendendamque sibi mordicus honestatem putet. Unde deliberandi iudicium multo est firmius multoque severius quoniam, quibus contigit suffragiorum redditio, nihil sibi ante oculos magis proponunt quam quod civitati conducat primum, non privato cuipiam. Quod tamen demum boni communitate singulis atque universis profuturum sit.

What is it in the things we have said about popular government   22
that they find so objectionable? Certain persons do not approve
the popular assembly, which we call the Great Council, on account
of its size, fearing, I believe, that no roof will be able to cover the
persons summoned, as we are told of the temple of Miletus that it
was so big that it remained without a roof.[21] In this they seem not
only to criticize the slowness and difficulty of convoking all these
people and the negligence with which public affairs are transacted,
but also that unworthy persons are convened to consult and delib-
erate. Before we discuss the difficulty of transacting business,
therefore, we shall discuss qualifications and the lack thereof.

First, who does not see that this is outstanding evidence of lib-   23
erty, if decrees of state are passed with many persons present, even
if that is more difficult and laborious? For nothing seems to invite
evil actions more than doors that are open to evil, as goes the old
and well-worn proverb about guarding the storehouse. What's
more, nothing seems better suited to foster correct deliberation
and finding out the truth than time, which usually resolves problems if you move a little more deliberately. Passions have less
power in a multitude than where just a few are deliberating, especially if the matter they are going to deal with is one of those
which provokes desire and anxiety. The people in general look
more to the common interest, in which they recognize their own.
For as the people hopes that something useful will accrue to itself
separately from decisions made in passion, it is far from hating
persons who would abuse power to seize all such things, and
thinks that honesty is something it must defend for itself, tooth
and nail. Hence decisions arrived at by [collective] deliberation are
more solid and strict, since voters have nothing more in view than
what is good for the city, and not for any private person. This in
the end benefits each and every person through the commonality
of good.

24   Nunc ad indignos, quos dicunt, transeamus. Qui mihi locus quam amplissimus videtur, qui non modo non carpi a malivolis, sed laudari magis a bonis viris debeat. Verum qui digni sunt quique indigni et quae vis verbo insit, dicendum est prius, ne implicata neque intellecta satis fluat oratio, si confusa nominis significatio extiterit. Est autem ea per se vox ambigua nisi res addatur qua quis dignus est. Ita fit honore dignos asseramus quosdam, alios poena dignos censeamus, quamvis dignitas, quae inde est loquendi consuetudine semper in laude est, ut et apud Graecos ἄξιος καὶ ἄξια. Igitur de dignitate disputaturi, quid ea tandem sit, aperiendum est. Quam quidem si velimus absolutam constituere aliquam virtutem, melius eam profecto mente cogitationeque comprehendemus quam experiri re possimus. Nam neque iustificabitur in conspectu Dei omnis vivens. Quamobrem communior quaedam atque ea quidem humana perquirenda est, in qua, etsi differentias esse complures oportet et quasi quosdam gradus dignitatum pro meritorum differentiis, tamen ut plures digni appellemus nomine, haud indignum erit. Non enim hi sumus qui bonorum inter se quique malorum discrimen esse nullum existimemus. Sed differre a bono meliorem, improbiorem autem ab eo qui minus habeat improbitatis ducimus. Neque item cum his sentimus qui nusquam centum re vera bonos reperiri statuunt, quod et ait Aristoteles libro quinto, quem de civitatibus scriptum reliquit. Asseruerim autem ea posthabita dignitate (nam eandem modo et virtutem et bonitatem appellamus) quae intelligi tantum, non etiam reperiri in quoquam datur. Asseruerim, inquam, vel in nostra civitate non centum modo reperiri posse, quos ille nusquam dicit, sed plures etiam quam centum centies, non tamen eiusdem omnes, sed diversae dignitatis homines, dignos tamen, quorum prudentia consiliumque etiam in republica non contemnatur.

Now let us look at the unworthy citizens they talk about. This   24
seems a large topic, which ought to be commended by good men
and not just carped at by men of ill will. First, we must consider
who is worthy and who is unworthy and what is the meaning of
this word [*dignus*], for our discourse will not flow in a coherent
and understandable way if there is confusion about the meaning of
this term. It is in itself a vague word unless the quality someone
has that makes him worthy is specified. Thus we declare some
worthy of honor, and we deem others worthy of punishment,
while according to our usual way of speaking, [the abstract noun]
"worthiness" is a word of praise, as among the Greeks the words
axios kai axia. So as we are going to discuss "worthiness," that is
the word we must explain. If we want to establish what worthiness
is as a virtue in the abstract, we shall better comprehend it in
mind and thought than we can through experience. "For neither
shall any living being be justified in God's sight."[22] Therefore we
must seek a more common, human virtue wherein, though many
differences must appear and varying degrees of worthiness in pro-
portion to varying sorts of merit, it will not be unworthy to call
many by the name "worthy." We are not one of those people who
think that there are no distinctions to be made within the classes
of good men and bad.[23] We think that better persons differ from
merely good ones, and more wicked persons from those of lesser
wickedness. Nor do we agree with those who judge that in reality
not a hundred truly good men can be found, as Aristotle says
in Book 5 of the *Politics* that he has left us.[24] I would assert that
this kind of worthiness (which is the same thing we call goodness
and virtue) should be laid aside; it can be understood in thought
but not found in any individual. I would assert, I say, that not only
can one find a hundred worthy men in our city — the number Aristotle says are to be found nowhere — but more than a hundred
times a hundred. Not all of the same degree of worthiness, but of
different degrees, yet worthy nonetheless, whose prudence and

Quid enim prohibet ut bono ingenio bonisque moribus, quales in nostra urbe multi sunt, etiam opifices, non et ipsi venire in partem debeant popularis administrationis? Cur eo quoque se adminiculo castrata (ut ita dicam) respublica volet, si erit inde, ut certe futurum est, aut consulendo aut agendo aliquid relatura commodi et ad bene rem gerendam facultatis. Et nobiles saepe et minus nobiles patriae profuere, neque in his minor laus quam in illis est, etsi census est ignobilior.

25   Neque vero nos sine discrimine, quod multi vituperant, ad deliberandum de rebus publicis omnes advenientes quasi in forum navaleque admittimus. Habetur enim vel diligentissima et civis et aetatis et legum ratio. Nec peregrino cuiquam (ut multi putant) venire in consilium licet, nedum suffragiorum latio permittatur. Minores triginta annis contione arcentur, ne tu deinceps puerilem hanc decernendi et agendi cum populo rationem voces. Leges etiam ipsae eximunt complures tributa non solventes, damnatos praeterea rerum capitalium, sacrilegos aut aliqua insigni alia nota legibus obnoxios. Nam temulenti, furiosi et quacunque insigniori quadam libidine minusque condonabili infames ne aspicere quidem quo convenitur sanctissimum illum publici consilii locum pro horrore possunt, ne quis indifferenter bonos malosque advocari recipique existimet. In nonnullos etiam, qui ab ea quam esse volunt omnes servatam rerum omnium integritatem, recessissent, severissime animadversum est, ut non iam maius aliquod inter se civibus sit quam de virtute honestateque certamen. Et spes est fore, his (quae maledico illi non probantur) artibus studiisque nostris, isto reipublicae administrandae genere, ut respiciat civitatem nostram aliquando Deus agatque nobiscum clementius, nec ut nos meriti fuerimus, verum secundum suam potius magnam misericordiam salvos nos faciat, quanquam etiam Deum ipsum ob depravatam in

counsel, even in public affairs, is not to be despised. What debars persons of sound intelligence and good character, of whom there are many in our city, even among the artisan classes, from serving as part of a popular government? Why would the state wish to be emasculated (as it were) of their aid, if it will derive therefrom, as surely it will, some advantage in counsel or action, some ability to conduct well its business? Both nobles and less noble persons are often useful to the country, nor are the latter less praiseworthy than the former, even if their rank is less exalted.

Nor is it true, as many people complain, that we exercise no   25 discretion and admit to public deliberation all comers, as though we were admitting them to the market place and the dockyards. For we have a set of well thought-out rules concerning citizenship and age and legal status.[25] Nor is any foreigner (as many suppose) admitted to council, let alone to the franchise. Men under thirty are excluded, so that you don't then voice puerile reasonings in the people's deliberations and decisions. The laws also exclude those who have not paid all their taxes, those who have been condemned for capital crimes, the sacrilegious and other persons liable to laws for other notorious acts. Drunkards, lunatics, and those infamous for any of the more notorious and less acceptable forms of lust may not even look upon that most holy place where the public council meets, out of a dread that someone might think we summon and receive good and bad men without discrimination. There is also rigorous admonishment of people who distance themselves from the kind of integrity that all wish to see preserved, so that there should be no greater rivalry among our citizens than rivalry in virtue and honor. And we hope that by these practices and efforts of ours—which are not approved by that slanderer—and with this kind of republican government, God may sometime take heed of our city and treat us with clemency, and that he may save us, not according to our merits, but according to his great mercy,

nobis neglectamque religionem (ut quidam narrant) esse infestum
putant.

26   Quae nobis pars modo restat, ut et de ea quid res habeat, non
multis verbis explicemus. Non est autem (ut mea fert opinio) in
bene instituendis civitatibus religionis vel non imprimis adhibenda
cura. Unde et nos sub primam reipublicae divisionem sacerdotes
collocavimus. Quos fuisse ab aliquibus qui de rebus publicis scripserunt fere neglectos, ne dicam praetermissos, vehementer miror.
Namque ad bene beateque vivendum, qui esse verus unicusque rerum omnium publicarum finis debet, nihil est religione et pietate
magis necessarium, sine qua ne homines quidem homines, nedum
civiles quidam ceteris praestantiores animalibus existimandi sint.
Nam in quo differamus a brutis, hoc uno omnium praeclarissimo
Dei sublato munere non video. Romani exactis regibus nomen tamen regium in civitate retinendum putaverunt transtuleruntque
ad sacra regem sacrificolum appellantes, qui praeesset curandis sacris. Hebraei autem, quos quidem nos his in negotiis quae ad religionem magis pertinent, sumus imitati magis, nonne quid simile
factitarunt? Levitarum apud illos id munus est, iam tum a principio, cum in duodecim tribus iuxta numerum filiorum Iacob omnis
Israelis populus tanquam in unam rempublicam divisus est, auctore etiam ipso et commonstratore Deo, Moyse autem sapientis-
simo illo duce atque felicissimo perficiente. Neque ulli usquam
populi gentesve adeo barbarae immanesque leguntur quae omni
penitus religione privarentur, utputa quae cum anima simul innas-
catur in corpus et cum aetate inolescat simul. Dividi autem commodissime in caerimonias et sacra solet. Dicant quid in nobis
potissimum notandum censent. Sit hoc dictum bona amicorum
venia: non consuevit Florentinus populus vel cultura sacrorum vel
eorum quae ad ornandam quoque modo religionem pertinent alicui cedere. Declarant id tot templa, tot aedes sacrae tanta ex-
tructae magnificentia et decore, ut merito in admirationem esse

although they think that even God himself is hostile to us owing to our abuse and neglect of religion (as certain men tell it).

This one part only still remains and we shall explain in few   26
words what that is about. For (in my opinion) it is not possible to constitute cities well without making the care of religion a primary concern. Hence we placed priests in our first division of the people in the republic. It amazes me that these have been pretty well neglected, not to say entirely left out, by those who have written on republics. For to live well and happily, which ought to be the sole and true purpose of all government, nothing is more necessary than religion and piety, without which men are not to be considered human, nor civil life superior to the life of brutes. For I do not see how we differ from the animals if one leaves out this most excellent of all services, the one we owe to God. The Romans, when they had expelled the kings, deliberately kept the title of king in the city and transferred it to the sacred realm, calling the man in charge of sacred rites the "king of sacrifices."[26] And the Hebrews also, whom we follow most in matters of religion, did they not do much the same? They assigned this duty to the Levites right from the start, when all the people of Israel were divided, as in a republic, into twelve tribes, according to the number of the sons of Jacob. And for this division the lawgiver was God himself, while Moses, their most wise and blessed leader, enacted it. Nor do we read of any people or nation so barbarous and cruel that they completely lacked religion, since the latter is born with the soul in the body and grows with it as one ages. It is customary and convenient to divide religion into ceremonies and sacred objects. Now let our enemies say what they deem is the worst charge against us. Let me reply with the permission of our friends and allies: the Florentine people are second to none in their care for sacred things or in everything that adorns religion. Our many temples show this, as do our many sacred shrines built with such magnificence and splendor that they deservedly command the ad-

queant omnibus hominibus. Confer cum nostris aliarum civitatum moles divinis dictatas nominibus. Nec numero nos nec nobilitate invenies inferiores.

27   Sed ista censeo minus reprehendunt, ne ab rebus ipsis, nobis etiam tacentibus, arguantur. Confusas esse magis apud nos distinctas, ut quidam putant, usu naturaque reipublicae partes non aequo animo ferunt; et sacerdotes etiam atque episcopos vocatos fuisse in administrandi res profanas societatem alienum putant. Decreta vero publica non iam senatu aut magistratu auctoribus, sed fratrum, sed praedicatorum auctoritate (quos vocant) rogarique et perferri aiunt; prophetas etiam nos excitavisse quosdam, qui rem Florentinam apud reliquos Italiae maxime populos ridiculam redderent. Acriora haec quidem et difficiliora propter eam quae de huiuscemodi rebus oboritur inter homines diversitatem. Itaque te mihi quam attentissimo opus est.

28   Enitar enim pro mea virili ut ne hoc quidem indiscussum indefensumque relinquatur. Separantur vero a sacris profana. Quis id negaverit? Verum esse ea inter se contraria, quae sub eodem genere numerentur, ut convenire nequeant nullus vel mediociter doctus concesserit. Quae igitur iniuria est si alterum genus alteri opituletur? Res vero publica unde unde potest utilitati consulat et saluti. Atque ut nunc quidem quid antiquitas servaverit praetermittamus, non soli nos hac tempestate talibus utimur ad recte gubernandum adminiculis, sed maximi etiam et religioni inprimis deditissimi reges et populi et principes idem extra omnem penitus vituperationem factitant. Illud acrius invehuntur, quod nostrarum iam legum atque decretorum fratres sint et praedicatores et peregrini quidam auctores, non cives, quod minus adeo damnandum fuisse arbitrantur. Dicant ergo cur fratris, cur praedicatoris nomina tantopere abhorreant. Fratris suavis est significatio, nec quam frater fratris propinquior esse proximitas cuiusquam potest. Unde et nomen est sortitus quod fere alter sit, qui frater est. Hoc

miration of all. Compare to ours the buildings devoted to holy
names in other cities. You will find ours inferior to none in their
number and nobility.

But this, I think, they are least inclined to criticize, as the facts   27
would refute them even if I remained silent. They are upset that
we confuse the parts of the republic that some regard as distinct
according to custom and nature; and they think it strange that
priests and bishops have been called to administer secular affairs.
They say that public decrees are now reviewed and passed not under the authority of the senate and the magistrates, but by the authority of friars and preachers (as they call them); and that we
have exalted certain prophets who make the Florentine state a
laughing stock, especially among the other peoples of Italy.[27] This
criticism is the more bitter and hard to deal with because men disagree strongly on just this subject. So I need your full attention.

I shall try as best I can not to leave this subject undiscussed and   28
undefended. Secular affairs are separate from sacred ones. Who
would deny that? In truth, as no moderately educated person
would concede, contrary things that may counted under the same
genus can be joined together.[28] What then is unjust about one genus assisting the other?[29] The state may draw on whatever source
it pleases to provide for its advantage and its welfare. And to omit
here the practice of antiquity, in our age we are not alone in using
such ministers in order to govern well, but even the greatest kings
and peoples and princes, and those most devoted to religion, have
constantly done the same without attracting criticism. Our critics
inveigh so bitterly against us because they say friars and preachers
and foreigners are writing our laws and decrees, rather than our
citizens, which they think would deserve less condemnation. Let
them say why they so fiercely hate the names of friars and preachers. The meaning of the word "friar" (*frater*) is a pleasant one, for
there can be no proximity closer than that of brother with brother.
Hence the brother (*frater*) is assigned his name because he is *fere*

enim magis modo placet quam quod quidam Graecarum assecta-
tores rerum putant, qui ἀπὸ τῆς φρήτρης fratrem dictum esse
voluerunt. Praedicatores autem Christus primus appellavit, qui,
ἀπὸ τῆς ἀρετῆς, 'Ite,' inquit discipulis, 'in universum mundum;
praedicate evangelium omni creaturae.' Nunquid igitur, si frater
erit, si praedicator, qui honestam rem aliquam utilemque monue-
rit, quia frater et praedicator est, non audietur? Si verbum Dei an-
nuntiaverit, ob appellationis odium non custodiemus? Nec beati
erimus, quod ille pollicetur Dei filius, qui in promissis fallere non
potest? Non videtur mihi is auctor fieri ferendae legis qui aliquid
quod lege dignum videatur in mentem eorum, qui constituenda-
rum legum habent in republica auctoritatem, induxerit, sed hi potius etiam legum supplicio afficiendi qui salutares huiusmodi voces
neglexerint. Nam quod de peregrina sapientia obloquuntur, multum quidem ab his differunt qui leges etiam ipsas e Graecia Romam advectas, non modo in civitatem, sed in duodecim etiam tabulas, quarum servaret scripta populus Romanus, congessere.

29   De prophetis nunc tandem restat locus, qui, etsi nonnulli aliter
forte iudicaverint, mihi tamen confutatu non admodum laboriosus
videtur, ut quod modo multi rident vertuntque partim levitati,
partim insaniae, mutata sententia admirentur atque vereantur.
Prophetae ergo nomen, ut hinc potissimum incipiamus, Graecum
est. Hebraei videntem dixere, nos vel divinatores vel vates, qui futura praedicunt, possumus (ut arbitror) appellare. Nequis existimet, etsi admiranda quaedam res est atque divina prophetia, ita
tamen hoc tempore subnasci apud homines novam, ut fictum id
esse aliquid fraudulentumque increduli et severiores nonnulli iudices et curiosiores rerum exquisitores ludant inque fabulam dedu-
cant. Apud omnes ferme gentes (nisi fallor) semper fuit opinio
aliqua praescientiae rerum futurarum. Unde sunt apud Graecos

alter, almost another self. This is more convincing than the notion
of some students of Greek, who maintain that *frater* derives from
apo tes phretres or "from the clan."[30] Christ was the first to name
preachers *apo tes aretes,* from their ability:[31] "Go," he said to his disciples, "into all the world; preach the gospel to every creature."[32]
So then, if it is a friar or a preacher who gives honorable and useful advice, should he go unheeded, just because he is a friar and
preacher? If he shall announce the word of God, shall we, out of
hatred for the name, not obey it? Shall we not be blessed, as the
very Son of God promises, who cannot fail to keep His word? I
do not think that man has the authority of a lawgiver who simply
puts into the mind of those who have legislative authority in the
republic something that seems worthy of becoming law. On the
contrary I think we should punish under the law anyone who rejects salutary advice of this kind. And in casting aspersions on
"foreign wisdom," they differ radically from the Romans, who collected laws imported from Greece into Rome, and not only into
the city but into the Twelve Tables which the Roman People preserved in written form.[33]

There remains the topic of prophets, concerning which many   29
may differ strongly from my view. But I do not think it difficult to
refute them; for while many laugh at prophecy, ascribing it either
to folly or insanity, yet they also change their minds and come to
admire and revere prophets. The word "prophet" — to begin with
this significant point — derives from the Greek.[34] The Hebrews
called them seers, and I think we can call those who foresee the future "diviners" and "soothsayers." Now, while prophecy is admirable and divine, let no one think that a new form of it has arisen
among the people of our own time, so that some skeptical and
austere judges consider it a fiction and a fraud, and some overly-
curious scholars mock it and reduce it to a myth.[35] Yet among almost all peoples (if I am not mistaken) there has always been
some belief in the foreknowledge of things to come. Whence

tanta in veneratione atque admiratione populorum tot oracula, tot cortinae, quercus quoque apud eos et columbae gentes ad se consulendum pertraxere. Atque haec quidem in Iovem, illa in Apollinem, atque alia etiam numina referentes, divinam eam esse vim, non hominum, significavere. Hinc vero Melampodes, Chalcantes, Amphiarai, Thyresiae et multi praeterea futura praedixerunt. Varro a Persis divinationem quae ex aqua fit originem habuisse testatur. Nam ab elementis quoque rerum naturalium atque a cadaveribus, ab alitibus earumque volatilibus, quae auguria nostri vocavere, divinationem petiverunt. Decem Varro Sibyllas enumerat, quas θεοβούλας appellant Aeolici genere sermonis. Cassandra item et Chryse, Iunonis virgines, divinant apud Homerum. Romani vix quicquam publici inauspicato aggrediebantur, atque inde quid esset eventurum praedicebant illi, quos vocabant augures. Dies nos deficiat, si cuncta divinationis et prophetiarum genera singillatim persequamur. Ad prophetas tantum Hebraeorum nostrosque revocetur oratio.

30   Deus semper humanum genus adamavit iuvitque inenarrabili atque incomprehensibili clementia divinae maiestatis suae adeo ut filium etiam suum morti tradiderit ignominiosissimae, ut ita nos a morte, quae per Adam irrepserat in homines, liberaret. Atque ut fragilitati opitularetur nostrae, ad praecavenda futura mala infortuniaque devitanda praesensionem quandam mentibus rerum futurarum immisit, ut per visa, per somnia, per nos ipsi aliquid provideremus, quaedam autem quae magis obscura forent delegit per quos ea significaret. Hos appellant Hebraei merito, ut supra dictum est, videntes, quorum per omnia tempora apud eos virtusque et numerus quam insignis fuit. Per istos populum suum de Aegypto eduxit, atque a Pharaone, crudelissimo Aegyptiorum rege, eiusque nequitia et persecutione liberavit. Per istos et in deserto deinde servavit, et ad ultimum usque prophetis semper admonen-

among the Greeks there was such popular veneration and wonder at the oracles and oracular tripods that those peoples even consulted oak trees and flocks of doves. And by ascribing the former to Apollo and the latter to Jupiter, and others to other divinities, they gave proof that the power of prophecy was divine and not human. Hence Melampus, Calchus, Amphiaraus, Tiresias and many others foretold the future. Varro bears witness that divination performed with water began with the Persians.[36] So divination was sought from natural elements and from cadavers and from the flight of birds, which our ancestors called auguries. Varro numbers ten Sibyls, whom the Aeolians in their dialect call *theoboulas*, "those who reveal the divine will." In Homer, likewise, Cassandra and Chryseis, virgins dedicated to Juno, practice divination. The Romans undertook almost no public action if the signs were inauspicious, and those whom they called augurs would predict outcomes. A day would not suffice for me to review all the kinds of divination and prophecies one by one. My discourse returns to the Hebrew and Christian prophets alone.

God has always loved and helped humankind through the un-   30
speakable and incomprehensible mercy of his divine majesty, even giving over his Son to a shameful death in order to free us from the mortality which through Adam entered into mankind. And to help us in our weakness, he sent to some minds warnings of evils and misfortunes to be avoided. Thus, through visions, dreams, and our own selves we could take precautions, but for matters that were more obscure He chose persons through whom he might make them known. These, as we have said, the Hebrews rightly called seers, and the power and number of Hebrew prophets was remarkable through all the ages. By these He led his people out of Egypt and liberated them from the wickedness and persecution of Pharaoh, the cruel Egyptian king. Through the prophets He ultimately saved them, even in the desert, and by the continual warnings of the prophets they conquered enemy armies, reached the

tibus, ipsi profligatis hostibus promissas terras et regna devicta possederunt. Non memoraverim hoc in loco Moysem aut eius successorem Iosue, filium Nun, aut Iudam aliosque complures, quorum nomina et res gestae et prophetiae nobiliores sunt. Septuaginta certe seniores praeter Hellad Medadque, qui in castris, cum illi a Moyse convocarentur, remanserant, omnes prophetarum simul acceperunt spiritum. In Ramatha quoque inter Samuelis discipulos nonne et tertii Saulis nuntii cum ipso tandem Saule, qui de se quoque fecit proverbium prophetaverunt?

31   Sed haec quidem vetustiora videri poterunt fortasse ac minus nostra. Verum nonne et Agabus Hierosolimitanus, ut est in libello de actibus Apostolorum scriptum, famem illam durissimam praenuntiavit, quae sub Claudio universum fere afflixit orbem? Quattuor etiam Philippi filiae prophetaverunt. Benedictus quoque abbas Totilam Italiae insultantem divina praemonitione deterruit. Antonius Arrianam praemonstravit haeresim, ut Iohannem iam Petrumque sileam heremitas, quorum ‹alter› cum Theodosio, cum Gotofrido alter hoc prophetandi divino munere claruerunt. Non est autem operae pretium, ut mihi videtur, ut plures enumererem ne scribere ad ostentandas historias magis quam ad veritatem atque necessitatem defensionis existimari possim. Cum et haec iam forsitan dicet aliquis: Quorsum tam multa de prophetis? Ut non adeo admirentur quidam ducantque inter ea quae fieri non possint, si nos quoque tempestate hac aliquem huiusmodi habuerimus, nec sit magis nostri nunc oblitus Deus, qui profitemur Christum, filium eius, quam olim Hebraeorum. Et profecto multa sunt praenuntiata nobis, quae et ita ut sunt praenuntiata evenere, quod tandem veri prophetae significatio est, ut in Deuteronomio scriptum legitur.

32   Velim vero dicant qui nos vituperant quid erremus. Prophetis credo dicent talibus non oportere fidem esse. At oportet profecto vera dicentibus credere, nisi velimus condemnari ab Abacuch pro-

promised land, and occupied the defeated kingdoms. I shall not mention here Moses, his successor Joshua, the son of Nun, Judah, or various others whose names and deeds and prophecies were more notable. Certainly the seventy elders who were convened by Moses all at once received the spirit of prophecy, except Eldad and Medad who remained in the camp.[37] In Ramah, also, did not the disciples of Samuel and the messengers sent three times by Saul prophesy, as well as Saul himself, who gave rise to the famous saying?[38]

But these might seem ancient examples and less than Christian 31 ones. But did not Agabus of Jerusalem, as is written in the Acts of the Apostles, foretell a terrible famine which afflicted the whole world under Claudius?[39] Four of the daughters of Philip were prophets.[40] The abbot Benedict, used a divine forewarning to deter Totila, who was attacking Italy.[41] Anthony foretold the heresy of Arius, but I shall say nothing now of John [of Egypt], and of Peter the Hermit, who were famous for their divine gifts of prophecy, the one in the time of Theodosius, the other in that of Godfrey.[42] It is not worthwhile, as I see it, to enumerate more examples, so that I don't give the impression that I'm writing to make a show of historical knowledge rather than to demonstrate the truth of my case. Perhaps someone is already going to say of this: Why write so much about prophets? Why? So that certain people may not be so astonished and believe it is impossible for us to have in our age have someone of this sort, nor think that God has forgotten us who confess Christ his Son any more than he forgot the Hebrews long ago. And indeed, we have heard many things predicted that have turned out as predicted which in the end, as we read in Deuteronomy, is the meaning of true prophecy.[43]

I wish our detractors would say where we are in error. I think 32 they would answer that there should be no credence given to prophets like this. But surely one should believe in those who

pheta, qui ait: 'Qui autem incredulus erit, non erit anima eius ius-
tificata in semetipso. Iustus autem ex fide vivit.' 'Iustus,' inquit, 'vivit ex fide:' ut vel hinc coniiciamus pseudoprophetis, idest, falsa
praedicentibus, negandum, ita assensum esse ut veris adhibenda
fides est. Praesertim cum nihil errari in ea re possit, Moyse do-
cente in Deuteronomio ut supra diximus, quibus credendum aut
non credendum sit. Tandem quomodocunque res habeat, hoc ego
ausim asserere. Nisi Deus noster, Deus misericordiarum et pietatis, Deus quietis et totius consolationis, per angelos, per prophetas, per visa, per quancunque virtutem salutis nostrae ineffabili nos
clementia admonuerit, periculum esse ne non modo ex his vitae
fluctibus non emergamus aliquando, sed ne stationem quidem aliquam, ubi consistamus, ne portum, dicam, et perfugium miseria-
rum harum respicere possimus. Nos certe in nostris periculis, quae
tam multa perpessi sumus, nullum fuimus experti praesentius
auxilium. Hinc, tyrannide amota, asseruimus nosmet in libertatem. Hinc diu eiectis afflictisque reddita tandem patria est optimis
civibus, neque aliam ullam ob causam, nisi ob invidiam et civium
inter se contentiones exulantibus. Hinc errata omnibus humanis-
sime condonata, ut lege etiam lata fieret omnium inter se civium
discordiarum odiorumque oblivio. Hinc reipublicae forma et gubernandi modus institutus. Hinc in dies, id est, admonitore et
monstratore Deo, multa domi forisque utiliter administrata. Hinc
spes est denique pristinam nos dignitatem non recuperaturos
modo, sed aucturos etiam et ornaturos, si aequitati causae confidendum est. Quoniam resistit Deus superbis, humilibus autem
dat gratiam, nec deserit sperantes in se, qui est benedictus in sae-
cula saeculorum.

33   Haec nunc habui, mi Trebati, quae ad te scriberem de rebus
nostris deque nostrae Reipublicae defensione. Quae si eam vim

speak the truth, unless we would be condemned by Habakkuk the prophet, who said: "If a man does not believe, his soul will not be justified for itself. But the just man lives by faith."[44] "The just man lives by faith," he says: just as we may gather from this that we should repudiate pseudo-prophets, that is, those who foretell falsely, so too must we have faith in true ones — especially since, to prevent our erring in this, Moses in Deuteronomy, as we have mentioned, teaches whom we should believe and whom not. In sum, however the matter stands, I would dare assert the following: If our God, the God of mercies and piety, the God of peace and of all consolation, does not by his unspeakable mercy warn us, for our salvation, through his angels, prophets, visions, and by all sorts of power, I say there is danger that we will never emerge from the stormy waves of life, nor find any solid ground on which to stand, nor any harbor and refuge from our afflictions. Surely amidst the many dangers which we have suffered, we have made trial of no more present help than this. It is thus that we have shaken off tyranny and claimed our liberty.[45] It is thus that our country is at last restored to her best citizens, long expelled and afflicted for no other reason than the envy and enmity existing among citizens. It is thus that all have been mercifully forgiven their errors, so that by law the discord and hatred among all our citizens is consigned to oblivion.[46] It is thus that the republic's form and way of being governed has been reformed. It is thus that daily, with God as our advisor and our guide, our affairs, at home and abroad, are usefully conducted. It is thus we have hope that we may at last not only recover our former prestige but also — if we may trust in the fairness of our cause — even augment and adorn it. For God opposes the proud and gives grace to the humble, nor does he desert those who hope in him, he who is blessed through all the ages.[47]

This, my Trebatius, is all I have to write to you in defense of   33 our affairs and our Republic. If these arguments have the force

habuerint quam illa habere debent, quae ex simplicitate cordis ve-
rique aperiendi affectu enuntiantur, nihil dubito fore ut hi saltem
quibus integra mens fuerit atque aliena a perturbationibus, aut ego
nimium sum falsus, persuadebuntur. Nam quid perturbati iudi-
cent, levior cura est et medicina difficilior. Neque nostrarum opus
virium aut huius temporis, in quo quidem magis quomodo armis
resistatur propulsenturque iniuriae procurandum videtur, quam ut
verbis contra ineptorum quorundam loquacitatem atque petulantiam, ipsi quoque inepti et facti sic scribendo procaciores conten-
damus. Vale. Kalen‹dis› Septembris MCCCCLXXXXVI.

34 Bartholomeus Scala eis qui legerint salutem dicit.

Scio nonnulli erunt qui mirabuntur qui solitus sim non probare
eos qui illa quae ipsi scripserint, modestiae (nisi fallor) transgressi
cancellos, informari patiuntur ut id quoque nunc mihi evenerit,
quod in aliis reprehenderim. Sed si intellexerint in publica me
nunc causa potius quam mea obsecutum me civibus meis, mutata
(ut arbitror) sententia, accipient magis aequo animo istam modo
parendi impositam necessitatem. Atque eos accusabunt potius qui
adeo maledicendo ambitiose et procaciter, ut nos publicam defensionem susciperemus, impulere. Nec vero amici quidam minus ad
cogendum valuerunt, quibus quidem nihil omnino tribuisse ple-
beium nimis videtur atque rusticanum. Quaedam vero negavisse
rude etiam inhumanumque atque ab omni amoris veri officio
multo maxime alienum est. Etsi enim tanta levitas praetereunda
forsitan silentio magis fuerit, tamen non fuit consilium, ut penitus
impune cederet. Neque ego non hanc saltem verborum et scripti
operam, qui maiora nequeam, rei nostrae publicae praestiterim, et
dicere quidem causam multo est quam agere condonabilius. Lacces-
situs vero, si propulset iniuriam, minus in culpa est, etsi dedisse
veniam divinius fuit. Valete.

they ought to have, spoken as they are from simplicity of heart and the desire to explain the truth, they will, unless I am completely deceived, doubtless persuade at least those of sound and dispassionate mind. What the passionate believe is of less concern and of more difficult cure. Nor is that the task facing our energies at this moment, when it seems that we should show more concern with how to mount armed resistance and repel injuries, than with how we may spar verbally against the verbosity and petulance of certain foolish people, when we ourselves are also foolish and made more doctrinaire by writing in this fashion. Farewell. 1 September 1496.

Bartolomeo Scala greets his readers.[48]   34

I know that some persons will be surprised that, while generally disapproving of those who (at least as I see it) overstep the bounds of modesty and allow what they have written to be printed, this now has happened to me as well—the very thing I have criticized in others. But once they understand that I am acting in the public interest rather than in my own, and for the sake of my fellow citizens, they will (I believe) change their minds and accept with equanimity the necessity to which I am now subjected. And they will rather blame those who have carried detraction so far, in their ambition and insolence, that they have compelled us to undertake a public defense. Nor were those friends least influential in deciding me, to whom it seems that nothing at all plebeian or rustic may be attributed.[49] To refuse certain things is rude and unkind and entirely foreign to every duty imposed by true love. Even if it might have been nobler to pass over great foolishness like this in silence, nevertheless, it did not seem advisable to let such things pass with impunity. Nor might I not offer our republic at least this effort of words and writing, I who am not capable of greater things; and to speak in a case is much more excusable than to be a party to it. The injured party is less at fault if he wards off an injury, although to forgive is more divine. Farewell.

Note on the Text

࿇࿇࿇

The Latin texts in this volume are based on those in *Bartolomeo Scala: Humanistic and Political Writings*, ed. Alison Brown (Tempe, Arizona: Medieval and Renaissance Texts and Studies, 1997), Part V, "Essays, Dialogues and Apologues" (pp. 251–305, 338–364, and 394–411). They are used by kind permission of Alison Brown and the publisher. The punctuation and paragraphing has occasionally been modified, and the names of the interlocutors inserted in Text 3 have been removed. Other, minor textual interventions have been recorded in the apparatus. Words in angle brackets have been supplied by the editor.

The two texts in Part V that have not been included in this volume, the *Apologi centum* and the *Apologorum liber secundus* and later apologues, may be found in translation in *Renaissance Fables: Aesopic Prose*, ed. David Marsh (Tempe, Arizona: Arizona Center for Medieval and Renaissance Studies, 2004).

Text 5, translated by David Marsh, was first published in *Cambridge Translations of Renaissance Philosophical Texts*, vol. 2: *Political Philosophy*, ed. Jill Kraye (Cambridge: Cambridge University Press, 1997), 174–194. It has been reprinted by kind permission of Cambridge University Press and the translator. Slight adjustments have been made to adapt the text to a bilingual format.

In the case of Texts 1–4 and 6 the Notes to the Translation are based primarily on those in the Brown edition, though they have been checked and in some cases supplemented. The notes to Text 5 are based on those in David Marsh's translation, pp. 194–199, as well as on the notes in the Brown edition; they have also been checked and in a few cases supplemented.

Notes to the Text

❧❧❧

1. non *bracketed in ed.*

2. WHETHER A WISE MAN SHOULD MARRY

1. Macedonem *ed.*

2. admittuntur *ed.*

3. DIALOGUE OF CONSOLATION

1. praefecerunt *ed.*

2. Aegaeotam *ed.*

3. aculeo *ed.*

4. occeperunt *ed.*

5. *Modern texts of Terence read* ingeniumst omnium hominum *for* Est enim hominum genus

6. tolle *Horace*

7. an *Horace*

8. oculos *ed.*: oculus *Vulgate*

9. ad aedificato *ed.*: exaedificavissent *Cicero*

4. PREFACE TO THE "COSIMO DE MEDICI" COLLECTION

1. Seleucos *ed.*

5. DIALOGUE ON LAWS AND LEGAL JUDGMENTS

1. *Omitted in Juvenal*

2. *Modern texts of Vergil read* ingens gelidum lucus *for* lucus ingens *and* cingunt *for* cingit

6. DEFENSE AGAINST THE DETRACTORS OF FLORENCE

1. quem *ed.*

2. agitur . . . maturat *ed.*

Notes to the Translation

꽃

ABBREVIATIONS

CIC   *Corpus iuris civilis*
PL   *Patrologiae cursus completus, series latina*, ed. J.-P.
            Migne, 221 vols. (Paris, 1844–91).

Complete citations of works referred to by author and title may be found in the Bibliography.

I. LETTER ON PHILOSOPHICAL SECTS

1. Scala's former patron in Milan, Filippo Borromeo, Count of Arona.

2. Cicero, *Tusculan Disputations* 2.1; *On the Orator* 2.156.

3. Leonardo Bruni, *Isagogicon moralis disciplinae*, in Bruni, *Opere letterarie e politiche*, ed. P. Viti (Turin, 1996), 195–241; English translation in *The Humanism of Leonardo Bruni*, ed. and tr. G. Griffiths, J. Hankins and D. Thompson (Binghamton, NY, 1987), 267–282.

4. I.e., moral philosophy, natural philosophy, and logic; see Cicero, *Academica* 1.19.

5. Augustine, *City of God* 19.1.

6. Cicero, *Academica* 1.15.

7. From the Greek *peripatein*, to walk around.

8. Ibid. 1.17.

9. Cicero, *On Ends* 1.17.

10. Augustine, *Against the Academics* 3.19.

11. Lucretius 1.830–844.

12. Diogenes Laertius 2.65, 105, 106, 125; 4.67; 6.1.

13. Cicero, *Academica* 1.33.

14. Ibid. 1.46.

15. Diogenes Laertius 4.59.

16. Cicero, *Academica* 2.69. The text is corrupt at this point but the sense is tolerably clear.

17. Augustine, *Against the Academics* 3.18.

18. Lactantius, *Divine Institutes* 7 (*PL* 5: 364).

19. I.e., physics, ethics and logic or dialectic.

20. Vergil, *Aeneid* 4.379–80 (trans. Dryden), words spoken derisively by Dido as she discounts Aeneus' claim that the gods have planned and ordered his departure; more literally: "Of course this will cost the gods some effort and these concerns will disturb their tranquillity!"

21. Compare Lucretius 3.425–669.

22. Scala here seems to have forgotten his earlier identification of dialectic as the third part of philosophy.

23. The more usual terminology, from Aristotle's ethics, is goods of the mind, body and external goods (i.e., those that support the best life of the organism), sometimes called the goods of fortune, as below.

24. Cicero, *Academica* 1. 25

25. Ibid. 1.41–42.

26. Cicero, *On Ends* 3.15

27. Cicero, *Academica* 1.38–39.

28. Augustine, *City of God* 2.14.

29. Psalm 14:1.

30. Vergil, *Aeneid* 6.719–21 (Dryden). More literally: "O Father, if souls can go from hence into the skies, would the sublime souls wish to return to their bodies?"

31. Augustine, *City of God*, 21.1; Plato, *Phaedo* 113e.

32. Vergil, *Aeneid* 6.617–18.

33. Genesis 1:26.

34. Basil, *De legendis libris gentilium* (*PG* 31: 570), which Scala no doubt knew in the popular translation of Leonardo Bruni.

2. WHETHER A WISE MAN SHOULD MARRY

1. The dedication is to Piero de' Medici (1416–1469), son of Cosimo de' Medici. Cosimo was the unofficial ruler of Florence from 1434 until his death in 1464. Piero succeeded him as head of the Medici party and first citizen of Florence in 1464. He married Lucrezia Tornabuoni in 1444, a woman of refined culture and a poetess.

2. Cicero, *Tusculan Disputations* 1.19.20; Augustine, *City of God* 8.3; but the story was widely circulated in antiquity and the Renaissance.

3. Cicero, *Tusculan Disputations* 5.9.

4. I Corinthians 1:20.

5. Jerome, *Adversus Jovinianum* 1.48. Many of the anecdotes and information in this essay come from this work of Jerome.

6. Statius, *Thebaid* 2.265–68. The story is told also in Jerome as cited in note 6, but without the curse on the necklace.

7. Jerome, *Adversus Jovinianum* 1.48.

8. Ibid.

9. This false view of Epicurus had been exploded by Leonardo Bruni in his *Isagogicon moralis disciplinae* (1424/26), which Scala cites in Text 1.2.

10. His name is formed from *theo*, "divine" and *phrasis*, "expression."

11. Ibid. 1.47, though Jerome cites Theophrastus as saying that the husband should be "of good health and ample means."

12. Juvenal 6.463.

13. Juvenal 6.47–49.

14. Jerome, *Adversus Jovinianum* 1.41–49.

15. Ibid. 1.47.

16. Augustine, *City of God* 5.18.

17. Ibid.

18. Cicero, *On Duties* 3.1.1.

19. Juvenal 6.268–9.

20. Jerome, *Adversus Jovinianum* 1.48; Diogenes Laertius 2.26. See also Giannozzo Manetti's *Life of Socrates* §33 in Manetti, *Biographical Writings*, ed. Stefano Baldassarri (Cambridge, Mass., 2003), 201.

21. Jerome, *Adversus Jovinianum* 1.48.

22. Juvenal 6.231.

23. Jerome, *Adversus Jovinianum* 1.48.

24. Ibid., citing Terence, *Hecyra* 201.

25. Jerome, *Adversus Jovinianum* 1.49.

26. Ibid.

27. Aulus Gellius, *Noctes Atticae* 1.6.1–2. In Gellius, Metellus Numidicus (censor 102 BC) is the speaker, not Cato the Elder, also a censor, who held the office about eighty years earlier.

28. Jerome, *Adversus Jovinianum* 1.48.

29. These marriage deities are listed in Augustine, *City of God* 6.9, where the list is attributed to Varro, who expresses disdain for rustic Roman superstition. Domiducus is an epithet of Jupiter and Juno, who as deities of marriage bring the bride to her husband's home in patrilocal marriage. Deus Domitius protects those married in the house. Virginensis presided over the loosening of the bridal girdle. Subigus ("conqueror") is the tutelary god that presided over the wedding night; Prema is the goddess presiding over newly-married persons; Pertunda is the goddess that presides over the loss of virginity.

30. A fragment of the poet Stesichoros (see *Poetae Melici Graeci*, ed. D. L. Page [Oxford 1962], 192) which appears in Plato's *Phaedrus* 243a. A large part of the *Phaedrus* was translated by Leonardo Bruni around 1424, including the hexameter verses quoted here. The translation is unpublished.

31. Cicero, *On Duties* 1.17.54.

32. Ibid. 1.28.100.

33. Jerome, *Adversus Jovinianum* 1.48.

34. Proverbs 31:10.

35. Juvenal 6.165.

36. Jerome, *Adversus Jovinianum* 1.41.

37. Ibid. 1.44. The detail that Artemisia drank Mausolus' ashes is not in Jerome, and may come from Boccaccio, *Famous Women*, ed. V. Brown (Cambridge, Mass., 2001), p. 233 (57.2) or one of Boccaccio's sources (see p. 493).

38. Ovid, *Heroides* 14; *Famous Women* 14.1–7.

39. Jerome, *Adversus Jovinianum* 1.46.

40. Ibid.

41. Macrobius, *Saturnalia* 1.11.37–40; see also Plutarch's *Lives*, *Romulus* 29.3–6.

42. Augustine, *City of God* 5.12.

43. Jerome, *Adversus Jovinianum* 1.45.

44. Ibid. 1.41.

45. Ibid. In Jerome's version they were ordered to engage in sexual acts with their captors, who were still covered with their father's blood.

46. Xenophon, *Cyropaedia* 6.4.2–11, cited via Jerome, *Adversus Jovinianum* 1.45.

47. Jerome, *Adversus Jovinianum* 1.41.

3. DIALOGUE OF CONSOLATION

1. Giovanni de' Medici, son of Cosimo, died on 1 November 1463; before his untimely death he was to have been Cosimo's successor as head of the Medici party and unofficial ruler of Florence. His death created a succession crisis to which Scala obliquely alludes.

2. Vergil, *Eclogue* 5.23.

3. *Iliad* 6.157–203, cited in Cicero, *Tusculan Disputations* 3.26.63. Cicero is offering a euhemeristic interpretation of Niobe's death, that her being turned to stone is a kind of metaphor for the silence into which she fell following the death of her children.

4. Ovid, *Metamorphoses* 1.83.

5. Cicero, *On Laws* 1.7.22.

6. Genesis 1.

7. I Corinthians 1:20.

8. Plato, *Apology* 21a.

9. Cicero, *On Friendship* 1.1.

10. *Theogony*, cited via Augustine, *City of God* 4.8–11.

11. Terence, *Eunuch* 245.

12. Augustine, *City of God* 6.2.

13. Eusebius, *The Preparation for the Gospel* 13.12, known to Scala in the translation of George of Trebizond (1448). See the edition of [Venice] 1470, sig.[o7]r.

14. *Corpus Hermeticum, Asclepius* 3.30 (ed. W. Scott, 1: 350).

15. Eusebius, *Preparation for the Gospel* 1.10, trans. Trebizond, ed. [Venice] 1470, sig.[b1]v.

16. Lactantius, *God's Creation (De opificio Dei)* §8.

17. Cicero, *Tusculan Disputations* 1.22.52; *On Laws* 1.23.61, but the saying "Know Thyself" is ubiquitous in ancient sources.

18. Plutarch, *Life of Alexander* 3; the same point, with different examples, is made by Cicero, *Tusculan Disputations* 1.46.111.

19. Livy 5.21.14–15.

20. Seneca, *Troiades* 1–4.

21. The insistence on the hereditary nature of Piero's gout is presumably intended to forestall criticism that his gout was the result of overindulgence.

22. Job 6:12–13 (Revised Standard Version)

23. Juvenal 15.131–33.

24. Cicero, *Tusculan Disputations* 2.25.60, quoting a line from a lost play of Aeschylus translated into Latin by Accius.

25. Augustine, *City of God* 19.1. See above, Text 1, §§3–4.

26. Cicero, *Tusculan Disputations* 3.11.25.

27. Ibid. 3.6.12.

28. John 11:33–35; Luke 22:42.

29. The victualling of armies in remote and mountainous areas was a notorious problem for Renaissance condottieri.

30. Genesis 1 passim, esp. 27–31, 2:7.

31. Luke 23:28–29, a particularly context-free citation.

32. Cicero, *Tusculan Disputations* 3.6.12; Diogenes Laertius 4.64–66.

33. See Ovid, *Letters From Pontus* 3.6.41–42: "clausos urere in aere uiros."

34. Diogenes Laertius 10.22; Cicero, *Tusculan Disputations* 2.6.15–18.

35. Seneca, *Trojan Women* 63–66 (tr. Frank Justus Miller in the Loeb Library).

36. Ibid. 83–87.

37. Ibid. 96–98. Scala skips the lines describing the baring and beating of breasts.

38. E.g. Ovid, *Metamorphoses* 13.400f.

39. Compare Seneca, *Moral Epistles* 107.11.

40. The argument against the security of human goods that follows seems in a general way indebted to Augustine's in *City of God* 19, passim.

41. *Andria* 77–78.

42. Ps. Diogenes, *Letters* 28, ed. Hercher, p. 242. The translation is not that of Francesco Griffolini.

43. Matthew 19:24; Mark 10:25; Luke 18:25.

44. Lucretius 2.34–36 (tr. William Ellery Leonard).

45. Cicero, *Tusculan Disputations* 5.21.61–62.

46. Lucretius 2.48–52 (tr. Leonard).

47. The most famous source for this common Greek classification of goods is Aristotle's *Ethics* 1.8, 1098b 10–18.

48. Pliny the Elder, *Natural History* 7.20.83. Strabo's *Geography* 6.1.12 (available to Scala in Guarino Veronese's translation) describes how Milo's strength was the cause of his own death: wandering in the forest, he tried to split a log asunder with his bare hands but instead became stuck in the cleft he had made and was eaten by wild beasts.

49. Lygdamus of Syracuse was the winner of the first *pankration* or combined wrestling and boxing championship in Olympia in 648 BC. See Solinus 74.

50. Pliny, *Natural History* 7.20.81.

51. Aulus Gellius 2.11 (Lucius Sicinius Dentatus); Pliny, *Natural History* 7.20.83 (Fufius and Athanatus); Pliny says 500 pounds, Scala 50.

52. Ibid. 7.20.81.

53. *Aeneid* 7.803–807 (tr. H. Rushton Fairclough in the Loeb Library).

54. Livy 9, passim.

55. Basil of Caesarea, *Epistula ad adolescentes* 9 (ed. Wilson, 33).

56. Probably thinking of (pseudo) Aristotle's *Economics*, a translation of which by Leonardo Bruni was dedicated to Cosimo in 1420.

57. Horace, *Letters* 1.12.3–6 (tr. John Conington).

58. Horace, *Satires* 1.1.76–78 (tr. Conington).

59. Ibid. 1.1.78–9.

60. Cosimo is implicitly comparing himself to Anchises, father of *pius Aeneas*, who carried his father on his shoulders out of burning Troy in *Aeneid* 2.707–725.

61. I.e. at the crossroads of life, where one chooses the path of virtue or of vice. See Servius's commentary on *Aeneid* 6.136.

62. Compare Juvenal 6.181.

63. Lucretius 2.14–16 (tr. Leonard).

64. *Phaedo* 67d; Cicero, *Tusculan Disputations* 1.3.74.

65. Job 7:1.

66. Cicero, *Tusculan Disputations* 1.48.116.

67. Ibid. 1.34.83.

68. Pseudo-Eusebius of Cremona, *De morte Hieronymi* 26 (PL 22: 263). On this text see Eugene F. Rice, *Saint Jerome in the Renaissance* (Baltimore, Maryland, 1985), 218–19.

69. Ecclesiastes 4:2–3.

70. Job 10:18.

71. Cicero, *Tusculan Disputations* 1.48.114.

72. Ibid. 1.47.113, 114.

73. Philippians 1:23.

74. Pseudo-Eusebius, *De morte Hieronymi* 26 (*PL* 22: 263).

75. Ibid., but full of images from the Song of Solomon.

76. Cicero, *Tusculan Disputations* 3.25.59–60. In Cicero the quotation is continued for another five lines.

77. Ibid. 3.25.60.

4. PREFACE TO THE
"COSIMO DE' MEDICI COLLECTION"

1. Lorenzo de'Medici, "the Magnificent" (1449–1492), son of Piero and grandson of Cosimo de'Medici, after 1469 the virtual ruler of Florence.

2. For a detailed study of this collection, see Brown, "The Humanist Portrait."

3. Hesiod, *Works and Days*, 288–90, almost certainly via St. Basil, *Ad adolescentes* 5 (ed. Wilson, 24), translated into Latin by Leonardo Bruni around 1400.

4. Source unknown; not in Diogenes Laertius or Diels-Kranz.

5. Plato, *Timaeus* 22b.

6. Sallust, *Jugurthine War* 1.1.

7. Quintilian, *Institutes* 9.4.41; 11.1.24; compare Juvenal 10.122.

8. On the library at San Marco in Florence, founded by Cosimo with books bequeathed by Niccolò Niccoli and Cosimo himself, see B. L. Ullman and P. A. Stadter, *The Public Library of Renaissance Florence* (Padua, 1982); see also Vespasiano da Bisticci, cited in note 11 below. On Cosimo's patronage in general, see Dale Kent, *Cosimo de' Medici and the Florentine Renaissance: The Patron's Oeuvre* (New Haven, 2000).

9. Plutarch, *Life of Sulla* 26, 468a.

10. Possibly Pollius Felix, a learned patron praised by Statius, *Silvae* 2.2.

11. Pope Nicholas V, who as Tommaso Parentucelli of Sarzana had advised Cosimo on the libraries of San Marco and the Badia at Fiesole before establishing the Vatican Library in Rome as pope; see Vespasiano da Bisticci's biography in *Le Vite*, ed. A. Greco (Florence, 1970), 1: 46–7, 63–69.

12. Possibly a reference to King Ladislas of Naples, who threatened Florence's existence as an independent republic in 1414, or Alfonso of Aragon.

13. Probably a reference to Duke (*dux*) Francesco Sforza of Milan, who as a result of Cosimo's diplomacy became an ally of Florence after 1450.

14. Presumably Venice, where Cosimo was an ambassador in 1438.

5. DIALOGUE ON LAWS AND LEGAL JUDGMENTS

1. Lorenzo left Florence for the Congress of Cremona on 12 February 1483; see Brown, *Bartolomeo Scala*, 289n.

2. Father of Niccolò, the famous political theorist.

3. On Scala's house, of which he was extremely proud, see Pellichia, "The Patron's Role."

4. Carnival in 1483 ran from 3 to 11 February.

5. Cosimo de'Medici (1387-1464), banker and stateman, unofficial ruler of Florence from 1434 to his death.

6. Niccolò da Uzzano (1359-1431), wealthy banker and stateman, a leader of the Florentine oligarchy, the regime that preceded the period of Medici rule.

7. *Liber Pontificalis* 9.2, but Scala could also be using Bartolomeo Platina's *Lives of the Popes* 9.2, published in Venice in 1479; see the edition and translation in this I Tatti series, ed. Anthony F. D'Elia (Cambridge, Mass., 2008). Telesphorus was pope from 125 to 136 AD.

8. *Liber pontificalis* 17.2; Platina, *Lives*, 17.2. Calixtus was pope from 217 to 222 AD.

9. The ancient codex of the *Pandects* or *Digest* (the most important part of the *Corpus iuris civilis* [CIC] or *Civil Law Code*, codified by the Emperor

Justinian in 533) was acquired from the Pisans after their defeat by Florence in 1406 and kept in the chapel of the Priors in the Palazzo Vecchio; the Florentines believed it to be the original codex redacted by the emperor's legal expert, Tribonian, although this is now regarded as dubious.

10. The two most famous jurists of the fourteenth century, Bartolo da Sassoferrato (1313/4–1357) and his pupil Baldo de Ubaldis (d. 1400); the controversy to which Scala refers must have occurred between 1351 and 1356, when both men were teaching in Perugia.

11. I.e., security for a loan or debt.

12. *CIC, Digest* 20.5.7. The Roman jurist Marcianus was an older authority often cited in the *Corpus*.

13. Giovanni Buongirolami of Gubbio (1381-1454), who worked in Florence and was sympathetic to the Medici party.

14. Otranto, on the southern tip of Italy, was captured and briefly held by the armies of the Sultan Mehmed II in 1480-81.

15. In fact the word is derived from the Turkish *bash* or head, whence the Latin *bassia*, the Italian *bascià*, and the English "bashaw" and "pasha."

16. King John II of Portugal, who reigned 1481-95, sponsored explorations including Diogo Cão's discovery of the Congo River (1482) and of the islands of Fernando Po and São Tomé (1483).

17. Lactantius, *Divine Institutes* 5.13.2.

18. Matthew 22:37-39 and Mark 12:30-31.

19. Matthew 22:40.

20. Franciscus Accursius of Reggio (1182-1260), the famous thirteenth-century glossator of the *Corpus Iuris Civilis*, and Cino da Pistoia (1270-1337), Latin commentator on the *Digest*; on Baldus and Bartolus, see note 10 above.

21. Ps.-Plato, *Hipparchus* 227e, a dialogue translated by Marsilio Ficino and presented to Cosimo de'Medici in the last year of his life.

22. *CIC, Digest* 44.1.2.1. The voluminous writings of the third-century jurist Ulpian were the source for nearly a third of Justinian's *Digest*.

23. Ibid. 44.1.2.3.

24. The *lex Cincia* of 204 BC imposed restrictions on the size of gifts to advocates; the emperor Claudius limited the permissable fee to 10,000 sesterces; see Tacitus, *Annals* 11.7.

25. Probably "fra i due litiganti, il terzo gode" (between two litigants it's the third who gains).

26. A Florentine word for a meeting of the 21 major and minor guilds.

27. Referring to a law passed in 1477 by which important cases could be appealed to the Merchants' Court in Florence.

28. Juvenal 6.240-241.

29. Plato, *Laws* 4, 711c, translated by George of Trebizond in 1450/51.

30. Aristotle, *Nicomachean Ethics*. 2.3, 1105a8-9.

31. Presumably a reference (added after the initial publication of the dialogue?), to the knighthood conferred on Scala by Pope Sixtus IV in 1484; see Brown, *Scala*, 98-99, 107-108.

32. Pandolfo Collenuccio of Pesaro (1444-1504), humanist; the ruler of Pesaro and captain-general of the Florentine military forces mentioned here is Costanzo Sforza (1447–1483).

33. Homer, *Odyssey* 11.568; compare Plato, *Minos* 319b, *Laws* 1.624b.

34. Homer, *Odyssey* 11.568-71.

35. Plato, *Gorgias* 524a.

36. Xenophon, *Cyropaedia* 1.2.14.

37. Juvenal 8.50.

38. This is the entire text of Scala's *Leges* (Laws), number XXVI in a collection of one hundred Latin apologues or fables written in 1481; see *Renaissance Fables*, tr. Marsh, in the Bibliography.

39. Livy 2.5.6.

40. CIC, *Institutes* 1.1.

41. Xenophon, *Spartan Constitution* 1.7-9.

42. CIC, *Institutes* 4.1.5.

43. Compare Herodotus 5.6, translated by Lorenzo Valla after 1453.

44. Compare Eusebius, *Preparation for the Gospel* 6.10.276.

45. Herodotus 1.197.

46. Ibid. 3.99.

47. *CIC, Institutes* 1.2.4-8.

48. Based on ibid. 1.2-7 (Gaius).

49. Ibid.; compare Cicero, *On Laws* 1.18.

50. Source unidentified. Bias was one of the Seven Wise Men of Greece, whose life is described in Diogenes Laertius 1.5.

51. See Aratus, *Phaenomena* 96-136.

52. Scala probably borrows the example of Phoroneus, found in Hyginus's *Fables* (143) from Poggio Braccciolini's *Historia convivalis*; see his *Opera omnia*, ed. R. Fubini (Turin, 1964-69), 1: 40.

53. Exodus 24:18, 32:15.

54. This and the following paragraph are dependant on (pseudo) Plato's *Minos*, translated by Marsilio Ficino for Cosimo de'Medici in 1464.

55. Ibid. 315a.

56. Livy 34.1.1 to 34.8.3.

57. Cicero, *On the Nature of the Gods* 2.25.64 and 3.24.62.

58. The following paragraph repeats the lawgivers and gods cited in Ficino's argument to the Minos, found in his *Opera omnia* (Basel, 1576), 2: 1135, as noted in Brown, *Scala*, 293. See also Ficino's *Lettere*, ed. S. Gentile (Florence 1990), 1: 17-18.

59. See J. Hankins, "Cosimo de' Medici and the 'Platonic Academy'," *Journal of the Warburg and Courtauld Institutes* 53 (1990): 144-162, on Cosimo's support for Platonic studies in Florence.

60. Also dependent on Ficino's argument to the *Minos* (note 58, above).

61. I.e., the virtue of justice; the title of Florence's ceremonial head of state was "Standard-Bearer of Justice" (*gonfaloniere della giustizia*).

62. Livy 3.33-58.

63. *CIC, Digest* 1.2.2 (twenty years); Livy 3.34 (thirty-two years, not thirty-eight).

64. Ibid. 3.32-37.

65. Cicero, *On the Nature of the Gods* 2.25.64.

66. Augustine, *City of God* 4.4, a famous quotation.

67. Compare Cicero, *On the Orator* 1.202.

68. An allusion to Horace, *The Art of Poetry* 413.

69. Vergil, *Aeneid* 6.258-9.

70. Cicero, *On the Nature of the Gods* 2.28.72.

71. Lactantius, *Divine Institutes* 4.28.3.

72. Lucretius 1.931-32.

73. Macrobius, *Saturnalia* 3.3.8-9.

74. Vergil, *Aeneid* 8.587-99.

75. James 1:26-27.

76. Genesis 1:26.

6. DEFENSE AGAINST THE DETRACTORS OF FLORENCE

1. This preface by Pietro Crinito and the following one by Crinito to Scala was placed at the beginning of the text in the first edition of 1496; see Brown, *Scala*, 125–127. Pietro Crinito (1475–1507) was a Florentine humanist of Medicean sympathies and a student of Poliziano, best known for his compendium *De honesta disciplina* (*Honorable Learning*) and for his *De poetis latinis* (*Lives of the Latin Poets*).

2. On this image see See Fritz Saxl, "Veritas Filia Temporis," in *Philosophy and History: Essays presented to Ernst Cassirer* (Oxford, 1936), 197–222.

3. The identity of the clearly pseudonymous "Trebatius" is not known. The name seems borrowed from that of Cicero's young protégé Gaius Trebatius Testa, who became a distinguished jurist. Brown in the footnotes to her edition of the text (p. 395) suggests Francesco Gualterotti or Giovanni Cerretani as possible candidates for the dedicatee.

4. Cicero, *On Ends* 1.20; *Tusculan Disputations* 1.42.

5. Vergil, *Georgics* 2.490–492.

6. I.e., Epicurus, Lucretius' philosophical master.

7. Macrobius, *Saturnalia* 5.16.8. *Tuche* is the Greek word for chance or fortune.

8. Pliny, *Natural History* 26.10.64, 100. Scala himself suffered severely from gout.

9. Juvenal 10.365–66.

10. Montepulciano and Pisa, acquired by the Florentine republic in 1388 and 1406, rebelled in 1494 after the French invasion and the fall of the Medici regime in Florence.

11. In 1261, after the defeat of the Guelfs by the Ghibellines at Montaperti in 1260. See Leonardo Bruni, *History of the Florentine People*, ed. and tr. J. Hankins (Cambridge, Mass., 2001–2007), 1: 174–76 (2.67–68), a text well known to Scala.

12. For Farinata degli Uberti's role at Empoli, see ibid. and Dante, *Inferno* 10.91–92.

13. On the siege of Colle Val d'Elsa in 1479, see Brown, *Scala*, 87–89. Colle was Scala's hometown.

14. The rebellion of Volterra in 1472 led to a massacre by the troops of Federigo of Montefeltro, who were in the employ of the Florentine state. Scala served as chancellor of the Florentine war commission during the rebellion.

15. Matthew 7:3–4, and Luke 6:41–42.

16. Matthew 7:2.

17. Plutarch, *Life of Lycurgus* 17.3.

18. Scala seems to be following Aristotle's distinction between an ideal constitution and the best one, relatively speaking, for most states, which is the mixed constitution; see Aristotle, *Politics* 4.1, 1288b; 4.11, 1295a–b. Following a common Renaissance view, Scala sees the ideal constitution as an exemplar by which to measure the excellence of a constitution rather than as a practical blueprint. See J. Hankins, *Plato in the Italian Renaissance* (Leiden, 1990), 1: 228–229.

19. I.e., deriving *senatus* from *senex*, old man.

20. Scala here seems to be describing a citizen army or militia.

21. The Great Council was created on 23 December 1494 and consisted of all those qualified for high political office; it was much larger and therefore more popular than the councils that had hitherto governed Florence. On the temple of Miletus, see Leon Battista Alberti, *De re aedificatoria* 7.3, who himself cites Strabo, *Geography* 14.1.5.

22. Psalm 142:2.

23. For example, the Stoics (see Cicero, *Stoic Paradoxes* 3), or the author of James 2:10.

24. Aristotle, *Politics* 5.1.8, 1302a.

25. The rules for attendance at the Great Council were not quite as Scala describes them: all citizens could be "imborsed," i.e. made eligible for sortition for office, at the age of 29, and 24 young men were qualified at the age of 24. Shortly after the *Defense* was written, the age of participation was lowered to 24 for all male citizens. See Scala, *Humanistic and Political Writings*, 406n.

26. Livy 2.2.1.

27. I.e., the Dominican prophet Savonarola. See Introduction.

28. Contrary (having some things in common) as opposed to contradictory (mutually exclusive): Scala makes use of basic logical terminology.

29. *A fortiori*, if two contrary species can come together, two genuses, such as religious and secular rule, can do so.

30. Etymologies from Paul's epitome of Festus, *De verborum significatu* 90 (ed. Lindsay, 80).

31. I.e., they were called *praedicatores* from their skill at "making known" (*praedicere*). The reference is to the Dominicans, Savonarola's order, known as the "order of preachers," the *ordo praedicatorum*.

32. Mark 16:15.

33. Livy 3.31.

34. Again from Paul's epitome of Festus, 90.

35. It may be noted that "curiosity" before the seventeenth century was ordinarily the name of a vice: the vice, specifically, of seeking to know things beyond one's concerns and ability to understand.

36. Isidore of Seville, *Etymologiae* 8.9.13.

37. Numbers 11:26.

38. "Is Saul also among the prophets?" I Samuel 19:19–24.

39. Acts 11:28.

40. Acts 21:8–9.

41. St. Gregory the Great, *Dialogues* 2.15.

42. St. Anthony Abbot of Egypt (251–356), one of the Desert Fathers, made famous by St Athanasius' biography, died some years before the reign of the emperor Theodosius (379–95). Peter the Hermit (d. 1115) was a contemporary of Godfrey, Count of Bouillon (c. 1060–1100), a hero of the First Crusade.

43. Deuteronomy 18:21–22. For the apparent fulfillment of Savonarola's early prophecies, see Donald Weinstein, *Savonarola and Florence: Prophecy and Patriotism in the Renaissance* (Princeton, 1970), 116–17.

44. Habbakuk 2:4.

45. I.e., through the expulsion of Scala's former patrons, the Medici.

46. Scala refers to the law of peace and amnesty passed as a result of Savonarola's influence on 19 March 1495.

47. James 4:6, Peter 5:5.

48. The letter to his readers follows the text of the *Defense* in the printed edition of 1496 and in at least one manuscript.

49. Evidently Scala regarded having one's writings printed to be degrading and self-aggrandizing.

Bibliography

꙲꙳

TEXTS

Scala, Bartolomeo. *Humanistic and Political Writings.* Edited by Alison M. Brown. Medieval and Renaissance Texts and Studies, 159 = Renaissance Society of America, Renaissance Texts Series, 16. Tempe, Arizona: Medieval and Renaissance Texts and Studies, 1997.

Renaissance Fables. Aesopic Prose by Leon Battista Alberti, Bartolomeo Scala, Leonardo da Vinci, Bernardino Baldi. Translated with an introduction and notes by David Marsh. Medieval and Renaissance Texts and Studies, 260. Tempe, Arizona: Arizona Center for Medieval and Renaissance Studies, 2004.

SECONDARY LITERATURE

Brown, Alison. "The Humanist Portrait of Cosimo de'Medici, Pater Patriae." *Journal of the Warburg and Courtauld Institutes*, 24 (1961): 186–221.

Eadem. *Bartolomeo Scala, 1430–1497, Chancellor of Florence: The Humanist as Bureaucrat.* Princeton: Princeton University Press, 1979.

Eadem. "Lucretius and the Epicureans in the social and political context of Renaissance Florence." *I Tatti Studies* 9 (2001): 11–62.

Garin, Eugenio. "The Humanist Chancellors of the Florentine Republic from Coluccio Salutati to Bartolomeo Scala." In idem, *Portraits from the Quattrocento*, tr. Victor A. Velen and Elizabeth Velen. New York: Harper and Row, 1972.

Pellecchia, Linda. "The Patron's Role in the Production of Architecture: Bartolomeo Scala and the Scala Palace." *Renaissance Quarterly* 42.2 (1989): 258–291.

Index

୬୧୨୫

Roman numerals (ix, xvi n3) refer to the text and notes of the Introduction. Two-part arabic numbers (5.27, 6.13) refer to the number and paragraph of Scala's essays. Arabic numbers with n (295n20) refer to the Notes to the Translation. Numbers in italics refer to the section (book, chapter, etc.) of works cited.

Publication of this volume has been made possible by

The Myron and Sheila Gilmore Publication Fund at I Tatti
The Robert Lehman Endowment Fund
The Jean-François Malle Scholarly Programs and Publications Fund
The Andrew W. Mellon Scholarly Publications Fund
The Craig and Barbara Smyth Fund
for Scholarly Programs and Publications
The Lila Wallace–Reader's Digest Endowment Fund
The Malcolm Wiener Fund for Scholarly Programs and Publications